POLISH & RUSSIAN
THE CLASSIC COOKBOOK

POLISH & RUSSIAN
THE CLASSIC COOKBOOK

70 TRADITIONAL DISHES SHOWN STEP BY STEP IN 250 PHOTOGRAPHS

Lesley Chamberlain & Catherine Atkinson

HH
HERMES
HOUSE

This edition is published by Hermes House, an imprint of Anness Publishing Ltd, Hermes House, 88–89 Blackfriars Road, London SE1 8HA; tel. 020 7401 2077; fax 020 7633 9499

www.hermeshouse.com; www.annesspublishing.com

If you like the images in this book and would like to investigate using them for publishing, promotions or advertising, please visit our website www.practicalpictures.com for more information.

Publisher: Joanna Lorenz
Editor: Margaret Malone
Photography: Ian Garlick
Styling: Shannon Beare
Food for Photography: Clare Lewis, assisted by Sascha Brodie
Illustrators: Angela Wood (artworks) and David Cook (map)
Production Controller: Claire Rae
Picture Credits: p 7 The Stock Market

ETHICAL TRADING POLICY
Because of our ongoing ecological investment programme, you, as our customer, can have the pleasure and reassurance of knowing that a tree is being cultivated on your behalf to naturally replace the materials used to make the book you are holding. For further information about this scheme, go to www.annesspublishing.com/trees

A CIP catalogue record for this book is available from the British Library.

Previously published as *From Borshch to Blinis*

NOTES
For all recipes, quantities are given in both metric and imperial measures and, where appropriate, in standard cups and spoons.
Follow one set of measures, but not a mixture, because they are not interchangeable.
Standard spoon and cup measures are level. 1 tsp = 5ml, 1 tbsp = 15ml, 1 cup = 250ml/8fl oz.
Australian standard tablespoons are 20ml. Australian readers should use 3 tsp in place of 1 tbsp for measuring small quantities.
American pints are 16fl oz/2 cups. American readers should use 20fl oz/2.5 cups in place of 1 pint when measuring liquids.
Electric oven temperatures in this book are for conventional ovens. When using a fan oven, the temperature will probably need to be reduced by about 10–20°C/20–40°F. Since ovens vary, you should check with your manufacturer's instruction book for guidance.
Medium (US large) eggs are used unless otherwise stated.

Main front cover image shows Russian Hamburgers – for recipe, see page 32

PUBLISHER'S NOTE
Although the advice and information in this book are believed to be accurate and true at the time of going to press, neither the authors nor the publisher can accept any legal responsibility or liability for any errors or omissions that may be made nor for any inaccuracies nor for any harm or injury that comes about from following instructions or advice in this book.

CONTENTS

INTRODUCTION

The region occupied by Russia, Poland and the Ukraine has a tradition of peasant cooking, defined by the tart flavours of sourdough rye bread, pickles and sauerkraut, and complemented by mushrooms, herring, onion and sausage. These simple foods reflect what the often poor soil yielded in the harsh climate, and what could be preserved by traditional means (in salt or vinegar or by drying) for year-round use. Hardy root and vegetable crops, a variety of grains, the flavours of garlic, mustard and horseradish, and sour dairy products, such as yogurt and buttermilk (the Russian *kefir*), were the region's staples. Cabbage and cucumbers, fresh or pickled, were the primary sources of vitamin C in what, for centuries, was a highly restricted diet.

RELIGIOUS INFLUENCES
In Russia and those parts of the Ukraine where the Russian Orthodox Church determined popular eating habits, at least until the beginning of the 20th century, the Church made a virtue out of economic necessity. It divided foods into two groups. For over half the days of the year only Lenten fare was allowed: vegetables, fish and mushrooms. Milk, eggs and meat were permitted on the remaining days.

The result of this intervention was a good number of simple, versatile recipes. A full meal might consist of a cabbage soup with a grain porridge called *kasha*. Meat, if available, would be cooked in the soup but served separately afterwards. On full fast days, mushrooms could be substituted for meat to give the soup flavour and perhaps to fill little pies or *pirozhki* to eat alongside it.

Buckwheat pancakes and soured cream, typical of the meat-free Carnival Week, now rank among the best-liked Russian dishes in the world. Russian Easter food, centred on roast suckling pig basted in soured cream and a cake, *kulich*, served with a sweet cream cheese, is a splendidly rich contrast with the simpler Lenten food that precedes it.

In Poland, there are 12 Lenten dishes – to equal the number of apostles – including a beetroot soup, herring, carp in black sauce and a mushroom dish. Christmas is an important time for the Roman Catholic Church and the elaborate Polish meal on Christmas Eve is gastronomically typical.

RECENT CHANGES
Two factors in the 19th century began to modernize the East European peasant diet. One was the industrialization that brought peasants into the towns and saw middle-class cooking influenced by cosmopolitan ideas. The other was the impact of the eating habits of the royal courts on the cuisines of both Russia and Poland, which eventually filtered down through the aristocracy to the bourgeoisie.

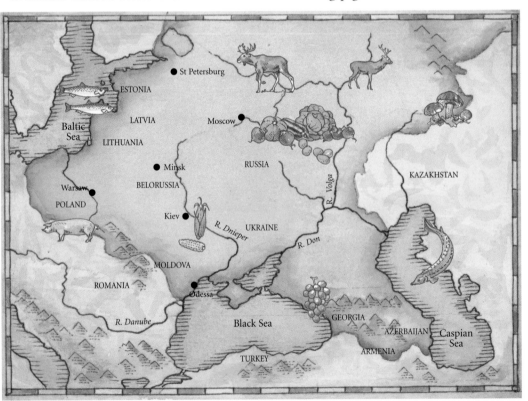

Left: The recipes in this book cover an area that stretches from the Baltic Sea in the north to the Caspian and Black Seas in the south. From Russia, the Baltic countries and Poland in the north, through the Ukraine and down to the edge of Turkey and the Middle East, these recipes reflect the wonderful diversity and the overall defining culinary characteristics of classic East European food.

Right: Open-air cooking on a large scale in Yakut, former USSR.

THE ROYAL COURTS

The Polish court flourished in the 16th century, when Poland's empire stretched from the Baltic to the Black Sea and the educated minority enjoyed an artistic and political culture, rich in contacts with Renaissance Europe. The Italian connection was particularly strong, due to the Italian-born Queen Bona Sforza who brought with her an entourage and ideas about cooking when she married King Sigismund in 1518. As a consequence, southern European vegetables were planted in the garden of the Royal Court at Krakow. Bona Sforza is also associated with Polish ice cream, pasta and cakes – Polish *babka* being really a first cousin to Italian *panettone*.

In the 19th century, access to French cookery books led to Polish cooking becoming richer than Russian in, for example, sauces and composite tastes. At the same time, however, the Russian upper classes also felt under constant pressure to "Frenchify" their own cooking, the court and aristocracy mainly employing French chefs to produce elaborate dishes, replete with butter and cream. Antonin Carême, as cook to Alexander I (Tsar 1801–25), began a task that was continued by four generations of foreign chefs up to the Russian Revolution.

Generally, however, there was always opposition to this outside influence, and patriotic palates preferred the traditional breads, grains and soups. One such example is *borshch*, the famous beetroot soup, whose origin cannot be fixed within any present-day national confines. It can be served as a consommé or as a thick soup.

By contrast the Russian cold table, originally borrowed from Scandinavia during the reign of the

great Westernizing Tsar, Peter I (1682-1725), has been wholly incorporated into the national cuisine as the classic first course. Comprising little open sandwich hors d'oeuvres, these *zakuski* dishes, which are washed down with ice-cold vodka, deserve their fame, especially as the jewel of the *zakuski* table is often caviare.

Ingredients

Vegetables and Mushrooms

Ridge cucumbers, with a firm texture and full flavour, are either used fresh in salads or pickled in bottles for winter. Other popular vegetables are beetroot, potato, carrots, parsnips and fresh cabbage, all of which grow well in a cold climate and can be stored all year round. Cabbage is also fermented in brine, with spices, to make the widely available sauerkraut. As for spring onions, both the white bulbs and the green tips contribute to the characteristic flavour of East European composite salads.

The romance of mushroom hunting belongs to the forests of Eastern Europe, where many varieties are found. Mushrooms are dried for use in soups and sauces, or salted or pickled for snacks with bread and vodka. They are also sautéed fresh in butter and herbs, or sauced with soured cream.

Top left, clockwise from left: pickled beetroot, sauerkraut, pickled cucumbers, dill pickles and caperberries.

Top right, clockwise: red and white cabbage, beetroot, cucumbers, mushrooms, parsnips, potatoes and carrots.

Right, from top left: Black and red lumpfish roe, salmon caviar, pike, salmon, carp and herring.

Fish

The most celebrated fish of this region belong to the sturgeon family. Of this family, both the beluga and the sevruga produce the highly prized black caviare. Freshwater salmon varieties are also very important, both for their firm flesh and for the "red" caviare so often seen on *zakuski* tables. Carp is traditional in Poland and is nowadays farmed. Herring is popular everywhere, although increasingly only the canned product is available. Pike, perch and pike-perch are the grand old river fish, yielding a firm white flesh that is suitable for pies and baked fish dishes.

Dairy Products

Soured cream takes the place of an oil in dressing East European salad of raw and cooked vegetables. It is the essential accompaniment to soups and pancakes and the basis for modern sauced dishes such as Beef Stroganov. It is also used in baking cakes and biscuits.

The traditional East European cheeses are made with cow's milk and are young and mild. Curd cheese is used to make savoury dip and *paskha*, the sweet Easter cream. Curd cheese can be used alone or with other ingredients to make savoury or sweet patties; it is also used to stuff pasta and pies, and forms the basis for the traditional cheesecake. *Brinza*, similar to Gree feta, is a brine cheese common all over Eastern and Central Europe, which appears in starters and pies.

Meat Dishes

Sucking pig is a traditional Russian delicacy, as is the game bird called *ryabchik*, or hazel-hen. Plentiful use is made of beef for braising and stewing. Polish sausage is made of top-quality pork and veal, flavoure with garlic and mustard seed.

GRAINS

The Russian word *kasha* and the related words in Polish and Ukrainian denote any cooked grain. Semolina, millet, oats and buckwheat are eaten at breakfast, usually cooked in water or milk and served with butter. Buckwheat, rice, millet or barley accompany savoury dishes. Buckwheat, actually a relative of the rhubarb family rather than a grain, is cooked into *kasha* and its flour is used to make traditional Shrovetide pancakes, or *blini*. It grows prolifically in Eastern Europe, and its recognizable smoky taste is characteristic of traditional peasant cooking.

Sourdough breads from this area have a distinctive, satisfying quality, thanks to their being made with rye flour by a sour fermentation process. This produces long-lasting loaves with excellent digestive properties, ranging from straw-coloured bread to the distinctly black Russian *borodinsky*, which is made with molasses and has its crust studded with coriander seeds.

HERBS, SPICES AND OTHER FLAVOURINGS

Dill, the most common herb in Eastern and Central European cooking, adds a distinct freshness to pickles as well as to salads and cooked dishes. The feathery leaves needed for authentic cooking lose much of their taste when dried so they should always be used fresh. The pungent seeds can be used in sauerkraut dishes and stews. Parsley, of the pungent, flat leaf variety, is also widely used in soups and salads and as a garnish, while the root adds flavour to stocks and soup bases. Fresh garlic adds piquancy to soups and stews, while mustard and horseradish give bite to fish and meat dishes.

FRUIT

East Europe has a strong tradition of domestic jam-making and bottling every available fruit and vegetable, from excellent plum jam to pickled spiced tomatoes. Less solid jams, which preserve the whole fruits, such as Russian

blackcurrant *varen'ye*, are traditionally served in a small saucer with tea, or to accompany a breakfast bowl of semolina *kasha*.

DRINKS

Russians drink tea that is either imported from the Far East or grown in Georgia. The tea is brewed in a small pot on top of the samovar, and diluted with water from the urn below. In Poland, under strong Central European and Italian influence, coffee is more popular. As for alcohol, both Poland and Russia claim to be the home of vodka, which has been made in Eastern Europe since at least the 15th century. Distilled, ideally from rye, it is then purified and water added. Small additions of barley, oats, buckwheat or wheat, herbs and tree bark give further flavour. Additions to the finished vodka make for specialities such as pepper vodka, which is used as a remedy for colds. Plain vodka is best for the *zakuski* table, however, served ice cold and downed in a single gulp.

Top, clockwise from back: dill, flat-leaved parsley, sour cream, cream, horseradish and fresh garlic bulbs.

Left, clockwise from top left: buckwheat flour, semolina, whole rolled porridge oats, pot barley, millet and raw buckwheat (centre).

SOUPS AND STARTERS

*The classic soups of Eastern Europe have remained unchanged for centuries.
Shchi, based on cabbage, is a north Russian speciality, while* borshch *is
made from beetroot and is popular in the south and throughout Poland and
the Ukraine. The balance of sweet and sour is typical, with the use of
fermented juice or pickled vegetables. Many hors d'oeuvres served in the west
originated as Russian starters. Caviare is probably the most famous of these,
traditionally served with small glasses of ice-cold vodka.*

Pea and Barley Soup

This thick and warming soup, *Grochówka*, makes a substantial starter, or it may be served as a meal in its own right, eaten with hot crusty bread.

INGREDIENTS

Serves 6
225g/8oz/1¼ cups yellow split peas
25g/1oz/¼ cup pearl barley
1.75 litres/3 pints/7½ cups vegetable or ham stock
50g/2oz smoked streaky bacon, cubed
25g/1oz/2 tbsp butter
1 onion, finely chopped
2 garlic cloves, crushed
225g/8oz celeriac, cubed
15ml/1 tbsp chopped fresh marjoram
salt and freshly ground black pepper
bread, to serve

1 Rinse the peas and barley in a sieve under cold running water. Put in a bowl, cover with plenty of water and leave to soak overnight.

2 The next day, drain and rinse the peas and barley. Put them in a large pan, pour in the stock and bring to the boil. Turn down the heat and simmer gently for 40 minutes.

3 Dry fry the bacon cubes in a frying pan for 5 minutes, or until well browned and crispy. Remove with a slotted spoon, leaving the fat behind, and set aside.

4 Add the butter to the frying pan, add the onion and garlic and cook gently for 5 minutes. Add the celeriac and cook for a further 5 minutes, or until the onion is just starting to colour.

5 Add the softened vegetables and bacon to the pan of stock, peas and barley. Season lightly with salt and pepper, then cover and simmer for 20 minutes, or until the soup is thick. Stir in the marjoram, add extra black pepper to taste and serve with bread.

Borshch

Beetroot is the main ingredient of *Borshch*, and its flavour and colour dominate this well-known soup. It is a classic of both Russia and Poland.

INGREDIENTS

Serves 4–6

900g/2lb uncooked beetroot, peeled
2 carrots, peeled
2 celery sticks
40g/1½oz/3 tbsp butter
2 onions, sliced
2 garlic cloves, crushed
4 tomatoes, peeled, seeded and chopped
1 bay leaf
1 large parsley sprig
2 cloves
4 whole peppercorns
1.2 litres/2 pints/5 cups beef or chicken stock
150ml/¼ pint/⅔ cup beetroot *kvas* (see *Cook's Tip*) or the liquid from pickled beetroot
salt and freshly ground black pepper
soured cream, garnished with snipped fresh chives or sprigs of dill, to serve

1 Cut the beetroot, carrots and celery into fairly thick strips. Melt the butter in a large pan and cook the onions over a low heat for 5 minutes, stirring occasionally.

2 Add the beetroot, carrots and celery and cook for a further 5 minutes, stirring occasionally.

3 Add the garlic and chopped tomatoes to the pan and cook, stirring, for 2 more minutes.

4 Place the bay leaf, parsley, cloves and peppercorns in a piece of muslin and tie with string.

5 Add the muslin bag to the pan with the stock. Bring to the boil, reduce the heat, cover and simmer for 1¼ hours, or until the vegetables are very tender. Discard the bag. Stir in the beetroot *kvas* and season. Bring to the boil. Ladle into bowls and serve with soured cream garnished with chives or dill.

— COOK'S TIP —

Beetroot *kvas*, fermented beetroot juice, adds an intense colour and a slight tartness. If unavailable, peel and grate 1 beetroot, add 150ml/¼ pint/⅔ cup stock and 10ml/2 tsp lemon juice. Bring to the boil, cover and leave for 30 minutes. Strain before using.

Fresh Cabbage Shchi

This version of Russia's national dish is made from fresh cabbage rather than sauerkraut.

INGREDIENTS

Serves 4–6
1 small turnip
2 carrots
40g/1½oz/3 tbsp butter
1 large onion, sliced
2 celery sticks, sliced
1 white cabbage, about 675g/1½lb
1.2 litres/2 pints/5 cups beef stock
1 sharp eating apple, cored, peeled and chopped
2 bay leaves
5ml/1 tsp chopped fresh dill
10ml/2 tsp pickled cucumber juice or lemon juice
salt and freshly ground black pepper
fresh herbs, to garnish
soured cream and black bread, to serve

1 Cut the turnip and carrots into matchstick strips. Melt the butter in a large pan and fry the turnip, carrot, onion and celery for 10 minutes.

2 Shred the cabbage, and add to the pan with the stock, apple, bay leaves and dill and bring to the boil. Cover and simmer for 40 minutes or until the vegetables are really tender.

3 Remove the bay leaves, then stir in the pickled cucumber juice or lemon juice and season with plenty of salt and pepper. Serve hot, garnished with fresh herbs and accompanied by soured cream and black bread.

Sorrel and Spinach Soup

This is an excellent Russian summer soup. If sorrel is unavailable, use double the amount of spinach instead and add a dash of lemon juice to the soup just before serving.

INGREDIENTS

Serves 4
25g/1oz/2 tbsp butter
225g/8oz sorrel, washed and stalks removed
225g/8oz young spinach, washed and stalks removed
25g/1oz fresh horseradish, grated
750ml/1¼ pints/3 cups *kvas* or cider
1 pickled cucumber, finely chopped
30ml/2 tbsp chopped fresh dill
225g/8oz cooked fish, such as pike, perch or salmon, skinned and boned
salt and freshly ground black pepper
sprig of dill, to garnish

1 Melt the butter in a large pan. Add the sorrel and spinach leaves and fresh horseradish. Cover and gently cook for 3–4 minutes, or until the leaves are wilted.

2 Spoon into a food processor and process to a fine purée. Ladle into a tureen or bowl and stir in the *kvas* or cider, cucumber and dill.

3 Chop the fish into bite-size pieces. Add to the soup, then season with plenty of salt and pepper. Chill for at least 3 hours before serving, garnished with a sprig of dill.

--- COOK'S TIP ---

Kvas is a Russian beer made by fermenting wheat, rye and buckwheat.

Mixed Mushroom Solyanka

The tart flavours of pickled cucumber, capers and lemon add extra bite to this rich soup.

INGREDIENTS

Serves 4
2 onions, chopped
1.2 litres/2 pints/5 cups vegetable
  stock
450g/1lb/6 cups mushrooms, sliced
20ml/4 tsp tomato purée
1 pickled cucumber, chopped
1 bay leaf
15ml/1 tbsp capers in brine, drained
pinch of salt
6 peppercorns, crushed
lemon rind curls, green olives and
  sprigs of flat leaf parsley, to garnish

1 Put the onions in a large pan with 50ml/2fl oz/¼ cup of the stock. Cook, stirring occasionally, until the liquid has evaporated.

2 Add the remaining vegetable stock with the sliced mushrooms, bring to the boil, cover and simmer gently for 30 minutes.

3 In a small bowl, blend the tomato purée with 30ml/2 tbsp of stock.

4 Add the tomato purée to the pan with the pickled cucumber, bay leaf, capers, salt and peppercorns. Cook gently for 10 more minutes.

5 Ladle the soup into warmed bowls and sprinkle lemon rind curls, a few olives and a sprig of flat leaf parley over each bowl before serving.

Grandfather's Soup

This soup derives its name from the fact that it is easily digested and therefore thought to be suitable for the elderly.

INGREDIENTS

Serves 4

1 large onion, finely sliced
25g/1oz/2 tbsp butter
350g/12oz potatoes, peeled and diced
900ml/1½ pints/3¾ cups beef stock
1 bay leaf
salt and freshly ground black pepper

For the drop noodles
75g/3oz/⅔ cup self-raising flour
pinch of salt
15g/½oz/1 tbsp butter
15ml/1 tbsp chopped fresh parsley,
   plus a little extra to garnish
1 egg, beaten
chunks of bread, to serve

1 In a wide heavy-based pan, cook the onion in the butter gently for 10 minutes, or until it begins to brown.

2 Add the diced potatoes and cook for 2–3 minutes, then pour in the stock. Add the bay leaf, salt and pepper. Bring to the boil, then reduce the heat, cover and simmer for 10 minutes.

--- COOK'S TIP ---

Use old potatoes, of a floury texture, such as King Edward or Maris Piper.

3 Meanwhile, make the noodles. Sift the flour and salt into a bowl and rub in the butter. Stir in the parsley, then add the egg to the flour mixture and mix to a soft dough.

4 Drop half-teaspoonfuls of the dough into the simmering soup. Cover and simmer gently for a further 10 minutes. Ladle the soup into warmed soup bowls, scatter over a little parsley, and serve immediately with chunks of bread.

Creamy Kohlrabi Soup

Kohlrabi has always been a popular Polish vegetable, since it tolerates frost and can be stored for a long time. *Zupa z Kalarepy* is a good example of how it can form the basis for simple, hearty dishes.

INGREDIENTS

Serves 4

450g/1lb kohlrabi
25g/1oz/2 tbsp butter
1 onion, roughly chopped
600ml/1 pint/2½ cups
  vegetable stock
600ml/1 pint/2½ cups milk
1 bay leaf
25g/1oz/¼ cup small pasta shapes
salt and freshly ground black pepper

1 Peel and dice the kohlrabi and set aside.

COOK'S TIP

Kohlrabi are usually sold trimmed; if you find them with leaves, shred them if large and use as a garnish, either raw or steamed.

2 Melt the butter in a large pan. Add the onion and cook gently for 10 minutes, or until soft. Add the diced kohlrabi and cook for 2 minutes.

3 Add the vegetable stock, milk and bay leaf to the pan. Bring to the boil, then cover and simmer for 25 minutes, or until the kohlrabi is tender. Let cool for a few minutes and remove the bay leaf.

4 Purée the soup until smooth (you may need to do this in batches) and season with salt and pepper. Bring to the boil, then sprinkle in the pasta. Cover and simmer for 10 minutes, or until the pasta is cooked. Serve with bread.

Creamed Mushrooms

This Russian starter, traditionally made with ceps, is delicious served with warm plain *blini*.

INGREDIENTS

Serves 4
450g/1lb/6 cups mushrooms
50g/2oz/4 tbsp butter
1 small onion, finely sliced
300ml/¹/₂ pint/1¹/₄ cups soured cream
30ml/2 tbsp chopped fresh dill
salt and freshly ground black pepper
warm, plain blini, to serve

1 Rinse the mushrooms under cold water. Drain well, then slice thinly.

2 Melt the butter in a frying pan and cook the sliced onion for 5 minutes.

3 Add the sliced mushrooms to the pan and cook over a high heat for 3 minutes, stirring all the time.

4 Stir in the soured cream and chopped dill. Season with plenty of salt and pepper. Bring to the boil and simmer for 1 minute. Serve immediately, with warm blini.

Eggs with Caviare

Caviare is the roe from the huge sturgeon fish that swim in the Caspian Sea. It is often served on its own, in a bowl set over crushed ice, with a glass of chilled neat vodka. Alternatively, it may be used sparingly, as in this Ukrainian recipe, as a garnish.

INGREDIENTS

Serves 4
6 eggs, hard-boiled and halved, lengthways
4 spring onions, very finely sliced
30ml/2 tbsp mayonnaise
1.5ml/¼ tsp Dijon mustard
25g/1oz/2 tbsp caviare or black lumpfish roe
salt and freshly ground black pepper
small sprigs of dill, to garnish
watercress, to serve

1 Remove the yolks from the halved eggs. Mash the yolks to a smooth paste in a bowl with the spring onions, mayonnaise and mustard. Mix well and season with salt and pepper.

2 Fill the egg whites with the yolk mixture and arrange them on a serving dish. Spoon a little caviare or roe on top of each before serving with watercress.

TYPES OF CAVIARE

Beluga is the largest member of the sturgeon family, and the eggs are a pearly-grey colour. **Oscietra** comes from a smaller sturgeon, and the eggs have a golden tinge. **Sevruga** caviare is less expensive than other types, as it produces eggs at a much younger age. **Lumpfish roe,** not a true caviare, has black or orange eggs. **Salmon roe**, from the red salmon, has large, translucent pinky-orange eggs.

Aubergine "Caviare"

The word "caviare" is used to describe spreads and dips made from cooked vegetables. The aubergine is the vegetable most widely used in this way, and many Ukrainian families have their own secret recipe.

INGREDIENTS

Serves 4–6
1.5kg/3lb aubergines
1 onion, very finely chopped
1 garlic clove, crushed
75ml/5 tbsp olive oil
450g/1lb tomatoes, peeled and chopped
5ml/1 tsp lemon juice
150ml/¼ pint/⅔ cup natural yogurt
5ml/1 tsp salt
freshly ground black pepper
spring onion slices, to garnish
toasted bread twists, to serve

1 Preheat the oven to 180°C/350°F/ Gas 4. Put the aubergines on an oiled rack over a roasting tin. Bake in the oven for 25–30 minutes, or until soft. Leave to cool.

2 Meanwhile, fry the finely chopped onion and garlic in 15ml/1 tbsp of the oil for 10 minutes.

3 Using a spoon, remove the baked aubergine flesh, then purée in a food processor until smooth. With the motor running, add the remaining oil.

4 Spoon into a bowl. Stir in the onions, tomatoes, lemon juice and yogurt, salt and pepper to taste. Cover with clear film and chill for 4 hours. To serve, garnish with spring onions and accompany with toasted bread twists.

Herring Pâté

Vast quantities of herring are fished in the Baltic Sea to the north of Poland. A traditional Polish hors d'oeuvre, *Pasta Śledziowa* is usually served with tiny glasses of ice-cold vodka.

INGREDIENTS

Serves 4
2 fresh herrings, filleted
50g/2oz/4 tbsp butter, softened
5ml/1 tsp creamed horseradish sauce
freshly ground black pepper

To serve
4 slices rye bread
1 small onion, cut into rings
1 red eating apple, cored and sliced
15ml/1 tbsp lemon juice
45ml/3 tbsp soured cream

1 Chop the herrings into pieces and put in a food processor with the butter, horseradish sauce and pepper. Process until smooth.

2 Spoon the herring pâté into a bowl. Cover with clear film and chill for at least 1 hour.

3 Serve the pâté on rye bread, add onion rings and apple slices, tossed in lemon juice. Top with a little soured cream and garnish with dill.

Little Finger Biscuits

These savoury Polish biscuits, *paluszki*, are delicious served warm or cold with soup or dips, or on their own as a snack.

INGREDIENTS

Makes 30
115g/4oz/8 tbsp butter, softened
115g/4oz/1⅓ cups mashed potato
150g/5oz/1¼ cups plain flour, plus
   extra for dusting
2.5ml/½ tsp salt
1 egg, beaten
30ml/2 tbsp caraway seeds

1 Preheat the oven to 220°C/425°F/ Gas 7. Put the butter and mashed potato in a large bowl. Sift the flour and salt into the bowl, then mix to a soft dough.

2 Knead the dough on a lightly floured surface for a few seconds, or until smooth. Wrap in clear film and chill for 30 minutes.

3 Roll out the potato dough on a lightly floured surface until 8mm/⅓in thick. Brush with beaten egg, then cut into strips 2 × 7.5cm/ ¾ × 3in. Transfer to an oiled baking sheet and sprinkle with caraway seeds.

4 Bake for 12 minutes, or until lightly browned. Transfer to a wire rack and leave to cool. Store in an airtight container.

Pirozhki

Homemade *pirozhki* are great favourites of old and young alike. They look splendid piled high and golden brown.

INGREDIENTS

Makes 35
225g/8oz/2 cups strong white flour
2.5ml/½ tsp salt
2.5ml/½ tsp caster sugar
5ml/1 tsp easy-blend dried yeast
25g/1oz/2 tbsp butter, softened
1 egg, beaten, plus a little extra
90ml/6 tbsp warm milk

For the filling
1 small onion, finely chopped
175g/6oz minced chicken
15ml/1 tbsp sunflower oil
75ml/5 tbsp chicken stock
30ml/2 tbsp chopped fresh parsley
pinch of grated nutmeg
salt and freshly ground black pepper

1 Sift the flour, salt and sugar into a large bowl. Stir in the dried yeast, then make a well in the centre.

2 Add the butter, egg and milk and mix to a soft dough. Turn on to a lightly floured surface and knead for 10 minutes, until smooth and elastic.

3 Put the dough in a clean bowl, cover with clear film and leave in a warm place to rise for 1 hour, or until the dough has doubled in size.

4 Meanwhile, fry the onion and chicken in the oil for 10 minutes. Add the stock and simmer for 5 minutes. Stir in the parsley, nutmeg and salt and pepper. Leave to cool.

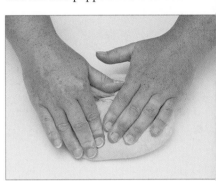

5 Preheat the oven to 220°C/425°F/ Gas 7. Knead the dough, then roll out until 3mm/⅛ in thick. Stamp out rounds with a 7.5cm/3in cutter.

6 Brush the edges with beaten egg. Put a little filling in the middle, then press the edges together. Leave to rise on oiled baking sheets, covered with oiled clear film, for 15 minutes. Brush with a little more egg. Bake for 5 minutes, then for 10 minutes at 190°C/375°F/ Gas 5, until well risen.

Buckwheat Blini

Traditionally eaten during the meatless week before Lent, both sweet and savoury toppings can be used; soured cream and caviare is the most famous.

INGREDIENTS

Serves 4
75g/3oz/²⁄₃ cup plain flour
50g/2oz/½ cup buckwheat or
  wheatmeal flour
2.5ml/½ tsp salt
5ml/1 tsp easy-blend dried yeast
175ml/6fl oz/¾ cup warm milk
25g/1oz/2 tbsp butter, melted
1 egg, separated
45ml/3 tbsp oil

For the toppings
150ml/5fl oz/²⁄₃ cup soured cream
30ml/2 tbsp chopped fresh dill
60g/2oz/4 tbsp red or black
  lumpfish roe
115g/4oz smoked mackerel, skinned,
  boned and flaked
60g/2oz/4 tbsp unsalted butter,
  softened
finely grated rind of ½ lemon
shredded lemon rind, to garnish
lemon wedges, to serve

1 Sift the flours and salt into a large bowl, adding any bran left in the sieve. Stir in the easy-blend yeast, then make a well in the centre.

2 Pour in the milk and gradually beat in the flour until smooth. Cover with clear film and leave to rise for 1 hour, or until doubled in size.

3 Stir in the melted butter and egg yolk. Whisk the egg white in a bowl until stiff and then gently fold in. Cover and leave to stand for 20 minutes.

4 Heat 15ml/1 tbsp of the oil in a large, heavy frying pan over a medium heat and drop in about 4 spoonfuls of batter. Cook for 1–2 minutes, or until bubbles appear on top.

5 Turn them over and cook for a further 1 minute, or until both sides are brown. Remove the blini from the pan and keep them moist in a folded clean dish towel.

6 Repeat the process with the remaining batter, adding a little oil to the pan when needed, to make about 24 blini. Allow to cool.

7 Arrange the blini on a serving plate. Use the soured cream and chopped dill to top half of the blini. Spoon 5ml/1 tsp lumpfish roe on top of the soured cream and dill.

8 In another bowl, mix the smoked mackerel, butter and lemon rind together and use to top the remaining blini. Garnish with shredded lemon rind. Serve with lemon wedges.

Olivier Salad

In the 1880s the French chef, Olivier, opened a restaurant in Moscow called the Hermitage. It became one of the most famous dining clubs in the city, where many innovative dishes were served. Olivier later published a book of everyday Russian cooking and gave his name to this elaborate salad.

INGREDIENTS

Serves 6

2 young grouse or partridges
6 juniper berries, crushed
40g/1½oz/3 tbsp butter, softened
2 small onions, each stuck with
   3 cloves
2 streaky bacon rashers, halved
10 baby potatoes, unpeeled
1 cucumber
2 Little Gem lettuces, separated
   into leaves
2 eggs, hard-boiled and quartered

For the dressing

1 egg yolk
5ml/1 tsp Dijon mustard
175ml/6fl oz/¾ cup light olive oil
60ml/4 tbsp white wine vinegar
salt and freshly ground black pepper

1 Preheat the oven to 200°C/400°F/ Gas 6. Put the grouse or partridges in a small roasting tin. Mix the juniper berries and the butter together and tuck half the juniper butter and one clove-studded onion into the vent of each of the birds.

2 Lay 2 bacon pieces over each breast. Roast for 30 minutes, or until the juices run only slightly pink when the thigh is pierced with a skewer.

3 Leave to cool, then cut the meat into 2.5cm/1in pieces.

4 Meanwhile, cook the potatoes in boiling salted water for about 20 minutes, or until tender. Allow to cool, then peel and cut into 1cm/½in slices.

COOK'S TIP

Cold roast beef can be used instead of the game, if you prefer.

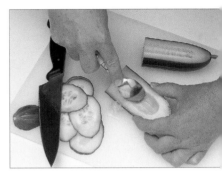

5 Cut a few slices of cucumber for garnishing and set aside. Halve the remaining cucumber lengthways, remove the seeds and dice.

6 To make the dressing, put the egg yolk, mustard and a little salt and pepper in a small bowl and whisk together. Add the olive oil in a thin stream, whisking all the time until thickened, then stir in the vinegar.

7 Put the pieces of meat, potato and cucumber in a bowl. Pour over half the dressing and mix carefully. Arrange the lettuce leaves on a serving platter and pile the salad in the middle.

8 Garnish with the reserved cucumber slices and the quartered hard-boiled eggs. Serve with the remaining dressing.

MEAT AND POULTRY

Although beef, poultry and game are eaten in Russia, Poland and the Ukraine, pork is by far the most popular meat. Whole joints are usually marinated to produce tender and succulent meat, and pork is the main ingredient of kielbasa, *the famous Polish sausage exported all over the world. Throughout the region, frequent food shortages in history have called for ingenuity in making a little go a long way, and many recipes reflect this by cleverly combining a number of meats with herbs, spices and pickled vegetables.*

Liver and Bacon Varenyky

There is an old Ukrainian superstition that if *varenyky* are counted, the dough will split and the filling spill out.

INGREDIENTS

Serves 4

200g/7oz/1¾ cups plain flour
1.5ml/¼ tsp salt
2 eggs, beaten
15g/½oz/1 tbsp butter, melted
beaten egg, for sealing
15ml/1 tbsp sunflower oil

For the filling

15ml/1 tbsp sunflower oil
½ small onion, finely chopped
115g/4oz smoked streaky bacon,
    roughly chopped
225g/8oz chicken or lamb's liver,
    roughly chopped
30ml/2 tbsp snipped fresh chives, plus
    extra for garnish
salt and freshly ground black pepper

1 Sift the flour and salt into a bowl. Make a well in the centre. Add the eggs and butter and mix to a dough.

2 Knead the dough on a lightly floured surface for 2–3 minutes, until smooth. Wrap in clear film and leave to rest for 30 minutes.

3 For the filling, heat the oil in a pan and cook the onion for 5 minutes. Add the bacon and cook for a further 4–5 minutes. Stir in the liver and cook for 1 minute, until browned.

4 Put the liver mixture in a food processor or blender and process until it is finely chopped, but not smooth. Add the snipped chives and season with salt and pepper. Process for a few more seconds.

5 Roll out the dough on a lightly floured surface until 3mm/⅛in thick. Stamp out rounds of dough with a 5cm/2in cutter.

6 Spoon a teaspoon of filling into the middle of each round. Brush the edges of the dough with beaten egg and fold in half to make half-moon shapes. Leave to dry on a floured dish towel for 30 minutes.

7 Bring a pan of salted water to the boil. Add the oil, then add the *varenyky*, in batches if necessary. Bring back to the boil and cook them at a gentle simmer for 10 minutes, until tender. Drain well and serve hot, garnished with snipped chives. Serve with fresh capers.

Roast Loin of Pork with Apple Stuffing

A spit-roasted sucking pig, basted with butter or cream and served with an apple in its mouth, was a classic dish for the Russian festive table. This roasted loin with crisp crackling makes a less expensive alternative.

INGREDIENTS

Serves 6–8

1.75kg/4lb boned loin of pork
300ml/½ pint/1¼ cups dry cider
150ml/¼ pint/⅔ cup soured cream
7.5ml/1½ tsp sea salt

For the stuffing

25g/1oz/2 tbsp butter
1 small onion, chopped
50g/2oz/1 cup fresh white
    breadcrumbs
2 apples, cored, peeled and chopped
50g/2oz/scant ½ cup raisins
finely grated rind of 1 orange
pinch of ground cloves
salt and freshly ground black pepper

1 Preheat the oven to 220°C/425°F/ Gas 7. To make the stuffing, melt the butter in a pan and gently fry the onion for 10 minutes, or until soft. Stir into the remaining stuffing ingredients.

2 Put the pork, rind side down, on a board. Make a horizontal cut between the meat and outer layer of fat, cutting to within 2.5cm/1in of the edges to make a pocket.

3 Push the stuffing into the pocket. Roll up lengthways and tie with string. Score the rind at 2cm/¾in intervals with a sharp knife.

COOK'S TIP

Do not baste during the final 2 hours of roasting, so that the crackling becomes crisp.

4 Pour the cider and soured cream into a casserole, in which the joint just fits. Stir to combine, then add the pork, rind side down. Cook, uncovered, in the oven for 30 minutes.

5 Turn the joint over, so that the rind is on top. Baste with the juices, then sprinkle the rind with sea salt. Cook for 1 hour, basting after 30 minutes.

6 Reduce the oven temperature to 180°C/350°F/Gas 4. Cook for a further 1½ hours. Leave the joint to stand for 20 minutes before carving.

Russian Hamburgers

Every Russian family has its own version of this homely hamburger. The mixture can also be shaped into small round meatballs known as *bitki*, which make irresistible snacks.

INGREDIENTS

Serves 4
115g/4oz/2 cups fresh white
   breadcrumbs
45ml/3 tbsp milk
450g/1lb finely minced beef, lamb
   or veal
1 egg, beaten
30ml/2 tbsp plain flour
30ml/2 tbsp sunflower oil
salt and freshly ground black pepper
tomato sauce, pickled vegetables and
   crispy fried onions, to serve

1 Put the breadcrumbs in a bowl and spoon over the milk. Leave to soak for 10 minutes. Add the minced meat, egg, salt and pepper and mix all the ingredients together thoroughly.

2 Divide the mixture into 4 equal portions and shape into ovals, each about 10cm/4in long and 5cm/2in wide. Coat each with the flour.

3 Heat the oil in a frying pan and fry the burgers for about 8 minutes on each side. Serve with a tomato sauce, pickled vegetables and fried onions.

Beef Stroganov

At the end of the 19th century, Alexander Stroganov gave his name to this now well-known Russian dish of beef and onions cooked with cream, and it became his signature dish when entertaining at his home in Odessa. Finely cut potato chips are the classic accompaniment.

INGREDIENTS

Serves 4
450g/1lb fillet or rump steak, trimmed
15ml/1 tbsp sunflower oil
25g/1oz/2 tbsp unsalted butter
1 onion, sliced
15ml/1 tbsp plain flour
5ml/1 tsp tomato purée
5ml/1 tsp Dijon mustard
5ml/1 tsp lemon juice
150ml/¼ pint/⅔ cup soured cream
salt and freshly ground black pepper
fresh herbs, to garnish

1 Place the steak between 2 oiled sheets of clear film. Gently beat with a rolling pin to flatten and tenderize the meat. Cut it into thin strips about 5cm/2in long.

2 Heat the remaining oil and half the butter in a frying pan and fry the beef over a high heat for 2 minutes, or until browned. Remove the strips of beef from the pan with a slotted spoon, leaving any juices behind.

3 Melt the remaining butter in the pan and gently fry the onion for 10 minutes, until soft.

4 Sprinkle over the flour then stir it in, followed by the tomato purée, mustard, lemon juice and soured cream. Return the beef to the pan and stir until the sauce is bubbling. Season to taste with salt and pepper, and then serve immediately, garnished with fresh herbs, with deep-fried potato chips.

Bigos

Poland's national dish, *bigos*, is best made a day in advance.

Ingredients

Serves 8

15g/¹⁄₂oz/¹⁄₄ cup dried mushrooms
225g/8oz/1 cup stoned prunes
225g/8oz lean boneless pork
225g/8oz lean boneless venison
225g/8oz chuck steak
225g/8oz *kielbasa* (see Cook's Tip)
25g/1oz/¹⁄₄ cup plain flour
2 onions, sliced
45ml/3 tbsp olive oil
60ml/4 tbsp dry Madeira
900g/2lb can or packet sauerkraut, rinsed
4 tomatoes, peeled and chopped
4 cloves
5cm/2in cinnamon stick
1 bay leaf
2.5ml/¹⁄₂ tsp dill seeds
600ml/1 pint/2¹⁄₂ cups stock
salt and freshly ground black pepper

1 Pour boiling water to completely cover the dried mushrooms and prunes in a bowl. Leave for 30 minutes, then drain well.

2 Cut the pork, venison, chuck steak and *kielbasa* sausage into 2.5cm/1in cubes, then toss together in the flour. Gently fry the onions in the oil for 10 minutes. Remove.

3 Brown the meat in the pan in several batches, for about 5 minutes, or until well browned; remove and set aside. Add the Madeira and simmer for 2–3 minutes, stirring.

4 Return the meat to the pan with the onion, sauerkraut, tomatoes, cloves, cinnamon, bay leaf, dill seeds, mushrooms and prunes. Pour in the stock and season with salt and pepper.

5 Bring to the boil, cover and simmer gently for 1³⁄₄–2 hours, or until the meat is very tender. Uncover for the last 20 minutes to let the liquid evaporate, as the stew should be thick. Sprinkle with chopped parsley. Serve immediately with boiled new potatoes, tossed in chopped parsley.

— Cook's Tip —

Kielbasa is a garlic-flavoured pork and beef sausage, but any similar type of continental sausage can be used. Use porcini mushrooms, if possible.

Kovbasa

These Ukrainian pork and beef sausages can be made several days ahead and kept refrigerated.

INGREDIENTS

Serves 6

450g/1lb pork, such as shoulder
225g/8oz chuck steak
115g/4oz pork back fat
2 eggs, beaten
30ml/2 tbsp *peperivka* (see *Cook's Tip*)
    or pepper vodka
2.5ml/¹/₂ tsp ground allspice
5ml/1 tsp salt
about 1.75 litres/3 pints/7¹/₂ cups
    chicken stock
fresh parsley, to garnish
mashed potato, to serve

1 Mince the meats and pork back fat together, using the coarse blade of a mincer, then mince half the mixture again, this time using a fine blade.

2 Combine both the meat mixtures with the eggs, *peperivka*, allspice and salt. Check the seasoning by frying a small piece of the mixture, then tasting it. Adjust if necessary.

───── COOK'S TIP ─────

Spicing whisky with peppers to make *peperivka* is an old tradition in the Ukraine. Add 3 whole cayenne peppers, pricked all over with a fine skewer, to 150ml/¹/₄ pint/ ⅔ cup whisky or bourbon and leave for at least 48 hours.

3 Form the meat mixture into 2 sausages, about 20cm/8in long. Wrap in double muslin and tie securely with string.

4 Bring the stock to a gentle simmer in a large pan. Add the sausages and simmer gently, turning frequently, for 35–40 minutes, or until the juices run clear when the sausages are pierced with a fine skewer.

5 Leave the sausages in the stock for 20 minutes, then remove and leave to cool. Remove the muslin and sauté the sausages in oil to brown them. Garnish with parsley and serve with mashed potato, topped with butter.

Field-roasted Lamb

This unusual recipe, originally for mutton slowly roasted over charcoal, comes from the Russian steppes.

INGREDIENTS

Serves 6
1.75kg/4lb leg of lamb
4 large garlic cloves, cut into slivers
5ml/1 tsp whole peppercorns
300ml/½ pint/1¼ cups natural yogurt
15ml/1 tbsp olive oil
15ml/1 tbsp chopped fresh dill
300ml/½ pint/1¼ cups lamb or
　vegetable stock
30ml/2 tbsp lemon juice
potatoes, spinach and carrots, to serve

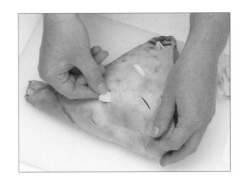

1 Make slits all over the lamb and insert generous slivers of fresh garlic into the slits.

2 Lightly crush the whole peppercorns in a pestle and mortar or rolling pin, if preferred.

3 Tip the yogurt, oil and crushed peppercorns into a bowl, then add the dill and mix together well.

4 Spread the yogurt paste evenly over the lamb. Put the lamb in a glass dish, cover loosely with foil and then refrigerate the lamb for 1–2 days, turning it twice.

5 Transfer the lamb to a roasting tin and let it come back to room temperature. Preheat the oven to 220°C/425°F/Gas 7. Remove the foil. Pour in the stock and lemon juice and cook, uncovered, for 20 minutes.

6 Reduce the oven temperature to 180°C/350°F/Gas 4 and continue roasting for a further 1¼–1½ hours, basting occasionally. Remove from the oven and keep covered in a warm place for 15–20 minutes before carving. Use the juices from the pan to make a gravy and serve with roast potatoes, boiled spinach and baby carrots.

Lamb Plov

Plov is the Russian name for this rice dish popular throughout Eastern Europe, known by different names – *pilau* in Turkey and *pilaf* in the Middle East.

INGREDIENTS

Serves 4
50g/2oz/scant ½ cup raisins
115g/4oz/½ cup stoned prunes
15ml/1 tbsp lemon juice
25g/1oz/2 tbsp butter
1 large onion, chopped
450g/1lb lamb fillet, trimmed and cut into 1cm/½in cubes
225g/8oz lean minced lamb
2 garlic cloves, crushed
600ml/1 pint/2½ cups lamb or vegetable stock
350g/12oz/scant 2 cups long-grain rice
large pinch of saffron
salt and freshly ground black pepper
sprigs of flat leaf parsley, to garnish

1 Put the raisins and prunes in a small bowl and pour over enough water to cover. Add the lemon juice and leave to soak for at least 1 hour. Drain, then roughly chop the prunes.

2 Meanwhile, heat the butter in a large pan and cook the onion for 5 minutes. Add the lamb fillet, minced lamb and garlic. Fry for 5 minutes, stirring constantly until browned.

3 Pour in 150ml/¼ pint/⅔ cup of the stock. Bring to the boil, then lower the heat, cover and simmer for 1 hour, or until the lamb is tender.

4 Add the remaining stock and bring to the boil. Add the rice and saffron. Stir, then cover and simmer for 15 minutes, or until the rice is tender.

5 Stir in the raisins, chopped prunes, salt and pepper. Heat through for a few minutes, then turn on to a warmed serving dish and garnish with sprigs of flat leaf parsley.

Golubtsy

These tasty Polish cabbage parcels are packed with a herby meat and grain stuffing. They are equally good made with minced lamb, beef or pork.

INGREDIENTS

Serves 4

1 large Savoy cabbage
30ml/2 tbsp sunflower oil
450g/1lb lean minced lamb, beef
   or pork
1 onion, finely chopped
5ml/1 tsp ground coriander
75ml/5 tbsp stock
115g/4oz/²/₃ cup cooked long-grain
   rice or buckwheat
30ml/2 tbsp chopped fresh parsley
25g/1oz/2 tbsp butter, melted
300ml/¹/₂ pint/1¹/₄ cups soured cream
30ml/2 tbsp tomato purée
1 bay leaf
salt and freshly ground black pepper

1 Preheat the oven to 180°C/350°F/ Gas 4. Carefully remove 12 outer leaves from the cabbage one at a time. Blanch them in a pan of boiling salted water for 4 minutes. Drain and pat dry on kitchen paper, then trim away the thick stalks.

2 To make the stuffing, heat half the oil in a frying pan. Add the meat and brown, stirring, for 5 minutes. Remove and set aside. Add the remaining oil and cook the onion for 5 minutes.

3 Stir in the coriander, then add the meat, stock, rice or buckwheat, half the parsley, salt and pepper. Simmer for 5 minutes.

4 Place 30ml/2 tbsp of stuffing on each leaf and wrap it up, tucking in the sides to make a parcel. Arrange in one layer in a greased ovenproof dish. Brush with melted butter.

5 Heat the soured cream, tomato purée and bay leaf gently, stirring until bubbling. Stir in the remaining parsley and season with salt and pepper.

6 Pour the sauce around the stuffed cabbage parcels and cover the dish with foil. Bake for 35 minutes, uncovering for the last 15 minutes, to allow the cabbage to brown.

COOK'S TIP

Instead of blanching the cabbage leaves in water, they can be softened by stacking them on top of each other, wrapping them in oiled foil, then baking at 180°C/350°F/ Gas 4 for 6 minutes.

Meatballs in Mushroom Sauce

These finely minced herby Russian meatballs, flavoured with vodka, are gently poached in a tasty stock.

INGREDIENTS

Serves 4

50g/2oz/4 tbsp butter
1 onion, roughly chopped
30ml/2 tbsp plain flour
150ml/¼ pint/⅔ cup milk
450g/1lb lean minced beef
30ml/2 tbsp vodka
1 egg
2.5ml/½ tsp salt
30ml/2 tbsp chopped fresh coriander
30ml/2 tbsp chopped fresh parsley
900ml/1½ pints/3¾ cups stock
2 bay leaves
freshly ground black pepper
sprigs of coriander, to garnish
plain boiled rice, to serve

For the sauce

25g/1oz/2 tbsp butter
115g/4oz/1½ cups small button mushrooms, halved
150ml/¼ pint/⅔ cup soured cream
salt and freshly ground black pepper

1 Melt the butter in a small pan and gently fry the onion for 5 minutes. Stir in the flour and cook for 2 minutes, stirring all the time. Remove the pan from the heat.

2 Gradually add the milk. Return the pan to the heat, bring to the boil and simmer for 2–3 minutes, until thick. Allow to cool for 10 minutes.

3 Tip the sauce into a food processor or blender. Add the minced beef, vodka, egg, salt and a little pepper and process until fairly smooth. Add the herbs and process for a few more seconds, until well mixed.

4 Bring the stock and bay leaves to the boil. Drop in 10 heaped teaspoonfuls of the meat mixture. Remove when they rise to the surface, then add the next batch. You will make about 30 meatballs.

5 To make the sauce, melt the butter in a large pan and fry the mushrooms for 5 minutes. Stir in the soured cream and bring to the boil. Season to taste. Add the meatballs to the sauce and warm through. Garnish with coriander and serve with boiled rice.

COOK'S TIP

The meatballs can be shallow fried in 2.5cm/1in sunflower oil, if preferred.

Chicken Bitki

Chicken is one of the most popular meats eaten in Poland. Use guinea fowl to mimic the gamey flavour of Polish chicken.

INGREDIENTS

Makes 12

15g/½oz/1 tbsp butter, melted
115g/4oz flat mushrooms, finely chopped
50g/2oz/1 cup fresh white breadcrumbs
350g/12oz chicken breasts or guinea fowl, minced or finely chopped
2 eggs, separated
1.5ml/¼ tsp grated nutmeg
30ml/2 tbsp plain flour
45ml/3 tbsp oil
salt and freshly ground black pepper
green salad and grated pickled beetroot, to serve

1 Melt the butter in a pan and fry the mushrooms for 5 minutes until soft and all the juices have evaporated. Allow to cool.

2 Mix the crumbs, chicken, yolks, nutmeg, salt and pepper and flat mushrooms well.

3 Whisk the egg whites until stiff. Stir half into the chicken mixture, then fold in the remainder.

4 Shape the mixture into 12 even meatballs, about 7.5cm/3in long and 2.5cm/1in wide. Roll in the flour to coat.

5 Heat the oil in a frying pan and fry the *bitki* for 10 minutes, turning until evenly golden brown and cooked through. Serve hot with a green salad and pickled beetroot.

Chicken Kiev

This popular recipe is a modern Russian invention. These deep fried chicken breasts filled with garlic butter should be prepared well in advance to allow time for chilling.

INGREDIENTS

Serves 4

115g/4oz/8 tbsp butter, softened
2 garlic cloves, crushed
finely grated rind of 1 lemon
30ml/2 tbsp chopped fresh tarragon
pinch of freshly grated nutmeg
4 chicken breast fillets with wing bones attached, skinned
1 egg, lightly beaten
115g/4oz/2 cups fresh breadcrumbs
oil, for deep frying
salt and freshly ground black pepper
lemon wedges, to garnish
potato wedges, to serve

1 Mix the butter in a bowl with the garlic, lemon rind, tarragon and nutmeg. Season to taste with salt and pepper. Shape the butter into a rectangular block about 5cm/2in long, wrap in foil and chill for 1 hour.

2 Place the chicken, skinned sides down, on a piece of oiled clear film. Cover with a second piece of clear film and gently beat the pieces with a rolling pin until fairly thin.

3 Cut the butter lengthways into four pieces and put one in the centre of each chicken fillet. Fold the edges over the butter and secure with wooden cocktail sticks.

4 Tip the beaten egg and the breadcrumbs into separate small dishes. Dip the chicken pieces first in the beaten egg and then in the breadcrumbs to coat evenly. Dip them a second time in egg and crumbs, then put on a plate and refrigerate for at least 1 hour.

5 Heat the oil in a large pan or deep fat fryer to 180°C/350°F. Deep fry the chicken for 6–8 minutes, or until the chicken is cooked and the coating golden brown and crisp. Drain on kitchen paper and remove the cocktail sticks. Serve hot, garnished with wedges of lemon and potato wedges.

Chicken and Pork Terrine

Serve this delicate Ukrainian pâté with warm, crusty bread.

INGREDIENTS

Serves 6–8

225g/8oz rindless, streaky bacon
375g/13oz boneless chicken
  breast, skinned
15ml/1 tbsp lemon juice
225g/8oz lean minced pork
½ small onion, finely chopped
2 eggs, beaten
30ml/2 tbsp chopped fresh parsley
5ml/1 tsp salt
5ml/1 tsp green peppercorns, crushed
fresh green salad, radishes and lemon
  wedges, to serve

1 Preheat the oven to 160°C/325°F/ Gas 3. Put the bacon on a board and stretch it using the back of a knife so that it can be arranged in over-lapping slices over the base and sides of a 900g/2lb loaf tin.

2 Cut 115g/4oz of the chicken into strips about 10cm/4in long. Sprinkle with lemon juice. Put the rest of the chicken in a food processor or blender with the minced pork and the onion. Process until fairly smooth.

3 Add the eggs, parsley, salt and peppercorns to the meat mixture and process again briefly. Spoon half the mixture into the loaf tin and then level the surface.

4 Arrange the chicken strips on top, then spoon in the remaining meat mixture and smooth the top. Give the tin a couple of sharp taps to knock out any pockets of air.

5 Cover with a piece of oiled foil and put in a roasting tin. Pour in enough hot water to come halfway up the sides of the loaf tin. Bake for about 45–50 minutes, until firm.

6 Allow the terrine to cool in the tin before turning out and chilling. Serve sliced, with a fresh green salad, baby tomatoes and wedges of lemon to squeeze over.

MEAT AND POULTRY 43

Roast Duckling with Honey

A sweet and sour orange sauce is the perfect foil for this rich-tasting Polish duck recipe, and frying the orange rind intensifies the flavour.

INGREDIENTS

Serves 4

2.25kg/5lb oven-ready duckling
2.5ml/½ tsp ground allspice
1 orange
15ml/1 tbsp sunflower oil
30ml/2 tbsp plain flour
150ml/¼ pint/⅔ cup chicken or
   duck stock
10ml/2 tsp red wine vinegar
15ml/1 tbsp clear honey
salt and freshly ground black pepper
watercress and thinly pared orange
   rind, to serve

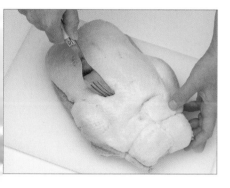

1 Preheat the oven to 220°C/425°F/ Gas 7. Using a fork, pierce the duckling all over, except the breast, so that the fat runs out during cooking.

2 Rub all over the skin of the duckling with allspice and sprinkle with salt and pepper.

3 Put the duckling on a rack over a roasting tin and cook for about 20 minutes. Next reduce the oven temperature to 190°C/375°F/Gas 5 and cook for a further 2 hours.

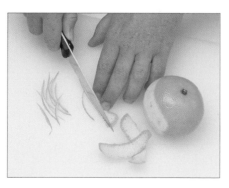

4 Meanwhile, thinly pare the rind from the orange and cut into very fine strips. Heat the oil in a pan and gently fry the orange rind for 2–3 minutes. Squeeze the juice from the orange and set aside.

5 Transfer the duckling to a warmed serving dish and keep warm. Drain off all but 30ml/2 tbsp fat from the tin, sprinkle in the flour and stir well.

6 Stir in the stock, vinegar, honey, orange juice and rind. Bring to the boil, stirring all the time. Simmer for 2–3 minutes. Season the sauce and serve the duckling with watercress and thinly pared orange rind.

FISH

The seas to the north and south and the vast lakes and the rivers that flow across this region provide an abundance of fish, which are cooked in wonderful ways. Russia's most famous export, caviare, comes from the huge sturgeon that swim in the Caspian Sea. The Baltic provides this region with herring, which is served in many guises throughout the year since it is well suited to pickling. However, freshwater fish predominate, including eel, perch, tench and salmon, but the favourites are pike and carp, which are always served on feast days.

Pike and Salmon Mousse

When sliced, this light-textured Russian mousse loaf, *Pate iz Shchuki*, reveals a pretty layer of pink salmon. For a special occasion, serve topped with red salmon caviare.

INGREDIENTS

Serves 8

225g/8oz salmon fillets, skinned
600ml/1 pint/2½ cups fish stock
finely grated rind and juice of
    ½ lemon
900g/2lb pike fillets, skinned
4 egg whites
475ml/16fl oz/2 cups double cream
30ml/2 tbsp chopped fresh dill
salt and freshly ground black pepper
red salmon caviare or dill sprig,
    to garnish (optional)

1 Preheat the oven to 180°C/350°F/ Gas 4. Line a 900g/2lb loaf tin with greaseproof paper and brush with oil.

2 Cut the salmon into 5cm/2in strips. Place the stock and lemon juice in a pan and bring to the boil, then turn off the heat. Add the salmon strips, cover and leave for 2 minutes. Remove with a slotted spoon.

3 Cut the pike into cubes and process in a food processor or blender until smooth. Lightly whisk the egg whites with a fork. With the motor running, slowly pour in the egg whites, then the cream. Finally, add the lemon rind, dill and seasoning.

4 Spoon half of the pike mixture into the prepared loaf tin.

5 Arrange the poached salmon strips on top, then carefully spoon in the remaining pike mixture.

6 Cover the loaf tin with foil and put in a roasting tin. Add enough boiling water to come halfway up the sides of the loaf tin. Bake for 45–50 minutes, or until firm.

7 Leave on a wire rack to cool, then chill for at least 3 hours. Turn out on to a serving plate and remove the lining paper. Serve the mousse cut in slices and garnished with red salmon caviare or a sprig of dill, if liked.

Salmon Kulebyaka

A Russian festive dish in which a layer of moist salmon and eggs sits on a bed of buttery dill-flavoured rice, all encased in crisp puff pastry.

INGREDIENTS

Serves 4

50g/2oz/4 tbsp butter
1 small onion, finely chopped
175g/6oz/1 cup cooked long-grain rice
15ml/1 tbsp chopped fresh dill
15ml/1 tbsp lemon juice
450g/1lb puff pastry, defrosted if frozen
450g/1lb salmon fillet, skinned and cut into 5cm/2in pieces
3 eggs, hard-boiled and chopped
beaten egg, for sealing and glazing
salt and freshly ground black pepper
watercress, to garnish

1 Preheat the oven to 200°C/400°F/ Gas 6. Melt the butter in a pan, add the finely chopped onion and cook gently for 10 minutes, or until soft.

2 Stir in the cooked rice, dill, lemon juice, salt and pepper.

3 Roll out the puff pastry on a lightly floured surface to a 30cm/12in square. Spoon the rice mixture over half the pastry, leaving a 1cm/½in border around the edges.

4 Arrange the salmon on top, then scatter the eggs in between.

5 Brush the pastry edges with egg, fold it over the filling to make a rectangle, pressing the edges together firmly to seal.

6 Carefully lift the pastry on to a lightly oiled baking sheet. Glaze with beaten egg, then pierce the pastry a few times with a skewer to make holes for the steam to escape.

7 Bake on the middle shelf of the oven for 40 minutes, covering with foil after 30 minutes. Leave to cool on the baking sheet, before cutting into slices. Garnish with watercress.

Braised Tench and Vegetables

Freshwater tench is the smallest member of the carp family, with a sweet firm flesh and few bones. In this simple Polish recipe, the combination of vegetables can easily be adapted to suit an individual's taste or seasonal availability.

INGREDIENTS

Serves 4
900g/2lb tench, filleted
  and skinned
15ml/1 tbsp lemon juice
75g/3oz/6 tbsp butter
1 onion, halved and cut into wedges
1 celery stick, sliced
1 carrot, halved lengthways and sliced
115g/4oz/1½ cups small button
  mushrooms, halved
50ml/2fl oz/¼ cup vegetable stock
salt and freshly ground black pepper

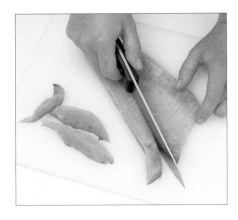

1 Cut the fish fillets into strips about 2.5cm/1in wide. Sprinkle them with the lemon juice and a little salt and pepper and set aside.

2 Melt the butter in a large flameproof casserole and cook the onion wedges for 5 minutes. Add the celery, carrot and mushrooms and cook for a further 2–3 minutes, stirring to coat in the butter.

3 Pour the stock into the pan. Place the fish on top of the vegetables in a single layer. Cover the casserole with a lid and cook over a very low heat for 25–30 minutes, until the fish and vegetables are tender.

VARIATION

Use small carp in this recipe if liked. Carp has a slightly earthier flavour.

Plaice in Polish Sauce

This sauce is Polish only in name, not in origin. A mixture of recipes, it is a quick and simple sauce to prepare, that goes well with any poached, grilled or steamed fish.

INGREDIENTS

Serves 4
4 plaice fillets, about 225g/8oz each
75g/3oz/6 tbsp butter
2 eggs, hard-boiled and
  finely chopped
30ml/2 tbsp chopped fresh dill
15ml/1 tbsp lemon juice
salt and freshly ground black pepper
lemon slices, to garnish
boiled baby carrots, to serve

1 Put the fish, skin side down, on a sheet of greased foil on a grill rack. Melt the butter in a small pan and brush a little over the fish. Season with salt and pepper.

2 Grill the fish under a moderate heat for 8–10 minutes, or until just cooked. Transfer to a warmed plate.

3 Add the eggs, dill and lemon juice to the melted butter in the pan. Heat gently for 1 minute. Pour over the fish just before serving. Garnish with lemon slices and serve with boiled baby carrots.

Fish Babka

This fish pudding is lightened with egg whites, giving it a soufflé-like texture. It is much more stable, however, and can be turned out to serve.

INGREDIENTS

Serves 4

350g/12oz white fish fillets, skinned and cut into 2.5cm/1in cubes
50g/2oz white bread, cut into 1cm/½ in cubes
250ml/8fl oz/1 cup milk
25g/1oz/2 tbsp butter
1 small onion, finely chopped
3 eggs, separated
1.5ml/¼ tsp grated nutmeg
salt and freshly ground black pepper
30ml/2 tbsp chopped fresh dill, plus extra to garnish
sliced courgettes and carrots, to serve

1 Preheat the oven to 180°C/350°F/ Gas 4. Base-line with greaseproof paper and butter a 1.5 litre/2½ pint/ 6¼ cup ovenproof dish.

2 Place the fish cubes in a bowl. Add the bread, then sprinkle over the milk and leave to soak while you cook the chopped onion.

3 Melt the butter in a small pan and fry the onion for 10 minutes, until soft. Cool for a few minutes, then add to the fish and bread with the egg yolks, nutmeg, dill, salt and pepper. Mix well.

4 Whisk the egg whites in a large bowl until stiff, then gently fold into the fish mixture.

5 Spoon the mixture into the dish. Cover with buttered foil and bake for 45 minutes, or until set.

6 Allow to stand for 5 minutes, then spoon out. Alternatively, loosen with a knife; turn out, remove the paper and cut into wedges. Garnish with dill and serve with courgettes and carrots.

Muscovite Solyanka

This layered fish and vegetable bake has the same name as one of Russia's classic soups. The name reflects the prevalent "sourness" of the ingredients.

INGREDIENTS

Serves 4

675g/1½ lb eel, skinned and boned
900ml/1½ pints/3¾ cups fish or
   vegetable stock
1.2 litres/2 pints/5 cups water
450g/1lb/4 cups shredded
   white cabbage
50g/2oz/4 tbsp butter
1 large onion, chopped
2 pickled cucumbers, sliced
12 green olives
15ml/1 tbsp capers, drained
75g/3oz/1½ cups fresh white
   breadcrumbs
salt and freshly ground black pepper

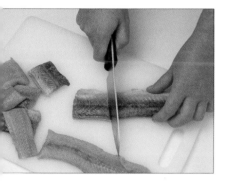

1 Cut the eel into large pieces. Bring the stock to a gentle simmer in a large pan, add the eel and cook for 4 minutes. Remove with a slotted spoon. Reserve 150ml/¼ pint/⅔ cup of the stock and set aside, leaving the remaining stock in the pan.

2 Pour the water into the pan of stock. Bring to the boil, then add the cabbage. Simmer for 2 minutes, then strain well.

3 Melt half of the butter in the pan. Fry the onion for 5 minutes.

4 Stir in the strained cabbage and reserved stock, then bring to the boil. Cover with a tight-fitting lid and cook over a low heat for 1 hour, until tender. Season with salt and pepper.

5 Preheat the oven to 200°C/400°F/ Gas 6. Spoon half the cabbage into a baking dish. Top with the eel and the cucumbers. Spoon over the remaining cabbage and any remaining stock.

6 Scatter the olives, capers and the breadcrumbs over the top. Melt the remaining butter and drizzle over the top. Bake for 25–30 minutes, or until lightly browned. Garnish with parsley sprigs and serve with boiled potatoes.

Rolled Fish Fillets

Whiting or sea perch can also be used in this dish. Their delicate flavour is complemented by the lemon and thyme.

INGREDIENTS

Serves 4

8 sole fillets, about 200g/7oz, skinned
45ml/3 tbsp olive oil
15ml/1 tbsp lemon juice
25g/1oz/2 tbsp butter
175g/6oz/2 cups button mushrooms, very finely chopped
4 anchovy fillets, finely chopped
5ml/1 tsp chopped fresh thyme, plus extra to garnish
2 eggs, beaten
115g/4oz/2 cups white breadcrumbs
oil, for deep frying
salt and freshly ground black pepper
grilled chicory, to serve

1 Lay the fish fillets in a single layer in a glass dish. Mix together the oil and lemon juice and sprinkle over. Cover with clear film and marinate in the refrigerator for at least 1 hour.

2 Melt the butter in a pan and gently fry the mushrooms for 5 minutes, until tender and all the juices have evaporated. Stir in the chopped anchovies, thyme, salt and pepper.

3 Divide the mixture equally and spread evenly over the fish. Roll up and secure with cocktail sticks.

4 Dip each fish roll in beaten egg, then in breadcrumbs to coat. Repeat this process. Heat the oil to 180°C/350°F/Gas 4.

5 Deep fry in 2 batches for 4–5 minutes, or until well browned and cooked through. Drain on kitchen paper. Remove the cocktail sticks and sprinkle with thyme. Serve with grilled chicory.

> —— COOK'S TIP ——
>
> To skin the fillets, slice the flesh away from the skin using a sharp knife. Keep the knife parallel to the fish and the skin taut.

Carp with Green Horseradish Sauce

Carp is a freshwater fish much used in Polish cooking, and it is traditional Christmas fare.

INGREDIENTS

Serves 4

675g/1½lb carp, skinned and filleted
45ml/3 tbsp plain flour
1 egg, beaten
115g/4oz/2 cups fresh white breadcrumbs
sunflower oil, for frying
salt and freshly ground black pepper
lemon wedges, to serve

For the sauce

15g/½oz fresh horseradish, finely grated
pinch of salt
150ml/¼ pint/⅔ cup double cream
1 bunch of watercress, trimmed and finely chopped
30ml/2 tbsp snipped fresh chives
2 eggs, hard-boiled and finely chopped (optional)

1 Cut the fish into thin strips, about 6cm/2½in long by 1cm/½in thick. Season the flour with salt and pepper. Dip the strips of fish in the flour, then in the beaten egg and finally in the breadcrumbs.

2 Heat 1cm/½in of oil in a frying pan. Fry the fish in batches for 3–4 minutes, until golden brown. Drain on kitchen paper and keep warm until all the strips are cooked.

3 For the sauce, put the horseradish, salt, cream and watercress in a small pan. Bring to the boil and simmer for 2 minutes. Stir in the chives and eggs, if using. Serve the sauce with the fish.

Baked Cod with Horseradish Sauce

Baking fish in a sauce keeps it moist. In this Ukrainian recipe, a second, tangy sauce is served alongside for added flavour.

INGREDIENTS

Serves 4
4 thick cod fillets or steaks
15ml/1 tbsp lemon juice
25g/1oz/2 tbsp butter
25g/1oz/¼ cup plain flour, sifted
150ml/¼ pint/⅔ cup milk
150ml/¼ pint/⅔ cup fish stock
salt and freshly ground black pepper
parsley sprigs, to garnish
potato wedges and chopped spring
    onions, fried, to serve

For the horseradish sauce
30ml/2 tbsp tomato purée
30ml/2 tbsp grated fresh horseradish
150ml/¼ pint/⅔ cup soured cream

1 Preheat the oven to 180°C/350°F/ Gas 4. Place the fish in a buttered ovenproof dish in a single layer. Sprinkle with lemon juice.

2 Melt the butter in a small heavy-based pan. Stir in the flour and cook for 3–4 minutes until lightly golden. Stir to stop the flour sticking to the pan. Remove from the heat.

3 Gradually whisk the milk, and then the stock, into the flour mixture. Season with salt and pepper. Bring to the boil, stirring, and simmer for 3 minutes, still stirring.

4 Pour the sauce over the fish and bake for 20–25 minutes, depending on the thickness. Check by inserting a skewer in the thickest part: the flesh should be opaque.

5 For the horseradish sauce, blend the tomato purée and horseradish with the soured cream in a small pan. Slowly bring to the boil, stirring, and then simmer for 1 minute.

6 Pour the horseradish sauce into a serving bowl and serve alongside the fish. Serve the fish hot. Garnish with the parsley sprigs and serve with the potato wedges and fried chopped spring onions.

Glazed Pike-perch

This Russian fish dish, with its glistening aspic coating, makes an impressive centrepiece for a formal occasion.

INGREDIENTS

Serves 8–10

2.25–2.75kg/5–6lb whole pike-perch
30ml/2 tbsp sunflower oil
2 bay leaves
8 whole peppercorns
1 lemon, sliced
300ml/½ pint/1¼ cups white wine
25g/1oz sachet aspic jelly
2 cucumbers, halved and thinly sliced
salt and freshly ground black pepper
dill sprigs and lemon wedges,
   to garnish
mayonnaise, to serve

1 Wash the pike-perch under cold running water. Snip off the fins with sharp scissors. Season the inside of the fish with salt and pepper. Brush the skin with the oil to protect it from the heat during cooking.

2 Put the fish on the trivet of a fish kettle or on a rack in a large roasting tin. Add the bay leaves, peppercorns and lemon slices. Pour over the wine and enough water to cover.

3 Cover with a lid or a piece of oiled foil. Bring to the boil and simmer very gently for 10 minutes. Turn off the heat and leave the pike-perch to cool with the lid still on. When cool peel the skin off the fish, leaving the head and tail intact.

4 Prepare the aspic with boiling water, according to the packet instructions. Cool and brush generously over the fish.

5 Arrange the cucumber slices over the fish, then brush again with aspic. Allow to set before serving, garnished with dill sprigs and lemon wedges.

--- COOK'S TIP ---

A whole fresh salmon or salmon trout can be cooked in exactly the same way.

VEGETABLES, GRAINS AND PASTA

Served on their own or as an accompaniment, vegetables in Russia, Poland and the Ukraine reflect the cold climate. Cabbage, beetroot, swede and turnip are the staples, often preserved by salting or pickling. Mushrooms are popular, too, since huge forests cover much of the region and gathering them is a favourite pastime. Potatoes also feature, particularly in Polish cooking, although grains, especially buckwheat, rye and barley, are more widely eaten. Surprisingly, stuffed pasta is traditional, usually with meat or cheese fillings.

Potato Cakes

Although not as widely used as cereals, potatoes feature often in Polish recipes. They were introduced during the reign of Jan Sobieski, in the 17th century.

INGREDIENTS

Serves 4

450g/1lb potatoes, peeled and cut into
 large chunks
25g/1oz/2 tbsp butter
1 small onion, chopped
45ml/3 tbsp soured cream
2 egg yolks
25g/1oz/¼ cup plain flour
1 egg, beaten
25g/1oz/½ cup fresh white
 breadcrumbs
salt and freshly ground black pepper

1 Preheat the oven to 180°C/350°F/ Gas 4. Cook the potatoes in a pan of boiling salted water for 20 minutes, or until tender. Drain well and mash. Allow to cool for a few minutes. Meanwhile, melt the butter in a small pan and fry the onion for 10 minutes, until soft.

2 Stir the butter and onion into the mashed potato and then mix in the cream and egg yolks.

3 Sift the flour over the potato mixture, then mix it in well. Season with plenty of salt and pepper. Shape into rounds, then flatten slightly to make about 16 "doughnuts" 6cm/ 2½in across.

4 Place the "doughnuts" on a lightly oiled baking sheet and brush with beaten egg. Sprinkle the tops with breadcrumbs. Bake for 30 minutes, or until browned.

Pampushki

When these crunchy Russian potato dumplings are split open, a tasty curd cheese and chive filling is revealed.

INGREDIENTS

Serves 4
675g/1½lb potatoes, peeled
225g/8oz/2⅔ cups cooked
  mashed potato
2.5ml/½ tsp salt
75g/3oz/scant ½ cup curd cheese
30ml/2 tbsp snipped fresh chives
freshly ground black pepper
oil, for deep frying

1 Coarsely grate the raw potatoes and squeeze out as much water as possible. Put them in a bowl with the mashed potato, salt and black pepper. Mix together. In another bowl, mix the curd cheese and chives together.

2 Using a spoon and your fingers, scoop up a portion of the potato mixture, slightly smaller than an egg, and then flatten to a circle.

3 Put 5ml/1 tsp of the cheese filling into the middle, then fold over the edges and pinch to seal. Repeat with remaining potato and cheese mixtures, to make about 12 dumplings.

4 Heat the oil to 170°C/340°F. Deep fry the dumplings for 10 minutes, or until deep brown and crisp. Drain on kitchen paper and serve hot.

--- COOK'S TIP ---

Pampushki are traditionally cooked in stock or water and served with soup. If you prefer to poach them, add 15ml/1 tbsp plain flour and 1 beaten egg to the mixture and poach the dumplings for 20 minutes.

Galushki

One of the most popular Ukrainian dishes, *galushki* are pieces of a pasta-like dough, cooked in milk or stock. Healthy and filling, they can be made from wheat flour, buckwheat flour, semolina or potatoes.

INGREDIENTS

Serves 4
225g/8oz/2 cups plain flour
1.5ml/¼ tsp salt
25g/1oz/2 tbsp butter, melted
2 eggs, beaten
1 vegetable stock cube
115g/4oz lardons or smoked streaky
  bacon, rinded and chopped,
  to serve

1 Sift the flour and salt into a bowl. Make a well in the centre. Add the butter and eggs and mix to a dough.

2 Knead on a lightly floured surface until smooth. Wrap in clear film and leave to rest for 30 minutes. Roll out on a lightly floured surface until 1cm/½in thick, and cut into 2cm/¾in squares using a sharp knife or a pastry wheel. Leave to dry on a floured dish towel for 30 minutes.

3 Crumble the stock cube into a pan of gently boiling water. Add the *galushki* and simmer for 10 minutes, or until cooked. Drain well.

4 Meanwhile, dry fry the lardons or bacon in a non-stick frying pan for 5 minutes, until brown and crispy. Serve scattered over the *galushki*.

Cheese Dumplings

Easily prepared, dumplings are common additions to soups throughout the Ukraine. They are also served with meats and on their own as a simple supper.

INGREDIENTS

Serves 4
115g/4oz/1 cup self-raising flour
25g/1oz/2 tbsp butter
25g/1oz/⅓ cup crumbled feta, dry
  brinza (sheep's milk cheese), or a
  mixture of Caerphilly and Parmesan
30ml/2 tbsp chopped fresh herbs
60ml/4 tbsp cold water
salt and freshly ground black pepper
parsley sprigs, to garnish

For the topping
40g/1½oz/3 tbsp butter
50g/2oz/1 cup slightly dry white
  breadcrumbs

1 Sift the flour into a bowl. Rub in the butter until the mixture resembles fine breadcrumbs.

2 Stir the cheese and herbs into the mixture. Season with salt and pepper. Add the cold water and mix to a firm dough; then shape into 12 balls.

3 Bring a pan of salted water to the boil. Add the dumplings, cover and gently simmer for 20 minutes, until light and fluffy.

4 For the topping, melt the butter in a frying pan. Add the breadcrumbs and cook for 2–3 minutes, until the crumbs are golden and crisp. Remove the dumplings with a slotted spoon and sprinkle with breadcrumbs. Serve garnished with parsley sprigs.

Drachena

A Russian cross between an omelette and a pancake, this is a savoury *drachena,* but it is often served as a dessert by leaving out the vegetables and sweetening with sugar or honey.

INGREDIENTS

Serves 2–3
15ml/1 tbsp olive oil
1 bunch spring onions, sliced
1 garlic clove, crushed
4 tomatoes, peeled, seeded
 and chopped
45ml/3 tbsp wholemeal rye flour
60ml/4 tbsp milk
150ml/¼ pint/⅔ cup soured cream
4 eggs, beaten
30ml/2 tbsp chopped fresh parsley
25g/1oz/2 tbsp butter, melted
salt and freshly ground black pepper
green salad, to serve

1 Preheat the oven to 180°C/350°F/ Gas 4. Heat the oil in a frying pan and gently cook the spring onions for 3 minutes. Add the garlic and cook for 1 more minute, or until the spring onions are soft.

2 Sprinkle the spring onions and garlic into the base of a lightly greased shallow 20cm/8in ovenproof dish and scatter over the tomatoes.

3 Mix the flour to a smooth paste in a bowl with the milk. Gradually add the soured cream, then mix with the eggs. Stir in the parsley and melted butter. Season with salt and pepper.

4 Pour the egg mixture over the vegetables. Bake in the oven for 40–45 minutes, or until hardly any liquid seeps out when a knife is pushed into the middle.

5 Run a knife around the edge of the dish to loosen, then cut into wedges and serve immediately with a fresh green salad.

Braised Barley and Vegetables

One of the oldest of cultivated cereals, pot barley has a nutty flavour and slightly chewy texture. It makes a warming and filling dish when combined with root vegetables.

INGREDIENTS

Serves 4

225g/8oz/1 cup pearl or pot barley
30ml/2 tbsp sunflower oil
1 large onion, chopped
2 celery sticks, sliced
2 carrots, halved lengthways and sliced
225g/8oz swede or turnip, cut into
  2cm/³⁄₄in cubes
225g/8oz potatoes, cut into 2cm/
  ³⁄₄in cubes
475ml/16fl oz/2 cups vegetable stock
salt and freshly ground black pepper
celery leaves, to garnish

1 Put the barley in a measuring jug and add water to reach the 600ml/ pint/2¹⁄₂ cup mark. Leave to soak in cool place for at least 4 hours or, preferably, overnight.

2 Heat the oil in a large pan and fry the onion for 5 minutes. Add the sliced celery and carrots and cook for 3–4 minutes, or until the onion is starting to brown.

3 Add the barley and its soaking liquid to the pan. Then add the swede or turnip, potato and stock to the barley. Season with salt and pepper. Bring to the boil, then reduce the heat and cover the pan.

4 Simmer for 40 minutes, or until most of the stock has been absorbed and the barley is tender. Stir occasionally towards the end of cooking to prevent the barley from sticking to the base of the pan. Serve, garnished with celery leaves.

Buckwheat Kasha

Kasha is a type of Russian porridge, made from a variety of grains including wheat, barley, millet and oats. The most popular is buckwheat, which has a distinctive nutty flavour.

INGREDIENTS

Serves 4
175g/6oz/scant 1 cup buckwheat
750ml/1¼ pints/3 cups boiling stock
25g/1oz/2 tbsp butter
pinch of freshly grated nutmeg
115g/4oz smoked streaky bacon,
  rinded and chopped
salt and freshly ground black pepper

1 Dry fry the buckwheat in a non-stick frying pan for 2 minutes, or until very lightly toasted. Add the stock.

2 Simmer very gently for 15–20 minutes, stirring occasionally to prevent it sticking. When almost dry, remove from the heat.

3 Add the butter to the buckwheat and season with nutmeg, salt and pepper. Cover the pan with a lid and leave to stand for 5 minutes.

4 Meanwhile, dry fry the bacon in a non-stick pan for 5 minutes, until lightly browned and crispy. Sprinkle over the kasha before serving.

—— COOK'S TIP ——

Buckwheat *kasha* is equally good with the addition of fried mushrooms and makes an excellent stuffing for roast chicken. Buckwheat is often sold already roasted, in which case there is no need to dry fry it before adding the stock.

Carters' Millet

This dish was originally cooked over an open fire by carters who travelled across the steppes of southern Ukraine.

INGREDIENTS

Serves 4
225g/8oz/scant 1¼ cups millet
600ml/1 pint/2½ cups
  vegetable stock
115g/4oz lardons or smoked streaky
  bacon, rinded and chopped
15ml/1 tbsp olive oil
1 small onion, thinly sliced
225g/8oz/3 cups small field
  mushrooms, sliced
15ml/1 tbsp chopped fresh mint
salt and freshly ground black pepper

1 Rinse the millet in a sieve under cold running water. Put in a pan with the stock, bring to the boil and simmer, covered, for 30 minutes, until the stock has been absorbed.

2 Dry fry the bacon in a non-stick pan for 5 minutes, or until brown and crisp. Remove and set aside.

3 Add the oil to the pan and cook the onion and mushrooms for 10 minutes, until beginning to brown.

4 Add the bacon, onion and mushrooms to the millet. Stir in the mint and season with salt and pepper. Heat gently for 1–2 minutes before serving.

Beetroot Casserole

This Russian vegetarian casserole can be served as a light meal in itself. Its sweet and sour flavour also makes it an ideal dish to serve with roasted chicken or game.

INGREDIENTS

Serves 4

50g/2oz/4 tbsp butter
1 onion, chopped
2 garlic cloves, crushed
675g/1½lb uncooked beetroot, peeled
2 large carrots, peeled
½ lemon
115g/4oz/1½ cups button mushrooms
300ml/½ pint/1¼ cups
    vegetable stock
2 bay leaves
15ml/1 tbsp chopped fresh mint, plus
    sprigs to garnish (optional)
salt and freshly ground black pepper

For the hot dressing

150ml/¼ pint/⅔ cup soured cream
2.5ml/½ tsp paprika, plus extra
    to garnish

1 Melt the butter in a non-aluminium pan and gently fry the onion and garlic for 5 minutes. Meanwhile, dice the beetroot and carrot. Finely grate the rind and squeeze the juice of the ½ lemon. Add the beetroot, carrots and mushrooms and fry for 5 minutes.

--- COOK'S TIP ---

Wear clean rubber or plastic gloves to avoid staining your hands when preparing beetroot. Cooking beetroot in aluminium pans may cause discoloration of pan and food.

2 Pour in the stock with the lemon rind and bay leaves. Season with salt and pepper. Bring to the boil, turn down the heat, cover and simmer for 1 hour, or until the vegetables are soft.

3 Turn off the heat and stir in the lemon juice and chopped mint, if using. Leave the pan to stand, covered, for 5 minutes, to develop the flavours.

4 Meanwhile, for the dressing, gently heat the soured cream and paprika in a small pan, stirring all the time, until bubbling. Transfer the beetroot mixture to a serving bowl, then spoon over the soured cream. Garnish with sprigs of mint and extra paprika, if liked, and serve.

Uszka

Uszka, meaning "little ears", are plump mushroom dumplings, traditionally served in Poland with clear soups. They are also delicious on their own, tossed in a little melted butter and chopped fresh herbs.

INGREDIENTS

Makes 20

75g/3oz/²/₃ cup plain flour
pinch of salt
30ml/2 tbsp chopped fresh parsley
1 egg yolk
40ml/2½ tbsp cold water
fresh parsley, to garnish
clear soup or melted herb butter, to serve

For the filling

25g/1oz/2 tbsp butter
½ small onion, very finely chopped
50g/2oz/1 cup mushrooms, finely chopped
1 egg white
15ml/1 tbsp dried white breadcrumbs
salt and freshly ground black pepper

1 Sift the flour and salt into a bowl. Add the chopped parsley, egg yolk and water and mix to a dough. Lightly knead the dough on a floured surface until smooth.

2 To make the filling, melt the butter in a pan. Add the onion and mushrooms and fry over a low heat for 10 minutes, or until the onion is very soft. Leave to cool.

3 Lightly whisk the egg white in a clean bowl with a fork. Add 15ml/1 tbsp of the egg white to the mushrooms, together with the dried breadcrumbs, salt and pepper. Mix together well.

4 Roll out the dough very thinly on a floured surface. Cut into 5cm/2in squares using a sharp knife or a pastry wheel, then lightly brush with the remaining egg white.

5 Spoon 2.5ml/½ tsp of mushroom mixture on to each square. Fold the dough in half to make a triangle, then pinch the outer edges together to seal them.

6 Bring a pan of boiling salted water or stock to a brisk boil. Gently drop in the dumplings a few at a time and simmer for 5 minutes. Drain and add to a clear soup or toss in melted herb butter and serve.

Cucumber Salad

Salting the cucumber draws out some of the moisture, thereby making it firmer. Make sure you rinse it thoroughly before using or the salad will be too salty. This popular Ukrainian dish is an ideal summer accompaniment to a main meal.

INGREDIENTS

Serves 6–8
2 cucumbers, decorated with a
   cannelle knife and thinly sliced
5ml/1 tsp salt
45ml/3 tbsp chopped fresh dill
15ml/1 tbsp white wine vinegar
150ml/¼ pint/⅔ cup soured cream
freshly ground black pepper
1 dill sprig, to garnish

1 Put the cucumber in a sieve or colander set over a bowl and sprinkle with the salt. Leave for 1 hour to drain. Rinse the cucumber well under cold running water, then pat dry with kitchen paper.

2 Put the slices of cucumber in a bowl, add the chopped dill and mix everything together well.

3 In another bowl, stir the vinegar into the soured cream and season the mixture with pepper.

4 Pour the soured cream over the cucumber and chill for 1 hour before turning into a serving dish. Garnish with a sprig of dill and serve.

Grated Beetroot and Celery Salad

Raw beetroot has a lovely crunchy texture. Here in this Russian salad, its flavour is brought out by marinating it in a cider dressing.

INGREDIENTS

Serves 4–6
450g/1lb uncooked beetroot, peeled
   and grated
4 celery sticks, finely chopped
30ml/2 tbsp apple juice
fresh herbs, to garnish

For the dressing
45ml/3 tbsp sunflower oil
15ml/1 tbsp cider vinegar
4 spring onions, finely sliced
30ml/2 tbsp chopped fresh parsley
salt and freshly ground black pepper

1 Toss the beetroot, celery and apple juice together in a bowl to mix.

2 Put all the ingredients for the dressing in a small bowl and whisk with a fork until well blended. Stir half into the beetroot mixture.

3 Drizzle the remaining dressing over the top. Allow the salad to marinate for at least 2 hours before serving, for the fullest flavour. Garnish with fresh herbs.

DESSERTS AND BAKES

Russians, Ukrainians and Poles all have a sweet tooth and this is reflected in the vast number and variety of desserts, cakes, pastries and breads. Special occasions are often marked with particular confections, such as Russian Paskha and Polish Babka. Honey and nuts are plentiful and feature in many sweet dishes. Other popular flavourings are cinnamon, cloves and cardamom, as well as candied fruits, vanilla and lemon peel. Fruit, especially orchard and soft fruit, can be of exceptionally high quality.

Kulich

Kulich is served only at Easter in Russia, often instead of bread. Slice in rounds from the top, with the first slice kept as a lid.

Ingredients

Serves 4
500g/1¼lb/5 cups strong white flour
pinch of salt
5ml/1 tsp ground cinnamon
75g/3oz/scant ½ cup caster sugar
50g/2oz/scant ½ cup raisins
50g/2oz/⅓ cup mixed peel
50g/2oz/⅓ cup almonds, chopped
7g/¼oz sachet easy-blend
   dried yeast
300ml/½ pint/1¼ cups milk
50g/2oz/4 tbsp butter
1 egg, beaten
jam, to serve (optional)

For the icing
115g/4oz/1 cup icing sugar
15ml/1 tbsp lemon juice

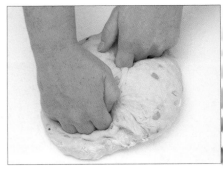

1 Sift the flour, salt and cinnamon into a large bowl. Stir in the sugar, raisins, mixed peel, almonds and dried yeast. Make a well in the centre.

2 Gently heat the milk and butter in a pan until melted. Allow to cool until tepid. Reserve 5ml/1 tsp of the beaten egg for glazing, then add the remainder to the dry ingredients with the milk and butter. Mix well to form a soft dough.

3 Knead the dough on a lightly floured surface for 10 minutes, or until smooth and elastic. Place in a clean bowl, cover with a damp cloth and leave in a warm place to rise for about 1 hour, or until doubled in size.

4 Preheat the oven to 190°C/375°F/ Gas 5. Grease and line a tall cylindrical tin or a deep 20cm/8in round cake tin with greaseproof paper. Turn the dough out and knead again until smooth. Place in the prepared tin, cover with oiled clear film and leave in a warm place until it has risen almost to the top of the tin.

5 Discard the cling film. Brush the top with the reserved egg. Bake for 50–55 minutes, or until a fine skewer inserted into the middle comes out clean. Cover with foil if the *kulich* begins to brown too much. Turn out on to a wire rack to cool.

6 For the icing, sift the icing sugar into a bowl. Add the lemon juice and mix to make a thick icing. Drizzle over the top of the *kulich* and leave to set. Spread with jam, if liked.

Paskha

Paskha is the Russian word for Easter and the name given to this rich curd cheese and candied fruit dessert, which celebrates the end of Lent. Traditionally, it is made in a pyramid-shaped wooden mould with the imprint of the Orthodox cross, but a clean, plastic flowerpot works equally well.

INGREDIENTS

Serves 6–8

115g/4oz/½ cup candied
   fruit, chopped
50g/2oz/scant ½ cup raisins
finely grated rind and juice of 1 lemon
5ml/1 tsp vanilla essence
675g/1½lb/3 cups curd cheese
25g/1oz/2 tbsp unsalted butter
150ml/¼ pint/⅔ cup soured cream
50g/2oz/¼ cup caster sugar
50g/2oz/¼ cup clear honey
50g/2oz/⅓ cup blanched
   almonds, chopped
candied fruits, lemon rind, angelica
   and honey, to decorate

1 Put the candied fruit, raisins, lemon rind and juice and vanilla essence in a small bowl. Stir, then cover and leave to soak for 1 hour.

— COOK'S TIP —

If preferred, drain the mixture for 1 hour in a muslin-lined sieve, before spooning into the lined pudding basin.

2 Meanwhile, line a 1.5 litre/ 2½ pint/6¼ cup plastic flowerpot with a double layer of muslin, allowing the edges to overhang the pot.

3 Put the cheese, butter and soured cream in a mixing bowl and beat until well blended. Add the sugar, honey, blanched almonds and soaked fruits and mix well.

4 Spoon the mixture into the lined flowerpot and fold the edges of the muslin into the middle. Cover with a small plate or saucer that just fits inside the flowerpot, then top with a 450g/ 1lb weight. Stand the flowerpot on a plate and refrigerate overnight.

5 Unfold the muslin, turn the paskha out on to a plate, then remove the muslin. Before serving, decorate with lemon rind, candied fruit and angelica, and drizzle with honey.

Polish Honey Cake

Many Eastern European cakes, like this Polish *Tort Orzechowy*, are sweetened with honey and made with ground nuts and breadcrumbs instead of flour, which gives them a delicious, rich, moist texture.

INGREDIENTS

Serves 12

15g/½oz/1 tbsp unsalted butter, melted and cooled

115g/4oz/2 cups slightly dry fine white breadcrumbs

175g/6oz/¾ cup set honey, plus extra to serve

50g/2oz/¼ cup soft light brown sugar

4 eggs, separated

115g/4oz/1 cup hazelnuts, chopped and toasted, plus extra to decorate

1 Preheat the oven to 180°C/350°F/ Gas 4. Brush a 1.75 litre/3 pint/ 7½ cup fluted brioche tin with the melted butter. Sprinkle with 15g/½oz/ ¼ cup of the breadcrumbs.

--- COOK'S TIP ---

The cake will rise during cooking and sink slightly as it cools – this is quite normal.

2 Put the honey in a large bowl, set over a pan of barely simmering water. When the honey liquifies, add the sugar and egg yolks. Whisk until light and frothy. Remove from the heat.

3 Mix the remaining breadcrumbs with the hazelnuts and fold into the egg yolk and honey mixture. Whisk the egg whites in a separate bowl, until stiff, then gently fold in to the other ingredients, half at a time.

4 Spoon the mixture into the tin. Bake for 40–45 minutes, until golden brown. Leave to cool in the tin for 5 minutes, then turn out on to a wire rack to cool. Scatter over nuts and drizzle with extra honey to serve.

Baked Coffee Custards

Unlike the Russians and Ukrainians, the Polish have a passion for coffee and use it in many of their desserts.

INGREDIENTS

Serves 4

25g/1oz/6 tbsp finely ground coffee
300ml/½ pint/1¼ cups milk
150ml/¼ pint/⅔ cup single cream
2 eggs, beaten
30ml/2 tbsp caster sugar
whipped cream and cocoa powder,
  to decorate

1 Preheat the oven to 190°C/375°F/ Gas 5. Put the ground coffee in a jug. Heat the milk in a pan until it is nearly boiling. Pour over the coffee and leave to stand for 5 minutes.

2 Strain the coffee-flavoured milk back into the pan. Add the cream and heat again until nearly boiling.

3 Beat the eggs and sugar in a bowl. Pour the hot coffee-flavoured milk into the bowl, whisking all the time. Strain into the rinsed jug.

4 Pour the mixture into 4 × 150ml/ ¼ pint/⅔ cup ramekins. Cover each with a piece of foil.

5 Stand the ramekins in a roasting tin and pour in enough hot water to come halfway up the sides of the ramekins. Bake for 40 minutes, or until lightly set.

6 Remove the ramekins from the roasting tin and allow to cool. Chill for 2 hours. Decorate with a swirl of whipped cream and a sprinkle of cocoa powder, if liked, before serving.

Tort Migdalowy

Almonds are in plentiful supply in Poland and are used in both sweet and savoury dishes. Here they are roasted, giving this coffee-cream-filled sponge a rich and nutty flavour.

INGREDIENTS

Serves 8–10

75g/3oz/½ cup blanched almonds
225g/8oz/1 cup butter, softened
225g/8oz/generous 1 cup caster sugar
4 eggs, beaten
150g/5oz/1¼ cups self-raising flour, sifted

For the icing

175g/6oz/1 cup blanched almonds
40g/1½oz/9 tbsp ground coffee
75ml/5 tbsp near-boiling water
150g/5oz/¾ cup caster sugar
90ml/6 tbsp water
3 egg yolks
225g/8oz/1 cup unsalted butter

1 Preheat the oven to 190°C/375°F/ Gas 5. Lightly grease and base-line 3 × 18cm/7in round cake tins with greaseproof paper.

2 Put the blanched almonds on a baking sheet and roast in the oven for 7 minutes, or until golden brown.

3 Allow to cool, then transfer to a processor or a blender and process until fine.

4 Cream the butter and sugar together in a bowl until pale and fluffy. Gradually add the eggs, a little at a time, beating well after each addition. Fold in the ground roasted almonds and the flour.

5 Divide the cake mixture evenly between the 3 prepared tins and bake for 25–30 minutes, until well risen and firm to the touch, swapping the position of the top and bottom cakes halfway through cooking. Turn out and cool on a wire rack.

6 For the icing, put the blanched almonds in a bowl and pour over enough boiling water to cover. Leave until cold, then drain the almonds and cut each one lengthways into 4 or 5 slivers with a sharp knife. Roast on a baking sheet for 6–8 minutes.

7 Put the ground coffee in a jug, spoon over the water and leave to stand. Gently heat the sugar and 90ml/ 6 tbsp water in a small heavy-based pan until dissolved. Simmer for 3 minutes, until the temperature reaches 107°C/ 225°F on a sugar thermometer.

8 Put the egg yolks into a bowl and pour over the syrup in a thin stream, whisking all the time until very thick. Cream the butter until soft, then gradually beat the egg mixture into it.

9 Strain the coffee through a sieve and beat into the icing. Use two-thirds to sandwich the cakes together. Spread the remainder over the top and press in the almond slivers.

Raisin Cheesecake

Cheesecakes were originally baked rather than set with gelatine. This Ukrainian dessert is an Easter speciality.

INGREDIENTS

Serves 8
115g/4oz/1 cup plain flour
50g/2oz/4 tbsp butter
15ml/1 tbsp caster sugar
25g/1oz/¼ cup almonds, very finely chopped
30ml/2 tbsp cold water
15ml/1 tbsp icing sugar, for dusting

For the filling
115g/4oz/8 tbsp butter
150g/5oz/¾ cup caster sugar
5ml/1 tsp vanilla essence
3 eggs, beaten
25g/1oz/¼ cup plain flour, sifted
400g/14oz/1¾ cups curd cheese
grated rind and juice of 2 lemons
65g/2½oz/½ cup raisins

1 Sift the flour into a bowl. Rub in the butter, until the mixture resembles fine breadcrumbs. Stir in the sugar and almonds. Add the water and mix to a dough. Lightly knead on a floured surface for a few seconds. Wrap in clear film and chill for 30 minutes.

2 Preheat the oven to 200°C/400°F/ Gas 6. Roll out the pastry on a lightly floured surface to a 25cm/10in circle and use it to line the base and sides of a 20cm/8in tart tin. Trim the edges of the pastry with a sharp knife.

3 Prick with a fork, cover with oiled foil and bake for 6 minutes. Remove the foil and bake for 6 more minutes. Allow to cool and reduce the temperature to 150°C/300°F/Gas 2.

4 For the filling, cream the butter, sugar and vanilla essence together. Beat in one egg, then stir in the flour. Beat the cheese until soft, then gradually mix in the remaining eggs. Blend this into the butter mixture. Stir in the lemon rind, juice and raisins.

5 Pour the filling over the pastry base. Bake in the oven for 1½ hours, until firm. Turn off the oven, leave the door ajar and allow to cool before removing. Dust with icing sugar.

Polish Pancakes

Fluffy pancakes are filled with a cheese and sultana mixture.

INGREDIENTS

Makes 6

115g/4oz/1 cup plain flour
pinch of salt
pinch of grated nutmeg, plus extra
  for dusting
1 egg, separated
200ml/7fl oz/scant 1 cup milk
30ml/2 tbsp sunflower oil
25g/1oz/2 tbsp butter
lemon slices, to garnish

For the filling

225g/8oz/1 cup curd cheese
15ml/1 tbsp caster sugar
5ml/1 tsp vanilla essence
50g/2oz/scant ½ cup sultanas

1 Sift the flour, salt and nutmeg together in a large bowl. Make a well in the centre. Add the yolk and half of the milk. Beat until smooth, then gradually beat in the remaining milk.

2 Whisk the egg white in a bowl until stiff. Fold into the batter.

3 Heat 5ml/1 tsp sunflower oil and a little of the butter in an 18cm/7in frying pan. Pour in enough of the batter to cover the base.

4 Cook for 2 minutes, until golden brown, then turn over and cook for a further 2 minutes.

5 Make 5 more pancakes in the same way, using more oil and butter as necessary. Stack up the pancakes and keep them warm.

6 To make the filling, put the curd cheese, sugar and vanilla essence in a bowl and beat together. Mix in the sultanas. Divide among the pancakes, fold them up and dust with grated nutmeg. Garnish with lemon slices.

Creamy Millet Pudding

The composer Rimsky-Korsakov enjoyed collecting Russian folk-tales. As millet was often featured in them, he famously incorporated the line *A my proso seyali, seyali* ("And we sowed and we sowed millet") into his opera *Snegurochka* (*The Snow Maiden*).

INGREDIENTS

Serves 4
115g/4oz/scant 1 cup millet flakes
600ml/1 pint/2½ cups milk
thinly pared strip of lemon rind
15g/½ oz/1 tbsp butter
30ml/2 tbsp granulated sugar
2 egg whites
plum or apricot jam, to serve

1 Preheat the oven to 180°C/350°F/Gas 4. Put the millet flakes and milk into a small pan. Add the lemon rind and butter, then bring to the boil.

2 Lower the heat and simmer gently for 10 minutes, stirring, until the mixture thickens. Stir in the sugar. Leave to cool for 10 minutes, then remove the lemon rind and discard.

3 Whisk the egg whites in a bowl until stiff. Gently fold into the millet. Spoon into a buttered shallow 1.2 litre/2 pint/5 cup ovenproof dish.

4 Bake for 40–45 minutes, or until the top is golden brown and puffy. Serve hot with plum or apricot jam.

Fruit and Nut Semolina Pudding

This layered dessert was apparently created by Russian Finance Minister, Dmitry Guriev, to honour his country's victory over Napoleon in 1812.

INGREDIENTS

Serves 4
350g/12oz fresh soft fruit, such as cherries or plums, stoned and chopped
25g/1oz/2 tbsp caster sugar
15ml/1 tbsp water
600ml/1 pint/2½ cups milk
5ml/1 tsp vanilla essence
90ml/6 tbsp semolina
15g/½ oz/1 tbsp soft light brown sugar
50g/2oz/½ cup chopped toasted hazelnuts or almonds, plus a few extra to garnish

1 Put the fruit in a small pan with the caster sugar and water. Cook over a low heat for 8–10 minutes, until the fruit is just soft.

2 Put the milk and vanilla essence in another pan and bring to the boil. Gradually sprinkle in the semolina, whisking all the time. Simmer for 7–8 minutes, or until thick and creamy.

3 Remove from the heat and stir in the soft light brown sugar and chopped nuts. Spoon half the semolina into four individual serving dishes, then top with half the stewed fruit.

4 Spoon over a second layer of semolina. Top with the remaining fruit and the extra nuts. Serve warm or cold.

Paczki

These doughnuts are traditionally eaten in Poland on Shrove Tuesday, at midnight on New Year's Eve, and also at Epiphany (6 January) when a coin is hidden in one of them.

INGREDIENTS

Makes 16
450g/1lb/4 cups plain flour
7g/¼ oz sachet easy-blend
   dried yeast
25g/1oz/2 tbsp butter
75g/3oz/scant ½ cup caster sugar
2 eggs, beaten
150ml/¼ pint/⅔ cup warm water
30ml/2 tbsp dark rum
90ml/6 tbsp plum jam, warmed
   and sieved
oil, for deep frying

For the coating
75g/3oz/scant ½ cup caster sugar
10ml/2 tsp ground cinnamon

1 Sift the flour into a large bowl and stir in the dried yeast. Rub in the butter until the mixture resembles fine breadcrumbs, then stir in the sugar.

2 Make a well in the centre of the mixture, then add the eggs, water and rum, and mix to a soft dough. Turn out on to a lightly floured surface and knead for 10 minutes, or until smooth and elastic.

3 Put the dough in a clean bowl, cover with oiled clear film and leave in a warm place to rise for 1 hour, or until doubled in size.

4 Knead the dough again for 1–2 minutes. Divide into 16 equal pieces and shape each into a ball.

5 Flatten each ball, put 5ml/1 tsp jam in the middle, then gather the edges together over the jam and pinch firmly to seal.

6 Place the dough balls well apart on greased baking sheets and cover with oiled clear film. Leave in a warm place to rise for 30 minutes.

7 Heat the oil in a large pan or deep-fat fryer to 170°C/340°F and fry the doughnuts, a few at a time, for 5 minutes, or until golden brown, turning once during cooking. Drain on kitchen paper.

8 Mix the caster sugar and cinnamon in a bowl. Add the doughnuts one at a time and toss in the mixture to coat. Serve warm.

COOK'S TIP

Allow the doughnuts to cool for at least 10 minutes before serving, as the jam inside will be boiling hot.

Apricot Treat

Fresh fruit was once scarce in Poland during winter, so dried fruits were often used. This rich apricot and almond dessert, a favourite in Poland, resembles the sweetmeats more common to the Balkan regions.

INGREDIENTS

Serves 6

225g/8oz/1 cup ready-to-eat
   dried apricots, chopped
45ml/3 tbsp water
50g/2oz/¼ cup caster sugar
50g/2oz/½ cup chopped almonds
50g/2oz/⅓ cup chopped candied
   orange peel
icing sugar, for dusting
whipped cream, to serve
ground cinnamon, to decorate

1 Put the apricots and water in a heavy-based pan. Cover and simmer, stirring, for about 20 minutes, until a thick paste forms.

2 Stir in the caster sugar and simmer, stirring, for a further 10 minutes until quite dry. Remove from the heat and stir in the almonds and chopped orange peel.

3 Using a knife, shape into a "sausage", about 5cm/2in thick, on a piece of greaseproof paper dusted with icing sugar.

4 Leave to dry in a cool place for at least 3 hours. Cut into slices and serve with whipped cream, sprinkled with a little cinnamon.

Dried Fruit Compote

Fruit grows in abundance in orchards throughout the Ukraine and dried fruits are used all year round. *Uzvar* is served on Christmas Eve and also at feasts at which the dead are honoured. This easy and delicious dessert is also made in Russia.

INGREDIENTS

Serves 6

350g/12oz/2 cups mixed dried fruits,
   such as apples, pears, prunes, peaches
   or apricots
1 cinnamon stick
300ml/½ pint/1¼ cups cider or water
65g/2½ oz/½ cup raisins
30ml/2 tbsp clear honey
juice of ½ lemon
mint leaves, to decorate

1 Put the mixed dried fruit in a large pan with the cinnamon and cider or water. Heat gently until almost boiling, then cover the pan, lower the heat and cook gently for 12–15 minutes, to soften the fruit.

--- COOK'S TIP ---

This compote will keep refrigerated for up to a week.

2 Remove the pan from the heat and stir in the raisins and honey. Cover the pan and leave to cool. Remove the cinnamon stick and then stir in the lemon juice.

3 Transfer the compote to a serving bowl, cover with clear film and keep refrigerated until needed. Allow the fruit compote to come to room temperature before serving, decorated with a few mint leaves.

Plum and Almond Tart

Plums and almonds have a natural affinity, and this Russian tart with its simple pastry case is a great way to serve them. Serve with home-made custard.

INGREDIENTS

Serves 6
175g/6oz/1½ cups plain flour
115g/4oz/8 tbsp butter, chilled
60ml/4 tbsp soured cream

For the topping
50g/2oz/4 tbsp butter, softened
50g/2oz/¼ cup caster sugar, plus
  30ml/2 tbsp for sprinkling
2 eggs, beaten
115g/4oz/1 cup ground almonds
about 6 plums, quartered and stoned
115g/4oz/scant ½ cup plum jam
60ml/4 tbsp flaked almonds

1 Sift the flour into a mixing bowl. Dice the butter and rub in until the mixture resembles fine breadcrumbs. Stir in the soured cream to make a soft dough. Wrap in clear film and chill for at least 30 minutes.

COOK'S TIP

Apricots can be used instead of plums, as an alternative, if liked.

2 For the topping, cream the butter and sugar until light. Add the eggs, alternating with the ground almonds.

3 Preheat the oven to 220°C/425°F/ Gas 7. Roll out the pastry on a lightly floured surface to a 30cm/12in round, then transfer to a large baking sheet. Prick all over.

4 Spread the almond mixture over the pastry, leaving a border of about 4cm/1½ in. Arrange the plums on top. Sprinkle with the 30ml/2 tbsp caster sugar. Turn in the border.

5 Bake the tart for 35–40 minutes, or until browned. Warm the plum jam in a small pan, press through a sieve and brush over the tart to glaze. Sprinkle flaked almonds on top to decorate.

VARIATION

The recipe could be used to make 4 individual tarts, like the one shown here. Thickly slice the plums instead of cutting them into quarters. Finish the tarts as above with the jam glaze and flaked almonds.

Lepeshki

With characteristic Russian preference for all things sour, these biscuits are shortened with soured cream instead of butter.

INGREDIENTS

Makes 24

225g/8oz/2 cups self-raising flour
pinch of salt
90g/3½oz/½ cup caster sugar
1 egg, separated
120ml/4fl oz/½ cup soured cream
2.5ml/½ tsp each vanilla and
   almond essence
15ml/1 tbsp milk
50g/2oz/½ cup flaked almonds

1 Preheat the oven to 200°C/400°F/ Gas 6. Sift the flour, salt and sugar into a mixing bowl and make a well in the centre.

2 Reserve 10ml/2 tsp of the egg white. Mix the remainder with the egg yolk, soured cream, vanilla and almond essences and milk. Add to the dry ingredients and mix to form a soft dough.

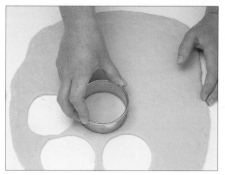

3 Roll out the dough on a lightly floured surface until about 8mm/⅓in thick, then stamp out rounds with a 7.5cm/3in cutter.

4 Transfer the circles to lightly oiled baking sheets. Brush with the reserved egg white and sprinkle with the flaked almonds.

5 Bake for 10 minutes, until light golden brown. Transfer to a wire rack and allow to cool. Store the biscuits in an airtight container.

Pyrizhky

These delicious Russian turnovers comprise a double helping of nuts: a buttery almond pastry with a walnut and rum filling.

INGREDIENTS

Makes 12
150g/5oz/1¼ cups plain flour
pinch of salt
65g/2½oz/5 tbsp caster sugar
50g/2oz/½ cup ground almonds
90g/3½oz/7 tbsp butter, cubed
2.5ml/½ tsp vanilla essence
1 egg, beaten, plus extra for sealing
    and glazing

For the filling
25g/1oz/2 tbsp unsalted butter,
    softened
50g/2oz/½ cup icing sugar, sifted
1 egg yolk
50g/2oz/½ cup walnuts, finely
    chopped
10ml/2 tsp rum

1 Sift the flour, salt and 40g/1½oz/ 3 tbsp caster sugar into a bowl. Stir in the ground almonds. Rub in the butter until the mixture resembles fine breadcrumbs. Make a well in the centre.

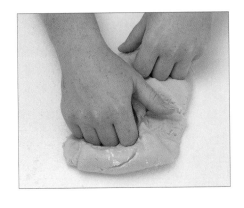

2 Add the vanilla essence and 1 beaten egg. Mix to a soft dough, then knead on a lightly floured surface for a few seconds until smooth. Wrap the dough in clear film and refrigerate for 40 minutes.

3 Meanwhile, for the filling, beat the butter and icing sugar together. Add the egg yolk and mix well. Fold in the walnuts and then stir in the rum.

4 Preheat the oven to 200°C/400°F/ Gas 6. Roll out the pastry 3mm/ ⅛in thick on a lightly floured surface. Cut into 7.5cm/3in squares, using a sharp knife or a pastry wheel.

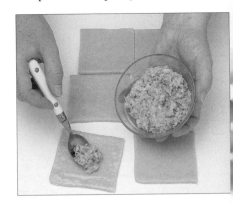

5 Brush the edges with beaten egg. Then place a spoonful of filling near one corner of each square.

6 Fold over the pastry to make triangles, then press the edges with a fork to seal. On a baking sheet, glaze with more egg and sprinkle with the remaining sugar. Bake for 15 minutes, until golden. Cool on a wire rack.

Babka

A typical Polish Easter menu is a grand affair and may include roast sucking pig, brightly coloured eggs and *Babka* – the word means "Grandmother". The cake was so named because it is made with gentleness and loving care.

INGREDIENTS

Serves 8
350g/12oz/3 cups plain flour
2.5ml/½ tsp salt
25g/1oz/2 tbsp caster sugar
5ml/1 tsp easy-blend dried yeast
115g/4oz/8 tbsp butter, softened
150ml/¼ pint/⅔ cup warm milk
4 egg yolks
115g/4oz/scant 1 cup sultanas
finely grated rind of 1 orange
60ml/4 tbsp clear honey, warmed
butter, to serve

1 Sift the flour, salt and sugar into a large bowl. Stir in the yeast, then make a well in the centre.

2 Add the butter, milk, egg yolks, dried fruit and orange rind. Mix to a dough. Turn out on a lightly floured surface and knead for 10 minutes, until smooth and elastic.

3 Put the dough in a well-greased 1.25kg/2½lb fluted cake tin. Cover with oiled clear film and leave in a warm place to rise for 1 hour, or until doubled in size.

4 Preheat the oven to 190°C/375°F/ Gas 5. Bake for 45–50 minutes, or until firm and a skewer inserted into the middle comes out clean.

5 Allow the cake to cool in the tin for 5 minutes. Turn out on to a wire rack and brush all over with the warmed honey. When cold, slice thickly and serve with butter.

Christmas Cookies

These spiced biscuits may be used as edible decorations: thread them with coloured ribbon and hang on the branches of the Christmas tree, as is traditionally done in the Ukraine.

INGREDIENTS

Makes 30
50g/2oz/4 tbsp butter
15ml/1 tbsp golden syrup or
   clear honey
50g/2oz/¼ cup soft light brown sugar
225g/8oz/2 cups plain flour
10ml/2 tsp ground cinnamon
5ml/1 tsp ground ginger
1.5ml/¼ tsp grated nutmeg
2.5ml/½ tsp bicarbonate of soda
45ml/3 tbsp milk
1 egg yolk
30ml/2 tbsp sugar crystals

1 Preheat the oven to 180°C/350°F/ Gas 4. Line 2 baking sheets with baking parchment. Melt the butter, syrup or honey and brown sugar in a pan. Leave to cool for 5 minutes.

2 Sift the flour, cinnamon, ginger, nutmeg and bicarbonate of soda into a bowl. Make a well in the centre. Pour in the melted butter mixture, milk and egg yolk. Mix to a soft dough.

3 Knead until smooth, then roll out between 2 sheets of baking parchment until 5mm/¼in thick. Stamp out rounds using biscuit cutters.

--- COOK'S TIP ---

Roll out the dough while it is still warm, since it becomes hard and brittle as it cools.

4 Place on the baking sheets. Make a hole in each with a skewer if you wish to hang them up later. Sprinkle with coloured sugar crystals. Bake for 10 minutes, until a slightly darker shade. Cool slightly, then transfer to a wire rack and leave to cool completely

Sour Rye Bread

Traditionally, the "starter" would be a little dough left over from a previous bread-making session, but it's simple to make your own. The starter gives this bread its delicious, slightly sour taste.

INGREDIENTS

Makes 2 loaves

450g/1lb/4 cups rye flour, plus extra
   for dusting (optional)
450g/1lb/4 cups strong white flour
15ml/1 tbsp salt
7g/¼oz sachet easy-blend
   dried yeast
25g/1oz/2 tbsp butter, softened
600ml/1 pint/2½ cups warm water
15ml/1 tbsp caraway seeds or
   buckwheat, for sprinkling (optional)

For the sourdough starter

60ml/4 tbsp rye flour
45ml/3 tbsp warm milk

1 For the starter, mix the rye flour and milk together in a small bowl. Cover with clear film and leave in a warm place for 1–2 days, or until it smells pleasantly sour.

2 To make the loaves, sift together the flour and salt into a large bowl. Next stir in the yeast. Make a well in the centre and add the butter, water and sourdough starter already prepared. With a wooden spoon mix well until you have a soft dough.

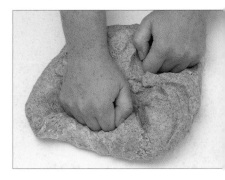

3 Turn out the dough on to a lightly floured surface and knead for 10 minutes, until smooth and elastic. Put in a clean bowl, cover with clear film and leave in a warm place to rise for 1 hour, or until doubled in size.

4 Knead for 1 minute, then divide the dough in half. Shape each piece into a round 15cm/6in across. Transfer to 2 greased baking sheets. Cover with oiled clear film and leave to rise for 30 minutes.

5 Preheat the oven to 200°C/400°F/ Gas 6. Brush the loaves with water, then sprinkle with caraway seeds or buckwheat, or dust with rye flour.

6 Bake for 35–40 minutes, or until the loaves are browned and sound hollow when tapped on the bottom. Cool on a wire rack.

--- COOK'S TIP ---

Sour rye bread keeps fresh for up to a week. This recipe can also be made without yeast, but it will be much denser.

Poppy Seed Roll

This sweet yeast bake with its spiral filling of dried fruits and poppy seeds is a wonderful example of traditional Polish cooking and is a firm favourite. The seeds have a gritty texture and keep the cake moist.

INGREDIENTS

Serves 12

450g/1lb/4 cups plain flour
pinch of salt
30ml/2 tbsp caster sugar
10ml/2 tsp easy-blend dried yeast
175ml/6fl oz/³⁄₄ cup milk
finely grated rind of 1 lemon
50g/2oz/4 tbsp butter

For the filling and glaze

50g/2oz/4 tbsp butter
115g/4oz/²⁄₃ cup poppy seeds
60ml/2fl oz/¹⁄₄ cup set honey
75g/2¹⁄₂oz/¹⁄₂ cup raisins
75g/2¹⁄₂oz/scant ¹⁄₂ cup finely
  chopped candied orange peel
50g/2oz/¹⁄₂ cup ground almonds
1 egg yolk
50g/2oz/¹⁄₄ cup caster sugar
15ml/1 tbsp milk
60ml/4 tbsp apricot jam
15ml/1 tbsp lemon juice
15ml/1 tbsp rum or brandy
25g/1oz/¹⁄₄ cup toasted
  flaked almonds

1 Sift the flour, salt and sugar into a bowl. Stir in the easy-blend dried yeast. Make a well in the centre.

2 Heat the milk and lemon rind in a pan with the butter, until melted. Cool a little, then add to the dry ingredients and mix to a dough.

3 Knead the dough on a lightly floured surface for 10 minutes, until smooth and elastic. Put in a clean bowl, cover and leave in a warm place to rise for 45–50 minutes, or until doubled in size.

4 For the filling, melt the butter in a pan. Reserve 15ml/1 tbsp of poppy seeds, then process the rest and add to the pan with the honey, raisins and peel. Cook gently for 5 minutes. Stir in the almonds; leave to cool.

5 Whisk the egg yolk and sugar together in a bowl until pale, then fold into the poppy seed mixture. Roll out the dough on a lightly floured surface to a rectangle 30 × 35cm/ 12 × 14in. Spread the filling to within 2.5cm/1in of the edges.

6 Roll both ends towards the centre. Cover with oiled clear film and leave to rise for 30 minutes. Preheat the oven to 190°C/375°F/Gas 5.

7 Brush with the milk, then sprinkle with the reserved poppy seeds. Bake for 30 minutes, until golden brown.

8 Heat the jam and lemon juice gently until bubbling. Sieve, then stir in the rum or brandy. Brush over the roll while still warm and scatter the almonds on top.

Braided Bread

This Ukrainian bread, *Kolach*, is served at many religious and family feasts. It is now usually only braided, but originally would have been shaped into a *kolo* (circle) – hence its name.

INGREDIENTS

Makes 1 large loaf
350g/12oz/3 cups strong white flour
5ml/1 tsp salt
5ml/1 tsp caster sugar
7g/¼oz sachet easy-blend dried yeast
150ml/¼ pint/⅔ cup milk
40g/1½oz/3 tbsp butter
1 egg, beaten, plus extra for glazing
10ml/2 tsp poppy seeds

1 Sift the flour, salt and sugar into a large bowl. Stir in the easy-blend dried yeast. Make a well in the centre.

2 In a pan, gently heat the milk with the butter until melted. Allow to cool until tepid, then add to the dry ingredients with the beaten egg. Mix to a soft dough.

3 Knead on a lightly floured surface for 10 minutes, or until smooth and elastic. Put in a clean bowl, cover with clear film and leave in a warm place to rise for 1 hour, or until doubled in size.

4 Preheat the oven to 200°C/400°F. Gas 6. Turn out the dough on a lightly floured surface and knead for 1 minute until smooth. Divide into 3 equal pieces. Roll each into a "sausage" about 25cm/10in long.

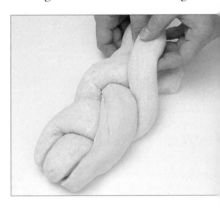

5 Braid the 3 strands together, starting with an outside strand, and working your way down. Stick the end under neatly at the end. Transfer to a lightly greased baking sheet. Cover with oiled clear film and leave to rise for 30 minutes.

6 Brush the loaf with beaten egg and sprinkle with the poppy seeds. Bake for 40–45 minutes or until golden brown. Cool on a wire rack.

Buckwheat Bread Rolls

These nutty-flavoured rolls are made using a mixture of flours, since buckwheat alone does not contain the gluten necessary for the bread to rise.

INGREDIENTS

Makes 16

350g/12oz/3 cups buckwheat flour
350g/12oz/3 cups strong white flour
10ml/2 tsp salt
7g/¼oz sachet easy-blend dried yeast
25g/1oz/2 tbsp butter, melted
about 600ml/1 pint/2½ cups
    warm water
30ml/2 tbsp olive oil
coarse salt, for sprinkling

1 Sift the flours and salt into a large bowl. Stir in the yeast and make a well in the centre. Add the butter and enough of the warm water to mix everything to a soft dough.

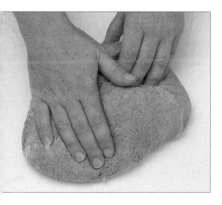

2 Knead the dough on a lightly floured surface for 10 minutes, or until smooth and elastic. Put in a clean bowl, cover with clear film and leave in a warm place to rise for 1 hour.

——— Cook's Tips ———

Buckwheat is a member of the rhubarb family and has triangular seeds, which produce a sweet and speckled flour.

3 Lightly knead the dough again until smooth. Divide into 16 equal pieces. Roll each into a ball and put on a greased baking sheet, leaving plenty of space between them.

4 Cover the rolls with oiled clear film and leave to rise for 30 minutes. Meanwhile, preheat the oven to 200°C/400°F/Gas 6.

5 Brush the rolls with the olive oil and sprinkle lightly with the salt.

6 Bake for 25–30 minutes, or until well risen and lightly browned. Cool on a wire rack, covering with a dish towel to keep the crust soft.

INDEX

Welcome!

To the start of your DJing career

DJing is no longer just the process of playing records. It's an incredibly addictive pastime that involves taking existing tracks and combining them to create something new and exciting. DJs such as Kissy Sell Out, James Zabiela and Eddie Halliwell regularly cut up and rearrange tracks live, as they play, using a variety of techniques. They might use hot cues, effects or music production techniques to create these edits and mash-ups.

Of course, it takes months, if not years, of hard work and dedication to become as skilled as those named above, but this MagBook is a great place to learn the basic techniques that will start you on your way to DJing superstardom.

We'll show you how to beatmix, how to DJ with Ableton Live and even what software and equipment is available for you to use, with reviews coming from the trusted and expert reviewers at DJ Worx. We've also got highly informative and inspirational interviews with top DJs such as Jordan Suckley, DJ Spoony and Amit, along with up-and-coming stars The Credence DJs.

We hope you'll have as much pleasure reading *How To DJ* as we did creating it, and get the best possible start to your DJing career, but don't stop there. Keep learning about the craft, keep experimenting and above all, have fun!

Andrew Unsworth
Editor

EDI
Edit
Andr
Production Editor
Steve Haines
Sub Editor
John Moore
Contributors
Anthony Enticknapp, Edward Jenkins, Desiree Oliver, Dominique Oliver, Mark Settle, Simon Rowbotham, Katie Wood
Special thanks
Tony Bellamy, James Bickerton, Johnathan Joseph, Amit Kamboj, Olly King, Sean Linney, Spencer Lowe, Steve Nash, Carl Nicholson, Jordan Suckley

ART & DESIGN
Art Editor Alex Westthorp
Cover Design Bill Bagnall
Photography Julian Velasquez, Henry Carter, Mark Settle

ADVERTISING & PRODUCTION
Senior Account Executive Matt Wakefield
0207 907 6617
Magbook Advertising Director Katie Wood
0207 907 6689
Digital Production Manager Nicky Baker

MANAGEMENT
MagBook Publisher Dharmesh Mistry
Operations Director Robin Ryan
MD of Advertising Julian Lloyd-Evans
Newstrade Director David Barker
Commercial & Retail Director Martin Belson
Chief Operating Officer Brett Reynolds
Group Finance Director Ian Leggett
Chief Executive James Tye
Chairman Felix Dennis

MAGBOOK

The MagBook brand is a trademark of Dennis Publishing Ltd, 30 Cleveland St, London W1T 4JD. Company registered in England.

All material © Dennis Publishing Ltd, licensed by Felden 2012, and may not be reproduced in whole or part without the consent of the publishers.

How To DJ ISBN 1-78106-095-9

LICENSING & SYNDICATION
To license this product, please contact Carlotta Serantoni on +44 (0) 20 7907 6550 or email carlotta_serantoni@dennis.co.uk.

To syndicate content from this product, please contact Anj Dosaj Halai on +44(0) 20 7907 6132 or email anj_dosaj-halai@dennis.co.uk.

LIABILITY
While every care was taken during the production of this MagBook, the publishers cannot be held responsible for the accuracy of the information or any consequence arising from it. Dennis Publishing takes no responsibility for the companies advertising in this MagBook.

The paper used within this MagBook is produced from sustainable fibre, manufactured by mills with a valid chain of custody.

Printed at BGP

Contents

Know Your Controller page 8

Know Your CDJ page 26

thedjguide.co

The Credence DJs **page 66**

Headphone Buying Guide **page 92**

Interview: DJ Spoony **page 104**

What is a DJ?

Technology has changed, but the role of the DJ is the same: to play music

Imagine a DJ at work, and what do you see? Once, you may have imagined an elderly baby boomer with a wacky beard and a penchant for charity, or some guy in a scary clown outfit begging young children to do The Superman. Nowadays, you're much more likely to imagine a stoned forty-something in Ibiza doing a Jesus pose behind a pair of Technics.

Since the likes of Fatboy Slim, Sasha and Paul Oakenfold ushered in the era of the superstar DJ, the public's perception of DJs and DJing has changed dramatically. Gone are the gaudy jumpers and shellsuits, having been replaced by ripped jeans and tight-fitting tops that really could do with a little slack. The modern perception of a DJ is as a highly paid god-like figure commanding the attention of thousands and sending them wild in ecstasy.

Yet despite what you may read in the press, hear on the radio and see on the TV, the art of DJing did not start with a superstar DJ using the latest gear in a vast superclub. The history of DJing is filled with ordinary men and women taking chances, making mistakes and, most importantly, making people dance.

Every superstar DJ – no matter how big their fanbase or how quickly they rose to fame – started somewhere. Every DJ had to learn to mix, get that all-important first gig and learn how to please a crowd.

In this MagBook we'll show you how to mix and how to use effects, hot cues and loops to create mash-ups and live remixes. We'll also show you the latest software and controllers available, how to get your first gig and even how to set up your own internet radio station – everything you need to know to get your DJing career started.

Practise non-stop, hone your skills and never say quit, even when there seems no hope of getting your big break, because you will get it. If you enjoy yourself, enjoy making other people happy and work hard you can become the next superstar DJ.

Know Your Gear

To be a world-class DJ, you obviously need to know your music, but unless you also know your gear inside out, you'll never be able to create exciting and unique mixes that tear the roof off the club.

In this chapter, we explain what a mixer, a CDJ and a controller do so you know exactly how your gear works. We also explain how to set up your computer for optimum performance, and advise you on what sound system you'll need.

Finally, we show you how to reduce the thing that vexes every digital DJ: latency. Latency is the time taken for something to happen when you've pressed a button, moved a jog wheel or activated an effect, and it can occur at many different places in your system. If you scratch a sample, for example, you want to hear the scratch instantly, not a few seconds after you've moved the jog wheel, because that might ruin your mix.

Knowing your equipment will enable you to unleash your creativity on the crowd and make you a better DJ. Read on to learn everything you need to know about your digital setup.

CHAPTER ONE

Know Your Controller

Want to create exciting and original mixes? Get to know your way around the most essential part of your kit, the controller

I f you want to get creative with your mixes like Eddie Halliwell and Kutski, then you need to know your controller inside out. There are two varieties of controller: modular and all-in-one. Modular controllers are designed to support DJs who need to control a specific subset of a software app, such as the mixer or effects sections. All-in-one controllers are designed to control the entire software application. They give you two or more decks, a mixer section and possibly an effects section so you can create mixes without having to touch your PC or laptop.

The controller shown here is the Denon MC2000, an all-in-one controller that lets you control effects, set loops and use 'hot cues' so that you can be as creative as you want to be.

The labels describe the common functions of a controller, some of which might not be available on the software you use with the MC2000.

Effects
DJs use effects to create tension, accentuate part of a track, mix out of a track and completely warp the original track. Popular effects include echo, flanger and filter, but unless your controller has a built-in effects processor, which is unlikely, the available effects will depend on the software you use.

Loop
The loop controls let you repeat sections of a track so that you can prolong mixes or layer the loop over another track. The best controllers also let you control the size of a loop while it's playing.

Jog wheels
DJs use jog wheels to scratch samples and move through tracks. Even though they look the same, the response of a jog wheel is different on each controller and depends on the technology and software used.

Pitch slider
The pitch slider lets you adjust the speed of a track so that you can get two or more tracks playing at the same speed.

Transport buttons
Transport buttons let you play and pause tracks, and set cue points.

Global controls

All controllers have a set of controls for specific functions, such as loading tracks in decks, browsing playlists and setting the behaviour of your decks. Some controllers have more global controls than others, and some controls are software-specific.

EQs

DJs adjust EQs to reduce or boost certain frequency bands. This lets DJs emphasise parts of a track or create smoother mixes. EQs let the DJ shape the sound subtly or boldly.

▲ Controllers let you make the most of your software

Hot cue buttons

Hot cues let you jump straight to a specific point in a track. This lets you change the order in which a track is played so that you can create a live edit. You can also use hot cues for drumming.

Faders

Faders are used to control the volume of your tracks. Channel faders (the four vertical faders shown here) control the volume of one specific channel, from no sound to full volume, while the crossfader (the single horizontal fader) is used to blend the output of two or more channels.

▲ Most controllers connect to a laptop via USB

Know Your Faders

These controls do far more than simply adjust the volume

Faders are the essential tools of the DJ's trade. Fundamentally, they control volume, but there's much more to faders than that. Different controllers and mixers have different types of fader, different fader sizes and different ways of releasing the sound. There are also a number of settings of which you must be aware.

Fader types

Your mixer or controller has two types of fader: the channel fader and the crossfader. The channel faders are used to control the volume of individual decks, while the crossfader is used to blend two tracks together, fading one track out while fading the other track in.

Some DJs prefer to mix using the channel faders only, while others ignore the channel faders completely, leaving them fully open and using only the crossfader. There's no right or wrong way.

Channel faders tend to have a longer throw, typically 60mm, whereas most crossfaders have a shorter throw, typically 45mm. The longer throw of the channel faders helps mix DJs combine and blend many tracks more harmoniously and with greater precision, while the shorter throw of the crossfader makes it perfect for scratch DJs, who can quickly throw it from one side to the other.

Style implies function

Your style of mixing has a massive bearing on the type of fader you need and the settings you should use. Do you scratch or

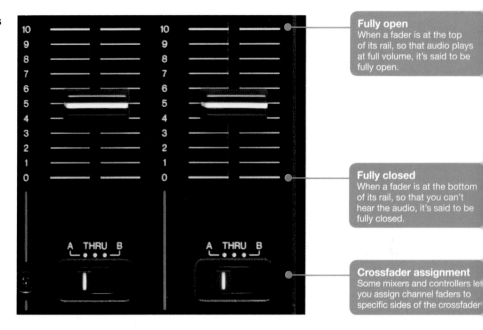

Fully open
When a fader is at the top of its rail, so that audio plays at full volume, it's said to be fully open.

Fully closed
When a fader is at the bottom of its rail, so that you can't hear the audio, it's said to be fully closed.

Crossfader assignment
Some mixers and controllers let you assign channel faders to specific sides of the crossfader

beatjuggle? Are you a club DJ mixing house or some other EDM genre?

Crossfaders, in particular, have a number of settings such as cut-in and curve, which can be altered to suit your style.

Cut-in refers to the point at which sound is heard when you open the crossfader, and can be as miniscule as 1mm so that the sound on the opposite deck is heard as soon as you move the crossfader, or as wide as 4mm or more. Regardless of your style, setting the cut-in to its shortest length seems like a common sense thing to do, but if it's too short you'll only have to nudge it slightly to release the tune playing on the opposite side of the crossfader. If you're beatmixing with your headphones on, you may not

notice, but your audience probably will, leading to much embarrassment.

Curve settings control the speed at which the full volume is released. If you take a regular channel fader as an example, moving it from the closed to the open position releases the volume in a steady, linear fashion. If you soften the curve, it takes longer for the fader to get to full volume. If you sharpen the curve, the fader reaches full volume within a shorter distance of fader travel. Sadly, not all mixers and controllers provide curve controls. If a mixer or controller has a curve control, it's usually for the crossfader.

If your mixer or controller has fader controls, play around with them to see which suits your style best.

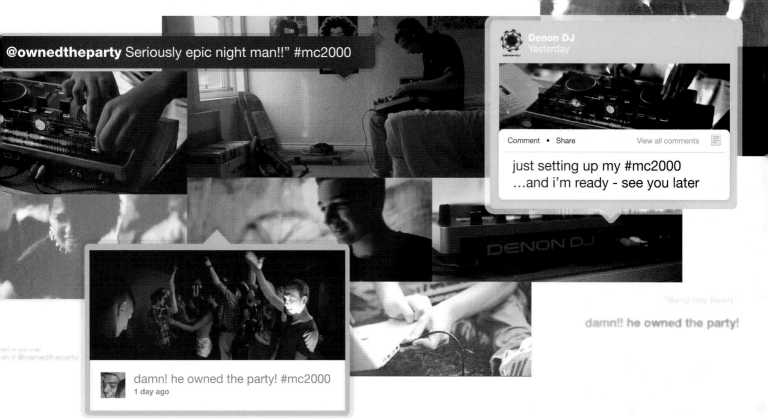

Own the party. #mc2000.

You want to lead the crowd - not just be part of it. Step up from the dance floor to the decks with the Denon DJ MC2000, the first truly affordable pro-grade DJ controller designed to get you filling the floor in no time at all. Hook it up via USB to your laptop, fire up the Serato DJ Intro software and you're ready to rock the room with dual deck control, built-in effects, loop points and advanced iTunes® integration.

Get ready at **denondj.com**

serato DJ INTRO

iTunes is a trademark of Apple Inc., registered in the U.S. and other countries.

Know Your DVS

Already own a set of turntables or CDJs? Digital vinyl systems let you combine your existing kit with creative DJing software

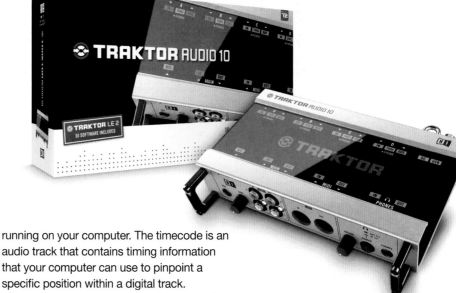

Carrying heavy record boxes and DJ equipment has never been popular with DJs, no matter how much they love their work, so it's no surprise that the digital vinyl system (DVS) was met with much enthusiasm.

The DVS is a bit of kit that lets DJs use their existing setup to control software in addition to playing regular CDs and vinyl. The DVS gives DJs the best of both worlds.

As vinyl became ever more expensive and legally downloading tracks became easier, the DVS became even more attractive.

If a DJ hears a killer track that they just have to use in their set, they no longer have to search for it on vinyl or CD, a task made all the more difficult if there's a limited number of CD and vinyl copies of the track in existence. DJs can download the track, play their set as normal and then, when they need to drop it, they can switch to the DVS and mix it in.

As DVSs have developed, many more features, such as loops, hot cues and effects, have been added. DVSs not only make DJing less painful and less expensive, they also open up a new vista of creativity that frees DJs from the shackles of a linear deck-to-deck style of mixing.

How the DVS works

Fundamentally, a DVS comprises an audio interface, timecode on vinyl or CD and a software application. The audio interface acts as a bridge between your existing turntable or CDJ setup and the software application

running on your computer. The timecode is an audio track that contains timing information that your computer can use to pinpoint a specific position within a digital track.

As an example, suppose you have a track loaded in deck A of the software application. The point at which the timecode begins is equivalent to the starting point of the track in deck A.

When you play the timecode, the software application translates it and plays the track at the exact time indicated by the timecode. If you play the timecode from the beginning, then the track in deck A will play from the beginning. If you hit play two minutes into the timecode, then the software application will play two minutes into the track in deck A.

Proprietary and open systems

Despite its name, you don't need traditional turntables to use a digital vinyl system. All you

need is some method of passing timecode to a software application running on a computer. Typically, you get a set of vinyl records and a set of CDs containing the timecode, but nowadays it's common to see DJs playing timecode from USB drives as well.

Even though all timecode does the same job, most of it is proprietary and will work only with specific software, such as Serato Scratch or Traktor Scratch Pro 2. There are, however, some software applications, such as Deckadance (**www.deckadance.com**), that you use different brands of timecode to control them. Such software systems are excellent value if you already have a decent audio interface and just want to try a DVS.

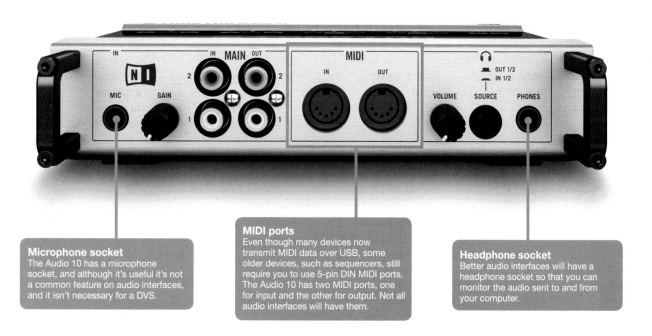

THE AUDIO INTERFACE IN DETAIL

The audio interface below is a Native Instruments Audio 10. It's designed to be used with Native Instruments' Traktor Scratch Pro 2, but you can also use it with software such as Deckadance or with music-production software such as Ableton Live 8.

The Audio 10 has five stereo input channels and five stereo output channels, which means you can control all four virtual decks in Traktor and still have a stereo input and a stereo output channel available for other uses. Other audio interfaces will have a different number of input and output channels, but they essentially work in the same way.

Ground screw
Analogue turntables are attached to ground posts in order to prevent ground hum, which manifests itself as an unpleasant humming noise. Ground hum interferes with a DVS's ability to translate timecode, so make sure your turntables are grounded.

USB port
Many years ago, FireWire ports were common, but this changed with the advent of USB2, and now most audio interfaces have USB ports. The USB port is used to transmit audio and MIDI data to and from your PC.

Input and output channels
The input channels are used to push audio from turntables, CDJs and musical instruments to your computer. The output channels return audio to your mixer from your computer.

Microphone socket
The Audio 10 has a microphone socket, and although it's useful it's not a common feature on audio interfaces, and it isn't necessary for a DVS.

MIDI ports
Even though many devices now transmit MIDI data over USB, some older devices, such as sequencers, still require you to use 5-pin DIN MIDI ports. The Audio 10 has two MIDI ports, one for input and the other for output. Not all audio interfaces will have them.

Headphone socket
Better audio interfaces will have a headphone socket so that you can monitor the audio sent to and from your computer.

Know Your
Connections

Unsure what the connections on your
mixer or controller do? Find out here

RCA connectors
RCA connectors are incredibly
versatile. They're used to input
and output audio and are used
with a variety of sources, such
as phono turntables, CDJs and
even musical instruments.

Y ou've got your mixer or controller, but how do you connect it to your laptop and your sound system? What's the difference between an XLR connector and an S/PDIF connector? Do those connectors even do the same thing?

The purpose of a controller is to receive data from a PC and send data back to it, and some controllers also have built-in audio interfaces that let them send and receive audio. The way in which the data is moved from one device to another is dependent on the controller and the connectors it has.

The connections shown here belong to the Pioneer DJM-900NXS, which has most of the connections DJs need. It's actually a digital mixer and controller combined, but it ably demonstrates most of the connection types you can expect to find on your controller or mixer.

Power connector
A small number of controllers
are powered by USB, but
most are powered from the
mains. Some have built-in
power supplies that use
'kettle-lead' connectors such
as this. Others have a figure-
of-8 power connector or a
round transformer jack.

XLR connectors
XLR connectors are
typically used to
output audio to a
power amp, as they are
here, or to receive input
from a microphone.

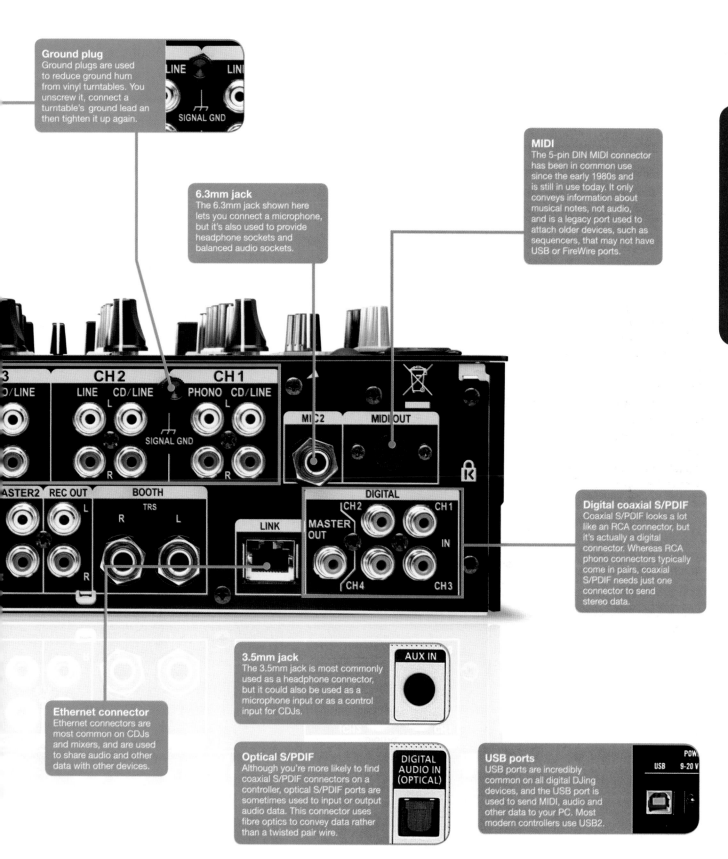

Ground plug
Ground plugs are used to reduce ground hum from vinyl turntables. You unscrew it, connect a turntable's ground lead an then tighten it up again.

6.3mm jack
The 6.3mm jack shown here lets you connect a microphone, but it's also used to provide headphone sockets and balanced audio sockets.

MIDI
The 5-pin DIN MIDI connector has been in common use since the early 1980s and is still in use today. It only conveys information about musical notes, not audio, and is a legacy port used to attach older devices, such as sequencers, that may not have USB or FireWire ports.

Digital coaxial S/PDIF
Coaxial S/PDIF looks a lot like an RCA connector, but it's actually a digital connector. Whereas RCA phono connectors typically come in pairs, coaxial S/PDIF needs just one connector to send stereo data.

Ethernet connector
Ethernet connectors are most common on CDJs and mixers, and are used to share audio and other data with other devices.

3.5mm jack
The 3.5mm jack is most commonly used as a headphone connector, but it could also be used as a microphone input or as a control input for CDJs.

Optical S/PDIF
Although you're more likely to find coaxial S/PDIF connectors on a controller, optical S/PDIF ports are sometimes used to input or output audio data. This connector uses fibre optics to convey data rather than a twisted pair wire.

USB ports
USB ports are incredibly common on all digital DJing devices, and the USB port is used to send MIDI, audio and other data to your PC. Most modern controllers use USB2.

KNOW YOUR GEAR

Know Your PC

A decent computer is essential for the smooth running of your digital DJ setup. Make sure you invest in a good PC to get the best out of it

The computer is the central nervous system of your digital DJing setup. It's the component that houses your tunes, runs your DJing software and lets you download videos of a monkey pulling a dog's tail, so it's tempting to rush out and buy the most expensive PC or, if you're anything like us, spend your money on sweets and coffee instead.

DJing software demands a lot of your computer, but that doesn't necessarily mean you need to have the latest state-of-the-art Core i7, 16GB number-crunching behemoth sitting on your laptop stand. Even a modest PC with a seemingly outdated spec is capable of running some DJing software, assuming you bought the PC in the last couple of years.

Keeping it dry

Even so, a DJing computer needs to do more than count numbers quickly and efficiently, especially if you're using it at a club or a house party. Drunken revellers are notoriously generous with their drinks, and will take every opportunity to share them with your equipment, especially if it's shiny and expensive. Even if your laptop isn't given a lager bath, it can still pick up grease and contaminants from grubby fingers covered in the residue of sugary liquids and bodily fluids.

And then there's the moisture. Never mind steaming hot superclubs clogged with the evaporated sweat of a thousand eager clubbers; even a pub can become a sweatbox once you've got an enthusiastic crowd dancing to your latest world-class dubstep set. Any laptop or PC you take to the venue needs to withstand the pressure of its environment or be something you can easily replace should it fail.

Throwing shapes

The other consideration you need to make is whether or not you need a laptop. They look cool, but if it's being used in your home studio, why not use a desktop PC instead? Desktop PCs tend to be more powerful and have greater amounts of RAM than their portable cousins, all of which makes them better able to deal with the stresses of your DJing applications. You're not restricted by screen size either, so you can spend the

ash you would have spent on a laptop on a
gh-quality 27in monitor instead. Then, you
on't have to squint to make out the title of
track in your software's browser.
There's always the option of a rack-
ounted PC, too. Rack-mounts are
esigned to be housed in a strong,
otective case, which makes them ideal
r DJing, as long as they're designed for
at purpose. Valeway Technology (**www.
lewaytechnology.com**) specialises in the
anufacture of specialist DJing computer
stems and can either build you a
ck-mount DJing PC or sell you a pre-
onfigured model.

omputers you can count on
onsumer PCs, both desktop and
ptop, are general-purpose machines.
hey're designed to suit the largest
umber of people and the widest range of
tivities. For that reason, they're largely
compromise. Some manufacturers may
roduce ranges that appeal to certain
udiences, but these are still pretty much
ased on existing models.
Workstations PCs, on the other hand,
e typically produced using higher-quality,
dustrial-grade components that are
esigned for reliability and stress. The
e thing you need from a laptop or PC
bove all else is reliability. You can have
e greatest, most expensive controller
vailable and you can have a thousand
cstatic ravers screaming your name, but
your PC fails the night's over, unless you
ave an iPod handy.
Most PC manufacturers have a
orkstation range, including Dell (**www.
ell.co.uk**), Lenovo (**www.lenovo.co.uk**)
d HP (**www.hp.co.uk**), but you can
xpect to pay more for such models
ecause of the higher-quality
omponents used.
Workstations can be
esktop or laptop
odels, so you
hould be able to
d a model to
it your needs.
s also a good
ea to check out the
arranty on such items to see if it
cludes on-site repair.

Balancing components
Laptops and desktops comprise many
different components, and some are
more important than others. We'll
go through them one by one
and explain which are most
relevant to digital DJing.

Processor
It's a regularly
used cliché, but
the processor,
or CPU, really is
the brain of your
computer. If your
CPU struggles to draw a dialog box, then
it's definitely going to struggle with Traktor,
so you need a decent one.
Only a few years ago, the CPU's clock
speed pretty much told you how powerful
it was, but with the proliferation of
multicore CPUs it has become a lot more
difficult to tell which is best. CPU naming
systems don't help much, either, although
they are getting better.
When it comes to DJing, the clock
speed is still important. The processor
must be able to process information quickly
in order to run your DJing software; any
delay and your sound and controls will
suffer. What's the point in practising that
killer drop if your laptop stalls the very
moment you try to execute it? It may work

perfectly a few seconds later, but by then
it's too late – your mix is ruined.
Native Instruments specifies a 2GHz Intel
Core 2 Duo or AMD Athlon 64 X2 CPU as
the minimum requirement for Traktor Pro
2, which is a specification that most recent
laptops will meet. Virtual DJ and Serato
Scratch also require similar CPUs.
Sadly, bare hardware doesn't mean you'll
get smooth performance. Your software
shares the CPU with your PC's operating
system, anti-virus software and whatever
else you have installed, and if any or all of
those applications demand more than their
fair share of CPU time the performance of
your DJing software may suffer.

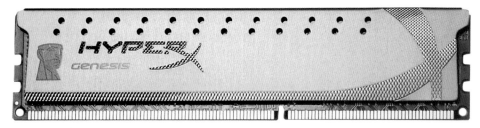

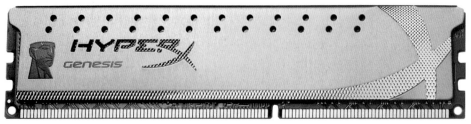

▲ More memory lets your computer run more plug-ins and more complex applications

Even so, you're much better off with a multicore CPU such as the Core 2 Duo than a single core CPU. Operating systems even the load over the many cores so that the CPU can effectively deal with many open applications. Certain DJing applications, such as Traktor Scratch Pro 2 and Ableton Live 8, can also use multiple cores to increase performance.

If you're in the market for a new laptop or CPU, check out Intel's Core ix CPUs. These CPUs are split into three ranges: Core i3, Core i5 and Core i7, with Core i3 CPUs being the entry-level models and Core i7 being the most powerful. Even though Core i3 is considered entry level, a fast Core i3 complemented by a decent set of components is good enough to run your DJing software.

If you're thinking of buying or upgrading your CPU then get the most powerful you can afford. Not because you need it now, but because it will be better able to process later revisions of your DJing software. This means you won't have to upgrade it as quickly.

Memory
The amount of RAM in your computer greatly affects the performance of your DJing software. Again, just because your DJing software says your system has the required amount of RAM, it doesn't mean that it will run smoothly if you also have other programs and services running in the background, such as anti-virus software and widgets.

The amount of memory needed is also dependent on your operating system. Modern operating systems are more complex and require more memory, whereas older operating systems such as Windows XP typically need a little less. It's a good idea to install as much RAM as you can, but that's going to be an expensive and, for the moment, unnecessary solution. As a general rule, if you're using a 64-bit operating system then you should aim for 8GB of RAM, but you should be fine with 4GB. If you're running a 32-bit Windows operating system, you're limited to around 3.2GB of RAM, even if you install 4GB in your PC. However, if you're running Windows XP 32-bit you might get away with 2GB of RAM, but whichever 32-bit Windows OS you're running, you're better off with 3GB, so get it installed if possible.

Different motherboards have different limits on the RAM capacity you can install. Laptops, especially, may limit you to a lower capacity, such as 3GB or 4GB. Check your PC system builder's website to see how much RAM you can install in your computer before you buy.

Hard disks and SSDs
There are two types of drive available for your computer: mechanical hard disks and solid-state drives (SSDs). Mechanical hard disks contain moving parts that read magnetic data off spinning platters, whereas solid-state drives read data stored in a form of persistent memory. Hard disks are much slower than SSDs but can store far more data, which makes them great for storing media such as your music and videos. SSDs, on the other hand, are extremely fast but offer much lower capacities for the same amount, which makes an SSD a great option for storing your operating system and DJing applications.

If your DJing computer is a desktop PC, you could always install an SSD for your OS and apps and a mechanical hard disk purely for your media, giving you the best of both worlds. If you do this, go for a 240GB SSD. This gives you plenty of space for your OS and applications now, and plenty of space for future expansion. If your budget can't stretch to a 240GB model (and 240GB SSDs are still expensive), you can get away with

◀ A fast graphics card isn't particularly important for DJing software

20GB. The mechanical hard disk can be a size appropriate to your library, but currently the best-value internal hard disks are 2TB models.

If you already have a laptop, your options are much more limited, and sticking with what you have is probably the best option. If you're buying a laptop, consider models with a solid-state drive. You'll lose out on capacity, but the speed advantage is worth it.

Some of the best places to buy drives, mechanical or solid state, are Scan (**www.scan.co.uk**), Dabs (**www.dabs.com**) and LambdaTek (**www.lambda-tek.co.uk**). Check out magazines such as *Computer Shopper* and *Micro Mart* and websites such as Expert Reviews (**www.expertreviews.co.uk**) to find the best models.

Sound card

Don't worry too much about the sound card in your laptop or PC, because chances are you'll use the audio interface in your controller to route audio to your speakers. If you don't have a controller yet, then two headphone outputs will be handy so that you have one output for your headphones and one for your speakers.

A dedicated DJing audio interface typically has better sound and is better able to meet the multi-channel requirements of DJing software than your computer's built-in sound card.

Sound advice

Something that isn't as important if you're using your computer in a club is sound-proofing, but it could be important if you're using it as your home-studio computer, especially if you use it to record your sets.

Computers, even laptops, can be noisy if you're using them to perform an intensive task such as running a digital vinyl system. The only way of silencing a laptop is to turn it off, but then it isn't much use. You can, however, sound-proof a PC to a degree.

You can do it one of two ways: by buying sound-deadening panels and attaching it to your PC's case, or by replacing your PC's components with quieter models. Components such as CPU coolers and graphics cards can be swapped for silent models, although you'll have to make sure there's enough room in your computer's case to accommodate a quiet heatsink for a powerful processor.

Sound-deadening panels cost around £10 from online stores such as Scan.

Graphics cards

You don't need the latest 3D gaming card to run DJing software. If you're upgrading or building a desktop system, get a decent passively cooled graphics card. Passively cooled graphics cards don't have noisy fans, so won't interfere with the sound of your DJing. If you have a laptop or if you're getting one, you'll be fine with its built-in graphics processor.

Windows or Mac OS?

With Apple producing Intel-based Macs, this age-old argument is more pointless now than it has ever been, and really comes down to personal preference. As long as your hardware's in good working order, both operating systems let you run DJing software reliably.

A case in point

To prove that you don't need an expensive Core i7 monster for DJing, take a look at our test laptop. It's a Samsung Q330 with a Core i3 CPU and 3GB of RAM. It has a mechanical hard disk and runs a 32-bit operating system. Despite its seemingly low specification, it runs Traktor Scratch Pro at very low latency settings. It's no longer on sale, but it proves that even a modest laptop can run a powerful digital vinyl system.

Scan 3XS systems

Scan has a good reputation as a supplier of PC components, but in recent years it has ventured into the sale of DJing controllers and accessories, as well as the sale of pre-built music-production PCs.

3XS, Scan's in-house system-building team, has produced a number of desktop and laptop models. At the time of writing, the cheapest was the 3XS S177 Tour RackDAW rackmount PC, at £1,078 inc VAT. It comprises a quad-core Intel Core i5 3550 CPU, a Noctua quiet CPU cooler, 4GB of RAM and sound-deadening panels.

As for 3XS's laptops, an example is the Scan Performance 17in laptop, which costs £1,405 inc VAT and comprises a 2.2GHz Intel Core i7 2720QM CPU, 8GB of RAM and a 7,200rpm

Seagate Momentus hard disk. For further details, check out the 3XS website at **www.scan.co.uk/shop/pro-audio**.

The Lowdown On Latency

Getting nasty noises? We show you
how to lessen latency for sweet sound

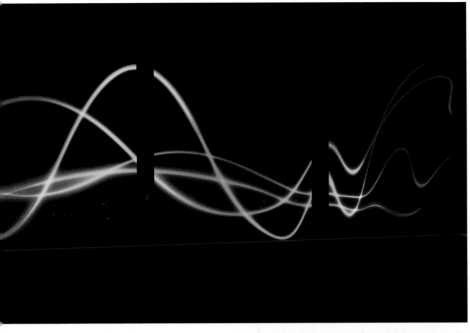

Ever had one of those dreams where you're being chased by a horde of zombies and you can't move until they're right on top of you, no matter how much you try to push yourself? A similar experience happens with your audio interface when there's too much latency in the connection. At least, it seems that way to us. For the data travelling from your device to your PC, it's probably a different story, one in which they meet some friends outside a pub, start drinking, lose track of time and end up at the PC after rolling out of a club at 3am.

You see, latency is the delay between you doing something on the controller and the effect of that action being heard. As an example, suppose you're playing a track and you move your controller's jog wheel to scratch part of it. If you scratch the sample and nothing happens for a while, that's latency, or a type of it. Latency occurs at different parts of the audio I/O process, and is caused for different reasons.

To give another, more concrete, example of latency, we once connected the record output of our mixer to a cheap audio interface in order to record our set. The audio interface was connected to a computer's speakers to monitor the mix being recorded. The latency between us scratching and eventually hearing the sound fed through the PC was so huge you could have knitted a jumper in it. In reality, it was two seconds, which is nothing if you're going about your normal everyday business, but that two-second delay between doing something on our decks and hearing the result of that action is much too large. DJs need to hear the results of their actions milliseconds later, not seconds.

Although the audio interfaces found on modern DJ gear are much better than they were just a few years ago, you still need to tweak latency for a number of reasons. Let's take a look at some of them.

Why does latency occur?

Latency occurs naturally because of the sequential nature of generating data and sending it somewhere. To output audio, your computer must retrieve audio data from its memory or hard disk, pass the data to its audio interface's digital-to-audio convertor (DAC) to turn the raw binary data into something you can hear, and then it sends the audio to an amplifier. Finally, the audio travels from a set of speakers to your ears. Each of these events adds time to the process. It may only be milliseconds, but these soon build up to produce a noticeable delay.

In the same way that you can't taste a cup of coffee till you've boiled some water, poured it on coffee granules and lifted the cup to your mouth, so you can't hear the audio until it's been through each stage of the process.

Latency occurs in both directions, too. You'll certainly notice this if you're using a DVS. With a DVS, you use timecode to send tracking data to your PC. This tracking data is then used to pinpoint an exact place in a track, and then your computer sorts out the audio generation. The computer has to process the audio coming in and going out, which adds even more time.

Another reason for latency, and one that can be controlled, is the way your computer deals with audio data. We refer to incoming and outgoing audio as streams of data, and it's good to imagine a stream of audio flowing along a channel, through your computer and out to your sound system. If that stream dries up, you'll have a drought of audio data and you'll encounter sound problems. You'll also have sound problems if you flood the computer with audio data.

The PC manages the flow of audio data with a sample buffer, which is a portion of memory in which the computer temporarily stores audio data. The size of a sample buffer is measured in samples. For DJs, an effective sample buffer is usually sized between 64 and 512 samples, with a lower buffer size providing lower latency and a higher buffer size providing higher latency. Given that fact, it's easy to assume you just need to set the sample buffer to its lowest size in order to acheive low latency, but unfortunately it isn't that simple.

If you set the sample buffer too high, you'll wait a lifetime before you hear anything, and if you set it too low your audio will be ruined by clicks, pops and other noises. The sample buffer you choose is dependent on a number of factors, such as the speed of your PC and the applications running on it.

Combating latency

Low latency is the goal of the digital DJ, and to find the lowest latency you need to adjust the sample buffer on a trial-and-error basis. We find that it's best to start with the lowest figure you can specify, which is usually a buffer of 64 samples. Typically, you set the sample buffer using the software utility that came with your controller, audio interface or mixer. Often, the sample buffer is controlled by a slider. Set the slider to the lowest point and then use your software. If your software produces sound that contains audible pops, clicks or other noises, increase the sample buffer by one notch and use your software again. When your mix is no longer ruined by noises, you've found the best latency setting for your setup.

SETTING THE SAMPLE BUFFER

Setting the sample buffer to the appropriate size for your setup is essential if you want the perfect combination of clean, glitch-free sound and a responsive system.

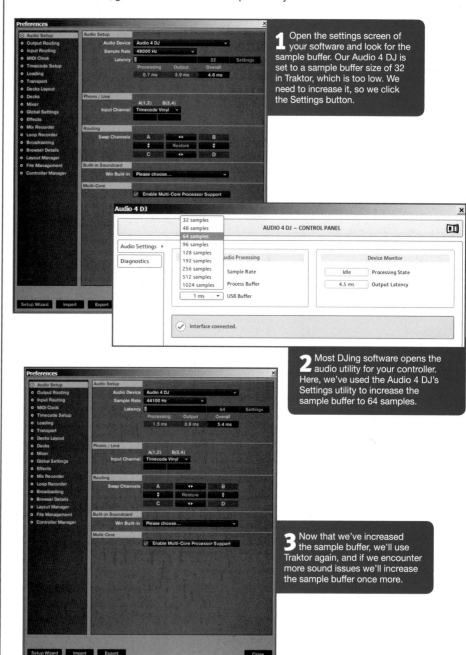

1 Open the settings screen of your software and look for the sample buffer. Our Audio 4 DJ is set to a sample buffer size of 32 in Traktor, which is too low. We need to increase it, so we click the Settings button.

2 Most DJing software opens the audio utility for your controller. Here, we've used the Audio 4 DJ's Settings utility to increase the sample buffer to 64 samples.

3 Now that we've increased the sample buffer, we'll use Traktor again, and if we encounter more sound issues we'll increase the sample buffer once more.

The sample buffer isn't the only factor affecting latency and your sound, however. Your USB ports and audio interface also have an effect, so make sure you're using the latest drivers for your gear. Just because your system plays Tetris, it doesn't mean it will get on with your audio interface, so check your audio interface or controller manufacturer's website to see if there's a newer version. Remember that just because a company releases a driver it doesn't mean it's stable. If you install a driver and then experience problems, don't be afraid of going back to the old one; just wind it back.

Know Your Sound System

Find out about the equipment you need to get sound from your setup

So you've got your controller, you've got your software and, most importantly, you've got your tunes. Before you can get your neighbours banging on the wall with excitement, though, you need to get some sound. Here we look at the equipment you need.

Home hi-fi

The type of sound system you use depends on the place in which your gear is used, and what gear you already have available. Chances are that you already have something you can use, such as a home hi-fi system, an iPod dock or an old amplifier. If you have one of these items, check to see if it has an auxiliary input. If it does, it will probably be a pair of RCA connectors, which is perfect for your needs. The vast majority of mixers and controllers have at least one set of RCA outputs, so you'll be able to plug your mixer or controller in to your hi-fi, iPod dock or amplifier and mix a killer set straight away.

Studio monitors

If you don't have any sound equipment at all, you have a number of choices. One option is to use studio monitors. These are speakers, typically bookshelf size, that are popular with many DJs because they're designed to give DJs and producers a clear impression of the audio they're playing through them.

Many manufacturers produce studio monitors. Some of the most well known names are KRK Systems (**www.krksys.com**), Genelec (**www.genelec.com**) and Yamaha (**uk.yamaha.com**).

Studio monitors can be passive or active. If you have no sound system at all, it's best to get active monitors, because they have an amplifier built in to each speaker. This means you don't have to buy an amplifier as well, or find space for it, but it does mean that the monitors are heavier and if something goes wrong with the amp then you lose a speaker.

Studio monitors can take a variety of inputs, typically RCA, 6.3mm jack and XLR, which offers users a great deal of flexibility when attaching equipment, because chances are your mixer or controller will have an output to match.

Amp and loudspeaker

Another option is to use an amplifier and a set of passive loudspeakers. With this option, you have the flexibility of replacing either the loudspeakers or the amplifier should you want to upgrade them or they break down. You can also buy a setup designed for the home, so that you can enjoy your music when not mixing, or for pubs and clubs.

If you're mixing in your home studio, then it makes sense to go for the consumer option. You'll get great hi-fi sound and you can plug other devices in to it, such as MP3 players and Blu-ray players.

If you only need a sound system for when you're playing in the pub or club, then you should look at a PA amp and speaker combo. PA systems are designed for high volume and for projecting sound over a large area, such as a dancefloor, and not necessarily for pleasing audiophiles, although some of the more expensive options do produce great sound.

When connecting your mixer or controller to a home hi-fi amp, you'll probably attach it using RCA cables, but some modern amps have digital S/PDIF inputs.

If your mixer or controller has a digital input, then you could always use that instead of RCA connections. The advantage of this is that you pass the digital audio straight to your amplifier, which then translates the digital audio in to analogue audio that you can hear. This means

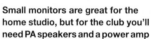

Small monitors are great for the home studio, but for the club you'll need PA speakers and a power amp

that you minimise sound degradation. You typically connect hi-fi speakers to your amplifier using banana plugs, but sometimes you just need to clip the bare speaker wire onto your speaker.

Power amps

With PA systems, it's a bit different. PA amps are power amps, and that means they don't do anything to the audio except amplify it and output sound to some speakers. Power amps usually have balanced XLR or 6.3mm TRS jack inputs. Essentially, the use of balanced connection types is used to minimise noise interference when using long cables, which is especially helpful when you're performing in a large pub or club.

At one time, only the most expensive mixers and controllers had balanced XLR or TRS outputs, but now it seems as if every other device has them. If the outputs on your mixer and controller match the input

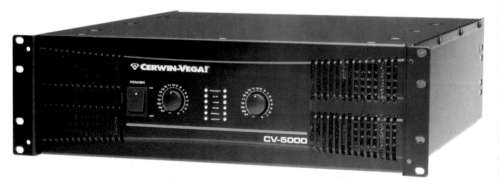

ACTIVE MONITORS IN DETAIL

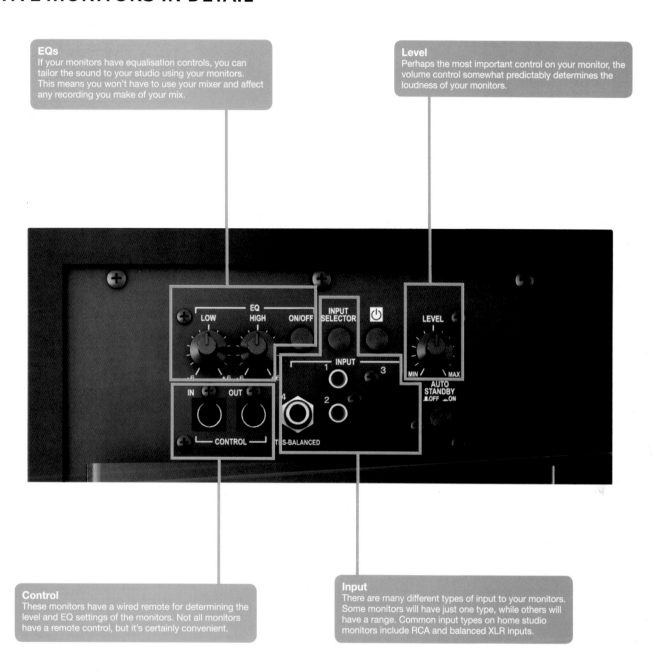

EQs
If your monitors have equalisation controls, you can tailor the sound to your studio using your monitors. This means you won't have to use your mixer and affect any recording you make of your mix.

Level
Perhaps the most important control on your monitor, the volume control somewhat predictably determines the loudness of your monitors.

Control
These monitors have a wired remote for determining the level and EQ settings of the monitors. Not all monitors have a remote control, but it's certainly convenient.

Input
There are many different types of input to your monitors. Some monitors will have just one type, while others will have a range. Common input types on home studio monitors include RCA and balanced XLR inputs.

---

your power amp, then you just need to
 the right cable, but if not, don't worry.
 easy to get hold of adaptors or leads
h TRS at one end and XLR at the other.
act, it's good practice to take adaptors
d cables with you when you go to gigs,
ause you never know what you'll find.
he contents of a DJ booth aren't nailed in

a rack, they'll go missing. You may turn up and find that someone's robbed the leads from the mixer to the power amp.

PA speakers
Although they do the same job as home hi-fi speakers, PA speakers are designed for durability and outputting loud volumes. As

a result, they have different connections to home hi-fi speakers, an example of which is the Speakon connector. This looks a bit like an XLR connector, but it's specifically designed for PA speakers, and it clips on to the speaker to prevent the connector pulling loose. Other connection types include 6.3mm jack and XLR.

Know Your CDJ

If you want to gig, you need to know the most popular DJing platform in clubland

Modern CDJs are much more than glorified CD players. They let you mix and scratch MP3s off a USB drive, control virtual decks in your favourite software and remix tracks on the fly. They're also all over clubland, so if you want to get gigging, you need to know your CDJ.

Initially, the CDJ took the basic controls of the classic Technics SL1210 (the pitch slider, forward and backward platter movement and play button) and applied it to a CD player. DJs didn't have to learn any new skills or techniques; they could get a pair of CDJs and apply the same techniques to mix CDs with regular vinyl and vice versa.

CDJs could do much more than play CDs at different speeds, however, and a series of innovations culminated in the release of the original CDJ-1000, a CDJ with a large jog wheel that let users perform genuinely good scratching and turntablist techniques. From there, CDJs have evolved to the point where they rival software applications for power and flexibility. Modern CDJs such as the Pioneer CDJ-2000 let you create loops with incredibly accurate timing, so you can create loops that stay in sync with other tracks for a long time. Some CDJs, such as the Pioneer CDJ-900, even let you set loops of a specific length with a single button.

Types of CDJ

The most popular brand of CDJ you'll see in clubs is Pioneer, which has been making CDJs for almost two decades. The current top of Pioneer's range is the CDJ-2000, but many clubs still use the CDJ-1000, which still a highly capable and versatile CDJ. You may also see the newer CDJ-900 and older CDJ-800 in clubland, too, but you're more likely to see these in bars. Other popular CDJ manufacturers include Numark, Denon, Gemini and Reloop.

Tabletop CDJs such as the CDJ-2000 are the most popular, but other types exist. Rack-mount CDJs are popular with mobile DJs because they can be combined with a mixer and amp in a single case that can be easily transported. Unlike tabletop CDJs, rack-mount CDJs have small jog wheels that are used to speed up or slow down tracks so you can get them in phase. They typically have loop controls too.

Another type of CDJ that's used by many mobile DJs is the all-in-one CDJ and mixer unit, a prime example being the Numark iCDMIX3. These all-in-one units are typically 19in in length, with a mixer interface and CDJ controls on the top panel and CDJ drawers at the front. These units are great if you regularly take your own gear to gigs and you don't want to scratch, because they're a self-contained unit. They're not too expensive, so you often see them in small venues. The drawback is that, like any other self-contained device, if one component breaks the whole thing won't work.

Mixing with CDJs

Fundamentally, mixing with CDJs is no different to mixing with anything else. You use the same beatmixing techniques and you use a jog wheel to speed up or slow down tracks to get them in phase. One

▼ The Numark iCDMIX3 combines an all-in-one CDJ and mixer unit in one device

▲ Some CDJs, such as the Denon SC3900, have spinning platters just like a traditional analogue turntable, so you can use them to practise your scratching technique

...erence is that, unlike software, not all ...Js display a waveform of the track ...'re playing. This means you need to ...ow a track inside out to know where the ...akdowns and other track events occur. ...n those that do display a waveform ...less detailed than software, with the ...veform just showing peaks and troughs. ...l, that's pretty much all you need to mix. ...ther than that, you need to make sure ...CDJ is set to the right platter mode ...d that you're happy with the pitch range.

The platter mode is especially important if you're mixing on Pioneer's CDJs. You switch platter mode using a push button, and either set it to CDJ mode or Vinyl mode; the former is best if you want to mix and the latter is good if you want to scratch.

The pitch range is the percentage by which you can adjust the speed of a track, and is usually a choice of 6%, 10%, 16% or 100%. If you play tracks with a similar BPM, it's best to use a lower pitch range. The reason for this is that any changes in pitch you make, such as going from 130bpm to 131bpm, are not continuous, and increase or decrease incrementally.

As an example, the CDJ-2000 increments or decrements the pitch in steps of 0.5% at a pitch range of 100%, 0.05% at a pitch range of 10% and 0.02% at a pitch range of 6%. That means you can perform much tighter beatmixes using the 6% pitch range, because you're increasing or decreasing the pitch by only 0.02% each time you move the pitch fader one step.

Similarly, it's much harder to get a tight beatmix when using the 100% pitch range, which means you'll have to match the speed of your tracks as closely as possible and then use the jog wheel to keep them in phase when they start to drift out of sync.

Scratching with CDJs

Scratching techniques were first developed using analogue turntables, but many of those techniques can be performed on tabletop CDJs, too. To make the transition from turntable to CDJ more natural, some CDJs have spinning jog wheels, but there

aren't that many. One good example is the Denon SC3900, which has a spinning platter driven by a high-torque direct-drive motor, just like you'd find on a vinyl turntable, as well as hot cue buttons, loop controls and the ability to control software via MIDI. Check out **tinyurl.com/bnbzwzo** to see talented turntablist DJ Switch perform a slick routine on a pair of SC3900s.

Even if you don't have a spinning platter, you can still pull off some amazing scratches and turntablist techniques with CDJs. The Pioneer CDJ-2000 and CDJ-900 models have excellent touch-sensitive platters and produce a realistic scratch sound. To see how good they are, check out **tinyurl.com/d5jhyzw** to see DJing legend Kutski put a pair of CDJ-2000s to good use.

Controlling software

As mentioned, many modern CDJs do much more than play CDs. One common feature is the ability to control software natively or with MIDI rather than a timecode CD. This gives you the best of all worlds, with some CDJs, such as the CDJ-2000, displaying data from Traktor or Serato Scratch onscreen.

If you're looking to buy a CDJ that can control your software, you should try to buy one that provides native control rather than MIDI. Native control is much tighter, whereas MIDI control can be subject to latency or poor response. You might, for instance, experience a lag between you moving the jog wheel and something happening in your software. That said, this is really only a problem if you scratch or use platter-based techniques.

CDJs IN DETAIL

USB/SD card ports
Some CDJs let you connect them to computers or play music from USB drives or SD cards.

Display
A CDJ's display gives you information about the state of a track. It tells you the name of the track, the current position within the track and the track time remaining. It may also display a waveform so you can see breakdowns and build-ups within a track.

Vinyl speed controls
Some CDJs let you set the start-up and braking speed of your CDJ to mimic an analogue turntable when it starts and stops. You can either have instant start-up or braking or you can have a slow start-up and braking. We prefer instant starts and a two-second brake.

Hot cues
Hot cues let you jump straight to a specific point within a track and are great for performing live edits and remixes. You can also use them percussively, as drum pads, for example.

Jog wheel
The jog wheel lets you speed up and slow down tracks, as well as scratch. Jog wheel sizes vary, but we find that the larger they are, the better they are for scratching. Some jog wheels are spun by motors, just like analogue turntables.

Transport controls
These controls let you start and pause tracks as well as set cue points and fast forward or rewind. Some CDJs also let you reverse the direction of play.

Loop controls
Most CDJs have loop controls that let you manually define the start an end points of a loo Some also let you set automatic loop of specific lengths Most let you store your loops so you can use them agai at a later date.

Sync/master tempo
Master Tempo keeps the pitch of a track the same when you adjust the speed of it and sync automatically beatmatches track

Pitch controls
The pitch controls let you change the speed of a track. You can also select the pitch range of the CDJ and select Master Tempo, whic maintains the origin pitch of a track ever though you adjust a track's speed.

CD slot
Insert your CDs here. Most CDJs let you use MP3 CDs as well as regular audio CDs.

thedjguide.co

Know Your MIDI

After almost 30 years, MIDI is still at the heart of music production and digital DJing

Almost 30 years have passed since the first Musical Instrument Digital Interface (MIDI)-enabled synthesisers were unveiled to the general public. Back then, in the era of bad circuits and undisciplined application make-up, no-one would have thought that a little-known and immature protocol for the control and generation of music would become so pervasive and indispensable. Indeed, the growth and development of MIDI technology has remarkable (in some places almost symbiotic) parallels with the development and adoption of the computers on which we rely for our digital DJing.

In fact, such is the flexibility and efficiency of MIDI that the protocol has been used in products and technology far removed from those envisaged by its original creators, from motion-capture suits to lighting controllers.

Back to the 80s

Officially, it was 1982 that saw the birth of the MIDI protocol, but the events that would eventually lead to the release of the first MIDI-enabled synthesisers occurred some years prior to that in the late 1970s. At that time, steps had already been taken to connect musical instruments, but these were proprietary affairs, limiting musicians who wanted to connect instruments from different manufacturers.

The move towards a universal communications protocol for the transmission and generation of musical data came about by commercial consensus, the electronics industry hoping that interoperability and connectivity would promote the use of electronic instruments among hobbyists and studio musicians alike. And it did. Within a few short years MIDI was as common as a cold and infinitely more appealing.

Although it was initially limited to music keyboards and synths, it wasn't long before other MIDI products emerged, such as the MIDI sequencer, an ingenious piece of equipment that records MIDI data. That data includes information about what notes to play, when to play them and what they should sound like. It revolutionised the way in which music was recorded and performed forever. It was reviled by bearded hippy luddites under the mistaken impression that the machine itself decided which note to play and when, not an original artist, but it was championed by those secure in their musical ability who relished the control sequencers gave them.

Such was the appeal of MIDI that it wasn't long before classic synths from the pre-MIDI era were retro-fitted with the technology. Classic bits of kit such as Roland's TB-303 bassline machine, which was much ridiculed and quietly killed off when released in the early 1980s because of its inability to produce any sound remotely like a traditional bass, experienced a sudden popularity boost in the late 1980s, when it became the cornerstone of the Acid House sound.

MIDI keyboards are compact and convenient

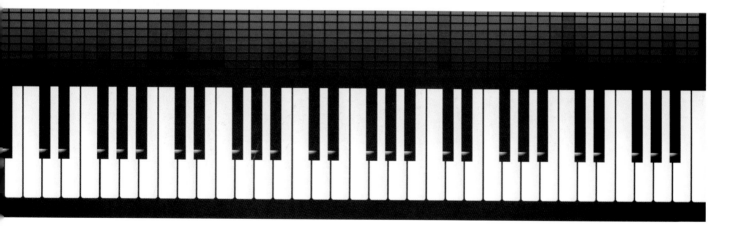

Other retro-fitted classics included Roland's TR series of electronic drum machines. Again, these were poorly received when released, but became ubiquitous in house, hip hop and electronic music from the late 1980s onward.

Perhaps the first true moment that MIDI made the irrevocable leap from hardware units to software was when Atari saw fit to include two MIDI ports on the side of its ST range of computers. The ST became a fixture in all good studios almost overnight as software sequencers that allowed musicians to visualise arrangements and hand-edit them with a mouse became available. Software sequencers were created to suit everyone, from free public domain releases for bedroom musicians to sophisticated and expensive Steinberg offerings for professional studios.

As time and computer technology has progressed, with Atari STs having been rendered obsolete by the IBM PC, MIDI has enabled the computer to become a sequencer, synthesiser, sampler and a means of distribution, bringing affordable, high-end music production to the masses.

In the early 1990s, a MIDI-based home studio was an expensive affair, with the keyboards and instruments themselves responsible for generating the sounds heard. Your tracks would either be output through your instruments' speakers or, if you could afford one, a mixer. Now all that's needed is a 'dumb' MIDI keyboard costing no more than £70. A musician can tap away on its keys (just as with any other keyboard), but it abdicates responsibility for the generation of sound to a PC or MIDI sound module. Instead of making a noise itself it sends MIDI data containing information about which keys have been pressed and for how long to the sound module or PC, which then interprets the data and uses a software synthesiser to generate the sounds that should be played. The sounds are then mixed using software and output through a pair of speakers. You really don't have to spend thousands on a workstation keyboard to make music.

Because of their use as a means of controlling software, many MIDI keyboards also come with faders and switches that can be used to control virtual mixing desks and EQ settings.

Arguably, this modern age of computer-based synths, sequencers and 'dumb' MIDI keyboards is directly attributable to the Atari ST and its built-in MIDI ports. Either way, we're grateful.

Music for the masses

Prior to the creation of MIDI, the playing of synthesisers and instruments was exclusively the domain of the musician, with the sonic output of the machines generated only by the hand of the person playing it. Entirely conventional, and for many people exactly the way it should be done, but this type of play does present some difficulty when it comes to recording the musical efforts of the performer. If you were a performer or composer and wanted to commit the sonic soundscapes you had created to a suitable medium so that your musical efforts might also be enjoyed by others, you had few choices. You could hire a studio and hire in session musicians at great expense to yourself, or you could painstakingly record multiple performances on to a multitrack tape, layering each instrumental to create a sonic whole, a process expensive in both time and money.

Take Mike Oldfield, for example, the hugely talented composer of the *Tubular Bells* series of albums. The recording of *Tubular Bells* is famous in musical history for both its complexity and the fact that Oldfield played every instrument heard on the record himself. It's a testament to the man's talent and ingenuity that the album exists at all, but would he still record it this way now? Of course not; he'd use a computer and MIDI technology. That doesn't make him any less of a musician or any less talented, it merely frees him from the drudgery and time-sapping tedium of repetitive tasks such as switching machinery on and off and setting up synths to concentrate on the most important and pleasurable aspect of musicianship: creating music.

Neither does MIDI technology prevent anyone from recording or playing music by traditional means. MIDI technology allows composers to use a computer as a 'scratchpad', a quick means of scoring a piece of music, the notation of which can be printed off as sheet music and given to an orchestra to perform. By combining a small, battery-powered MIDI keyboard with a laptop, a musician can compose, edit and record music anywhere, whether on a train, a beach or in orbit.

Since its beginnings in the early 1980s, MIDI technology has made the complete music-production process available to anyone with the time to devote to it. And thanks to the proliferation of MIDI technology, you no longer need to be rich or in possession of a 100-piece orchestra to compose multi-voiced symphonies or rich musical soundscapes. You need only a MIDI instrument, a MIDI sequencer and a humble PC.

MIDI CONNECTIONS

The most common MIDI connector is the 5-pin DIN socket, which has been in use since the first MIDI instruments. Thanks to its chunky size it's difficult to damage and resistant to being accidentally disconnected, important factors when using them in 'live' situations. Traditionally, MIDI instruments and equipment have been graced with three 5-pin DIN sockets, labelled In, Out and Thru, as can be seen on the Xone 1D controller (right).

In recent years, as both music and computer technology have matured, manufacturers have incorporated USB and

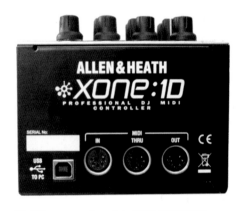

FireWire connections into their equipment because of their universality, high bandwidth and small size.

ADVANCE YOUR ART

TURNTABLISM IS ALIVE AND MORE CREATIVE THAN EVER.

Introducing the Sixty-One and Sixty-Two from Rane – two revolutionary new mixers that tightly integrate with leading digital DJ solution, Serato Scratch Live.

The Sixty-One is a plug-and-play mixer offering two-deck digital DJing, software effects and all the record and playback channels you need.

The Sixty-Two is an advanced two channel, two USB port mixer with dedicated controls for over 40 Scratch Live features, including cues, loops and the SP-6 sample player.

Genre-bending musical pioneer Z-Trip co-designed the Limited Edition Sixty-Two Z Mixer, which features a face plate designed by renown artist Shepard Fairey and high-quality custom purple cables.

www.serato.com   www.rane.com

Sixty-One   Sixty-Two   Sixty-Two Z

serato™ SCRATCH LIVE

Create Your Own MIDI Maps

A major advantage of digital DJing gear is its ability to be customised to work how you want. MIDI mapping is an essential part of that process

1 Open Traktor's Settings screen and select the Controller Manager option. Make sure that your controller is selected in the Device drop-down menu.

W e're all individuals, or so we're told, and that's certainly the case when it comes to DJing hardware. No matter how many controls manufacturers pack into their controllers and no matter how much time they spend mapping those controllers to our favourite software, we're still not happy with them. Luckily, we don't have to live with it. Most controllers let you remap them so they work exactly as you want them to.

With Novation's Dicer controllers, you can easily and conveniently control software without having to touch your computer. The Dicer is well-mapped out of the box, and lets you set and trigger hot cues, set loops and control effects, but you there's still scope for customisation.

We've connected a pair of Dicers to a laptop running Traktor Scratch Pro 2, and we want to configure the Dicers so that we can move through and select items in the browser. MIDI mapping in Traktor and other software might be daunting, but all you need to do is practise, and remember – if you make a mistake you can always delete it afterwards and start again.

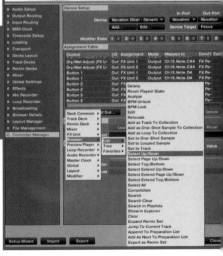

2 Next, you need to select the Traktor function that you want to map to your controller. Click the Add In button and navigate to the control you wish to map. We've selected Select Up/Down (Browser List) from the Browser menu.

032

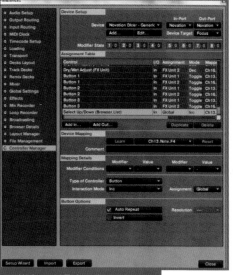

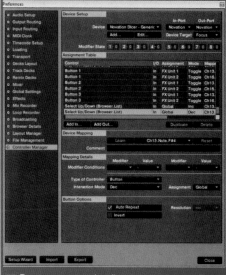

5 We've told Traktor that we're using a physical button, which means we also need to tell it in which direction the button moves through the list. Up or down? We've selected increase (Inc), which moves down through the list. We may want to move through the list quickly, so a good option to check is Auto Repeat, which is in the Button Options group. This means we can keep the control held down and the cursor will continue to move through the browser list.

7 Because we occasionally want to move up a list, we need to configure another Dicer button to do just that. We repeated steps one to five but we selected decrease (Dec) for the button's Interaction Mode. Now our Dicer lets us move through the browser window so that we can select our tracks, except that we don't have a button to load the selected track in to a deck.

3 We need to tell Traktor which physical control we want to map. Make sure the Traktor function you wish to map is selected. Click the Learn button on Traktor's Controller Manager screen and then press the controller button that you wish to use with the selected Traktor function. The MIDI value of that controller button is then displayed next to the Learn button.

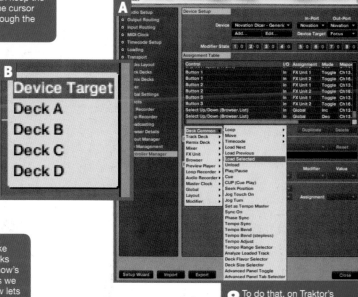

8 To do that, on Traktor's Controller Manager screen, add the Load Selected function (A). Click the Learn button and map the physical control you want to use. Traktor recognises it as a button, so we just need to tell it to which deck we need to load it (B). Using the Assignment drop-down menu, select the deck. We chose deck A.

4 Make sure you turn Traktor's Learn button off, otherwise you'll overwrite the MIDI value if you press any other button on your controller. We've mapped the control, but we still have some work to do. At the moment, Traktor thinks the control is a fader or pot, so we need to tell it we're pressing a button. Open the drop-down menu labelled Type of Controller and select Button.

6 You now need to make sure your control works the way you expect, so now's the time to test it. Just as we hoped, our controller now lets us move down through the list.

How To Mix

Ever gone to a club and been blown away by a DJ's mix? How did they get that breakbeat to drop at that exact moment, getting everyone's hands in the air and putting wide smiles on their faces? Hang on a minute, that's a vocal from Mainline, isn't it? Those bits aren't in the original track – how did they do that?

If you want to have clubbers screaming your name and going nuts, you need to learn how to mix effectively and creatively. You need to cultivate your own unique mixing style and do more than simply start one track as the other ends.

This chapter gives you all the skills you need to beatmix, create live edits and use samples to produce a set that keeps your audience guessing and interested. Giving them something that other DJs can't is more likely to get you more gigs and greater success, so follow our guides and then use your skills to wow the crowds with your unbridled creativity.

CHAPTER TWO

Beatmixing
The Essential Guide

If you want to be a DJ, you need to know how to beatmix. Here we show you how to master the art

Chances are that you've never seen a herd of elephants stampeding a kettle factory, but you've probably heard something like it many times before in pubs, clubs and house parties all over this green and pleasant land. It seems everyone thinks that mixing simply involves playing music and pushing a crossfader occasionally, until they try it and the venue rattles to the sound of 1,000 angry elephants trying to make a brew.

Whether you're into dubstep, electro house or minimal techno, you have to master beatmixing if you want to sound good and be taken seriously as a DJ. Gone are the days when beatmixing meant riding a fine line between perfection and disaster, but aligning beats so that mixes sound smooth and natural is still undoubtedly the most important mixing technique a DJ can master.

It's also much more than getting two or more tracks playing at the same speed. It's about choosing the right intro points, making sure the tracks are harmonically compatible and knowing when to complete the mix. Over the next few pages we'll teach you everything you need to know about beatmixing, from musical theory to aligning BPMs and finding a track's key so that you can mix harmonically. Beatmixing isn't hard to understand, but making it second nature takes practice, so power up your controller, pump up the bass and rock the place.

Four for your floor
You don't have to be Beethoven to mix beats, but knowing how tracks are constructed is essential for dropping tracks at the right time for maximum effect. Most modern dance tracks, whether they're hip-hop, house or techno in style, have a 4/4 time signature. Indeed, it's very rare for dance tracks to have any other time signature, and those tracks that do are probably intended for the home rather than the dancefloor.

Even if you've never heard of a time signature, you probably recognise it in the music you listen to. Common house tracks, such as David Guetta's *Every Time We Touch* or Tensnake's *Coma Cat* have a 4/4 time signature, but what does that mean? Well, for a DJ it essentially means that each 4/4 track has a regular recurring beat that acts as a pacemaker for the DJ and for those dancing. This means that DJ can easily discern the tempo of a track and align beats when mixing.

If you play the Extended Mix of David Guetta's *Every Time We Touch* from the

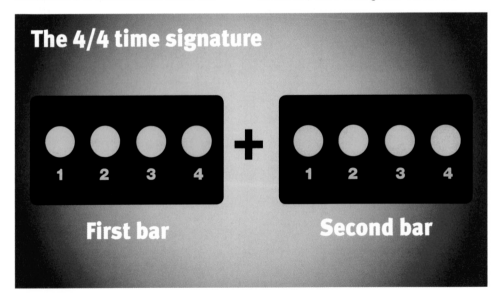

The 4/4 time signature

① ② ③ ④
1   2   3   4
First bar

+

① ② ③ ④
1   2   3   4
Second bar

036

thedjguide.co

PHRASING

The screenshots below show how phrases of two tracks match up. In the first two screenshots, Every Time We Touch is started at the moment One kicks back in from its breakdown. Doing this means that Every Time We Touch properly kicks in at the very moment One ends. Timing your tracks like this is important for creating natural-sounding mixes.

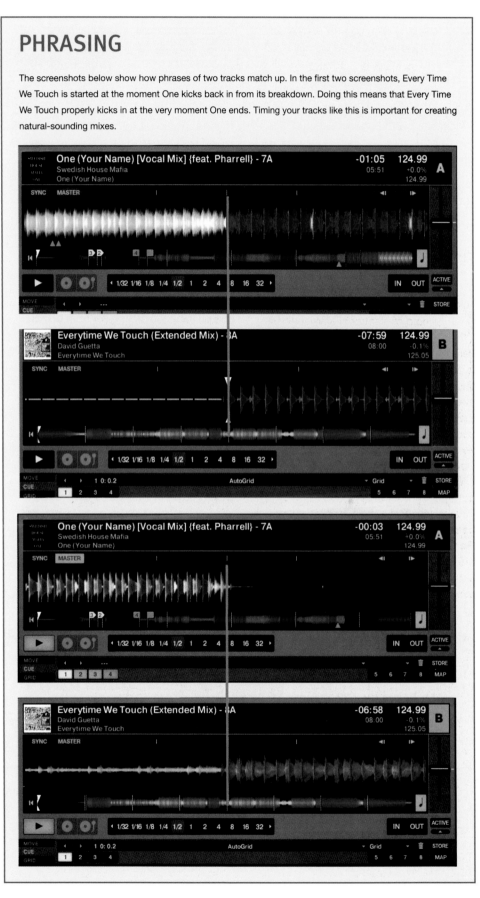

ginning, you'll notice how the bass drum
ps regularly and to a certain time. Listen
it again, and this time count the beats in
ur head. Say to yourself, "one, two, three,
r," at the exact moment that each of the
st four beats play. After you've counted
ur beats, start at one again, so that you
y "one" on the fifth beat you hear.
Each four-beat section is known as
ar, and music producers use bars
building blocks for full songs. When
u say "one" on the fifth beat you hear,
u're starting a new bar. Producers
ckage these bars into multiples of four,
d these packages are called patterns.
ese patterns are cyclical, so once
u've reached the end of a pattern it'll be
eated from the beginning.

hrasing

w play *Every Time We Touch* again, but
s time fast-forward to around a minute
o it, just as the drum beat kicks back in

after the breakdown. As soon as that first kick drum plays, get counting. Notice the change at the end of the four-bar block? That is, after 16 beats? That's the end of the pattern, but notice how the beats continue and a new pattern starts. Once you get a certain number of patterns together, DJs refer to that collection of bars as a phrase. Put simply, a phrase is a large section of track in which something happens. You might, for example, have a piano riff that's 32 beats (8 bars) in length. That's a phrase. You can take that phrase and use it again and again, or use a different phrase once it's come to the end.

When you're DJing, you can use phrases to mix out of one track and then mix in to another one. As an example, the Extended Mix of *Every Time We Touch* has a 32-bar intro. When it gets to the end of that 32-bar phrase, the track kicks in properly and you hear the bass. In order to mix this track in to another one, all we have to do is find a track with a 32-bar outro and start *Every Time We Touch* just as the other track enters the 32-bar outro sequence.

For example, load the Vocal Mix of Swedish House Mafia's *One* into one of your software's decks. Fast-forward to the last breakdown in the track, around 4 minutes and 45 seconds in to it. If you play *Every Time We Touch* from the point at which the bass drum kicks back in on *One*, *Every Time* would be introduced fully to your audience just as *One* ends. You wouldn't even have to move the crossfader from the middle position to complete a blend. You can let *One* finish and then push the crossfader back to the *Every Time* side at your leisure.

Phrasing is an important part of beatmixing because it lets you combine tracks in a way that makes your mixes sound natural and exciting. Instead of just matching the BPMs of a couple of tracks and pushing the crossfader from one side to the other, phrasing lets you mix tracks over meaningful segments of tracks. Think about the tracks you're mixing and see which phrase would be the best place to mix out from on the outgoing track and which phrase would be best to mix into on the incoming track.

Phasing

Once you've got your beats correctly matched and you've decided the exact point at which you're going to mix in your next track, you still have a job to do. When you play the incoming track, it's unlikely to play exactly on beat with the track you're currently playing. You need to speed it up or slow it down momentarily to get both tracks in phase, which is a shorter way of saying we need to get both tracks playing beats at the same time.

There are a couple of ways of doing this depending on your setup. If you're using software, there are usually a couple of buttons with arrows on them. These are pitch-bend buttons. Press them and you'll notice that the track on that deck increases or decreases in speed, depending which button you've pressed, adjusting the timing of that track in relation to the other deck.

If you're using a controller, you can use its jog wheels to do the same thing. You move the jog wheel clockwise to speed up a track and anti-clockwise to slow it down. Some controllers even have pitch bend buttons as well as jog wheels, so you choose the method you prefer.

Be careful when getting tracks in phase, though. When you're learning to mix, there's a tendency to confuse the process of getting BPMs matched and the process of getting tracks in phase. If you get the two tracks in phase and they quickly fall out of phase, you still need to match their BPMs. If they sound out of phase, but they're consistently off-beat so that the mix doesn't sound like a train-wreck, you need to adjust the phasing of the tracks.

EQing

So you've got the BPMs matched, the tracks are in phase and your phrasing is perfect, but your mixes still don't sound fantastic. Perhaps one track is louder than the other, or perhaps the sound of the bass drum occasionally disappears or sounds hollow. What's wrong?

An important part of the mixing process is managing your EQs and sound levels. When you mix two tracks together, it's unlikely that they'll sound completely perfect together. Certain frequencies will clash and may sound muffled or distorted.

PFL CUEING

When we mix, we let the audience dance to one track while we cue the other in our headphones, but what do we mean by cueing? Put simply, cueing is the act of preparing the next song for play. You load a song into a deck and place a cue marker at the location in the track where you want it to play when you press the Play button.

Fundamentally, that's all cueing is, but the digital DJ does much more than that. The digital DJ must beatmatch the BPMs of two or more tracks in their headphones, as well as set any loops or effects they may want to use. Again, the audience mustn't hear any of this, so most controller and mixers have a control that lets you crossfade between the track playing to the audience and the track playing in your headphones.

The control is called a pre-fade listen (PFL) crossfader, and it serves two purposes. Not only does it let you match BPMs of tracks, it also lets you practise crossfading the

tracks. The PFL crossfader works best when you wear your headphones over both ears, and fading between tracks lets you make sure that you've matched the BPMs of the tracks properly. If one track has a heavy bass drum or percussion then it might dominate and drown out the track from which you're trying to mix out of or into. If you crossfade the track using the PFL control, you can hear how the tracks sound as their volume is increased and decreased in the mix. The track with the dominant bass drum might not be correctly beatmatched, and if you decrease that track's volume using the PFL crossfade and increase the volume of the other track, you might be able to hear that. You can then sort it out before you play those tracks to the audience, preventing any embarrassment.

SPLIT-CUEING

You may have seen quite a few DJs mixing with one ear covered by a headphone and the other ear uncovered, but what are they doing? Although you can quite easily mix with your headphones on both ears and use the PFL crossfader to make sure BPMs are matched, some DJs prefer to have one track playing in one ear and another track playing in the other ear.

When you see DJs with only one ear covered by headphones, they're using a technique known as split-cueing. There are couple of ways of doing this. The most basic is to cue the track you want to bring in to the mix and listen to it through one headphone while listening to the track already playing on your speaker system. It takes a bit of practice, but you

can hear the difference in phasing and BPMs this way. If you're in your home studio, your monitors or speakers will be close so you can hear both sources clearly, but if you're in a club, you'll need to focus your uncovered ear on the DJ booth's monitors.

The other way of split-cueing is dependent on your mixer. A lot of modern mixers, such as the Rane MP26 and Pioneer DJM-900NXS, have a split-cue function that splits audio so that one headphone plays the cued track and the other headphone plays the track already playing through your speaker system. We find that when split-cueing with one headphone on and the other off, the phasing of beats can be off because of the difference in the time it takes for your ears to hear tracks. One track is played straight in to your covered ear, while the other

one must reach your uncovered ear from a speaker. This produces a type of latency. Having both tracks pumped straight in to both ears, albeit with a specific track for each ear, makes it easier to get tracks in phase so that your mix sounds perfect as soon you drop the incoming track.

It's best to practise different cueing techniques, because you never know what equipment you'll be using in a club or bar. Just because your home mixer or controller lets you PFL crossfade in your headphones it doesn't mean that the mixer in a club or bar will let you do the same. You may have to split-cue. If you've already practiced split-cueing in your home studio, you won't have a problem doing it when mixing live in front of an audience.

e clash may prove distracting to the tener, focusing attention on the sounds irritating your audience so much they ave the club and never come back. To event this happening, you need to use just your EQs as you mix to smooth out e sound so that the mix sounds natural. DJ controllers and mixers typically have ree-band EQs, which means they can t or boost high-end, mid-range and low- d frequency bands, with the devices ving a control to adjust each band. DJing ftware often apes this setup, and also ers DJs a three-band EQ section for ch channel, although some applications ovide greater flexibility. Traktor Pro 2, instance, lets you use a four-band EQ ction for each channel, and Ableton Live s you control up to 16 bands. For most Js, though, a three-band EQ is enough.

The most important band for DJs is e low frequency band. When you mix o tracks without first adjusting your Qs, you'll find that it's totally obvious to eryone that you're bringing a new track to the mix and it sounds amateurish, or u might notice a big increase in volume at may even distort the sound of your mix. hen mixing two tracks, it's a good idea to duce the bass frequencies of the incoming ck and then gradually increase them as ur mix progresses. Make sure you cut the ss frequencies of the outgoing track as u increase those of the incoming track. s worth noting that you'll sometimes want

to increase the bass frequencies of the incoming track for effect. Perhaps you're mixing a quiet intro of one track in to a breakdown of another. If the drums of the incoming track kick in just as the breakdown of the outgoing track ends, you may want to boost the bass a little to provide a bit of post-breakdown energy.

Keep practising!

Over the next few pages, we'll guide you through mixing on different setups so that you can follow the guides and learn the processes involved in mixing. Be warned: learning to mix isn't easy, but it is fun and rewarding. Don't give up, keep practising, and you will learn how to mix.

How To
Beatmix

You can follow this guide with a controller or your laptop and mouse. We've used Traktor Pro 2.5, but these techniques can equally be used with other software

Test yourself!

When you can match beats effortlessly using many different tracks, remove the phase meter so that you have to use your ears to tell if a track's faster or slower. Also move the pitch slider on deck A to add variation. You're doing this for your own benefit, not to please an audience, so don't worry about the tracks sounding too fast or too slow.

1 The first thing you need to do is load two tracks in to decks A and B, so right-click on a track in the browser and load it in to Deck A. Do the same for deck B. If you're learning to beatmix, the best thing to do is choose two 4/4 tracks that have basic intros with a just a bass drum and a snare or hand clap on the second and fourth beats. That way, you can more easily tell when your beats are synchronised.

2 The next thing you need to do is turn off the BPM counter. It's an incredibly handy tool and something you should use when you're more confident at beatmixing, but when you're starting off it's all too easy to use the BPM counter instead of your ears. Click the Cog icon at the top right of the screen to open the Settings screen, then select the Decks menu. Click the box that says BPM and select Off from the drop-down list. Turn the BPM counter off on both decks.

3 Next, you need to adjust each deck's fine pitch control. The pitch slider increases the BPM of a track by too large a degree, even when you have the tempo range set to 8%. You need fine control to get the beats matched as closely as possible, so hover your cursor over the base of each deck's pitch slider until plus and minus icons appear then right-click them. Select 'Min' from the menu that appears.

4 Set a 16- or 32-beat loop on the track in deck A then press Play. If your track has a long drum-based intro, then set a longer loop. If not, choose a shorter one. At this point, you just want to match beats with as clean a track as possible.

5 Press play on deck B when the loop on deck A starts at the first beat. The beats may start in time, but they'll soon drift apart. Use the deck's pitch bend buttons to get them back in phase. The button you press is dependent on the speed of the track in deck B. If it's faster, you need to press the left-hand button. If it's slower, you need to press the right-hand button. Traktor's phase meter shows you which track is faster. If deck B's phase meter is moving to the left, the track's too slow; if it's moving to the right, it's too fast.

6 At the same time, use deck B's pitch slider to increase or decrease the speed of the track. This is an iterative process, so you may need to stop and start deck B's track a number of times until you've matched the two BPMs. The two BPMs are matched if you no longer have to use the pitch bend buttons to keep the tracks synchronised. If you're new to beatmixing it will take some time, so keep practising. It's worth it.

How To Use Effects

Effects create excitement in your mixes and let you make natural and creative transitions. We show you how to make the most of them

Sound effects are an important weapon in the digital DJ's arsenal. Effects can completely change the way a track sounds, or they can build tension in a mix. They can be a great way of getting rid of an outgoing track and are an important tool when creating your own on-the-fly mixes.

There are many different types of effects, and the way you use them and the control you have over them changes with each effect, but there are some controls that are common to every effect. Every effect has a means of turning it off and on, some means of controlling the amount of effect applied and some means of changing the timing or behaviour of the effect.

As an example, the flanger effect alters the phasing of a track to give it a jet-like whooshing effect. Most flanger effects modulate the pitch of the effect, so that it cycles through high and low frequencies. This brings the effect to life and ever so slightly changes the mood of your music. You can usually change the length of this cycle so that you either have the flanger effect applied over longer periods, perhaps 32 beats, or over shorter periods, so that the flanger effect applies a kind of short, squelchy sound to your track.

Effect controllers

Although there are many common types of effect, such as Echo, Flanger and Reverb, the way you control them depends on your software, mixer or controller. Many mixers and controllers provide a number of buttons and potentiometers for effect control, but others may provide sliders or an X/Y pad.

The X/Y pad works like a graph, and is a square area that you press with your finger. When you press the X/Y pad you set a coordinate that dictates the amount of the effect to be applied to a track, the timing of the effect and any other parameters that may be applicable. X/Y pads let you quickly apply an effect or alter effects settings. X/Y pads offer great versatility. You can use it t alter an effect's settings subtly in a smooth and slow manner, building tension or excitement, or you can use it to alter effec settings quickly to create instant, dramatic changes. X/Y pads are most common on dedicated outboard effects units such as the Korg Kaoss Pad Quad, although some MIDI controllers, such as the mixer/controller hybrid that is the DJM-2000, als have an X/Y pad.

You can do the same with a collection of pots and buttons, but they're generally located very close together so that you need to use both hands to change effects settings and clash fingers when you do so. Even so, pots are fantastic for individually specifying the value of an effect's paramet such as the amount of the effect's feedbac or its timing. You'll find that most controlle use pots and buttons as their effects controls because they save space and mo closely resemble the controls of popular software applications such as Traktor Pro and Virtual DJ.

If your MIDI controller has a collection of pots and buttons and your software has an X/Y pad to control effects, don't panic. More than likely, your software will let you assign two of your pots to control the X and Y axes, so that you can use them in conjunction with each other to specify coordinates on the X/Y pad.

▲ Effects can be used for a number of different purposes

COMMON EFFECTS

Some effects are more popular and common than others. Here's a selection of effects that you'll find in most software apps and on most controllers.

ECHO

The Echo effect does exactly what you think: it repeats part of a track and slowly fades it out so you get an echo effect. It's an extremely versatile effect. One way of using it is to apply a soft echo to an acapella or a breakdown to add depth and a dream-like quality. It's also great if you want to mix out a track or stop your set without it sounding as if you've ejected a CD. To do this, set the timing of your effect to ½-beat, engage the effect and quickly close the fader. To make this technique sound natural, you need to do it at the end of a bar or phrase, otherwise your audience will wonder why the music has stopped.

REVERB

The Reverb effect mimics the acoustics of different environments, such as a living room, a concert hall or a cavern. Indeed, some effects units let you choose presets that take a source sound and apply the effect to make it sound as if your track is playing in that environment. Most, however, will give you the controls to shape the sound yourself, making it sound as deep or as shallow as you like. The reverb effect is great for making your own breakdowns or for emphasising a vocal.

FLANGER

Wherever you find an effects unit you'll find a flanger. This effect is incredibly popular because it's so simple, yet it adds an exciting dimension to a mix. The Flanger effect adjusts the phasing of the source sound passed through it so that you get a whooshing effect that's similar to the sort of sound you hear when a jet passes you from travelling one end of a runway to the other. It's worth noting that you can actually make your own flanger effect by loading the same track in two decks and playing them at the same time. Even if they appear to be perfectly in phase you'll still hear a flanger effect. Adjust the jog wheel slightly to alter the phasing and you'll hear the intensity of the flanger effect increase.

The Flanger effect can be used liberally, but apply it subtly or your audience will soon tire of it and leave your club for another one. It sounds best when applied to vocal-led breakdowns, acapellas and intros.

FILTER

The Filter effect is also pretty self-explanatory. It takes a sound and subtracts certain frequencies from it. A Filter is similar to EQs in this respect, except that the filter gives you a bit more control. There are many different types of Filter effect, but most let you specify the exact bands you want to filter. A high-pass filter lets you hear higher frequencies, and you can specify the frequencies to be heard using a pot or some other control. A low-pass filter blocks high frequencies, and you can also specify the frequencies that can be heard using a pot or some other control. A high-pass filter is great for integrating orchestral or vocal-led led music with other tracks, while the low-pass is great for emphasising drums and basslines, or creating your own breakdowns.

re- and post-fader effects

ot only does the way you interact with ects differ depending on your hardware d software, but you also need to become miliar with the idea of pre-and post-fader ects. Pre-fader effects are applied to source before it hits a fader, so moving e fader has no bearing on the effect. st-fader effects, on the other hand, still ect your tracks after you've moved the er. It may not sound like much of an ue, but it does have an impact the way u interact with your effects. A pre-fader ho effect, for example, wouldn't be heard

if you closed the fader, whereas if you drop the fader on a post-fader echo you'd still hear the echo fade out even though you'd no longer hear the source track. For some effects, it doesn't matter if your effects unit is working pre- or post-fader, but many people prefer their echo and reverb effects to work post-fader.

Some applications, such as Traktor Pro 2, use pre-fader effects but also provide alternative controls that simulate post-fader effects. The Traktor Pro 2 Echo and Reverb effects, for example, have a Freeze button. Press this and you hear just the effect,

not the underlying track. This is a good compromise and can be very effective.

Effects parameters

The two most important parameters used to control effects are depth and timing. The Depth control, also known as the Dry/Wet control, dictates the level of effect that is applied to your mix. This lets you apply effects subtly to slightly enhance mood and anticipation, or dramatically to give your mix a new direction or shock your audience. As for timing, that's usually specified as a beat fraction, such as a quarter of a beat or two bars. Timing is important because it dictates the length of time for which the effect is active. A 1/8-beat echo, for example, will be shorter and punchier than a two-bar echo, which echoes a longer portion of a track.

Be creative!

When you're using effects, don't be afraid to be creative, especially if you're trying them out in your home studio. Some of the best uses for effects that you'll ever hear have been the result of mistakes that unexpectedly sound great.

The best way to learn how your mixer or software application's effects work is to select them and use them on a track you know inside out. Try using them on the point at which that track breaks down to see how it can emphasise or accentuate the breakdown, then see how well it works on vocals and percussion.

When planning mixes, think how you can use effects to make the transition from one track to the other more natural or exciting. Perhaps you want to mix two tracks, but the transition isn't that interesting or it sounds forced. Try using an Echo or Reverb effect on it to see how it sounds.

Finally, don't let effects them dominate your tracks. People want to enjoy your mixes, but they also want to dance to tunes they recognise. Use your effects to tease and excite the audience or make your transitions sound fresh, but don't ruin everyone's favourite track by applying a five-minute echo over it.

DEDICATED EFFECTS UNITS

Digital DJs are massively spoiled by the wealth of effects in software applications such as Traktor Pro 2, Virtual DJ, Itch and Deckadance, but there are some occasions when it's handy to use a dedicated effects unit that you plug in to your mixer or controller.

Perhaps you get a gig in a club and the mixer doesn't have onboard effects, or perhaps you want to combine software and hardware effects to transform tracks out of all recognition. You could attach a dedicated outboard effects unit to the club's mixer so that you can still get creative and spice up your mixes, or patch it in to your home studio to support the rest of your setup.

To get the best out of a dedicated effects unit you need to attach it to your mixer's Send and Return ports. These ports let the mixer send and receive audio to and from the effects unit. Send and Return ports are usually 6.3mm TRS jacks, but occasionally a mixer will use RCA connectors instead. Once connected, you control the amount of effect applied using the mixer or controller's Effect Loop controls. The exact controls you'll see vary from mixer to mixer. Some let you set the level sent to the effects unit and the amount returned, while some only let you control the amount of the effect applied to a track.

THE THREE GOLDEN RULES OF EFFECTS USE

1 Less is more
Don't go overboard with your effects; use them sparingly. Don't have a flanger running permanently in the background because you'll either annoy people or have them thinking there's something wrong with the sound system.

2 Keep an eye on your levels
Sometimes, applying an effect can increase the volume of the affected track, and the jump in volume can make your mix sound amateurish. Make sure you keep an eye on the volumes of your Send and Return loop and your mixer channels.

3 Keep an eye on your controls
In the heat of a mix, it's easy to forget about your effects controls, especially if your mind is focused on something else or you've cued up an incoming track in your headphones, but make sure you've turned off the effects when you've finished with them. Otherwise, you might still have a high-impact echo effect still running, which will annoy your audience.

EFFECTS PANEL IN DETAIL

Mixer-based effects units might look scary, but they're actually straightforward and simple once you get used to them. Pioneer's DJM mixers are incredibly popular, and you'll often come across them in clubs. Each new DJM offers something different, but essentially they all work the same way and offer similar controls.

Effects display
The effects display shows you the currently selected effect, the channel to be affected, the currently selected beat fraction, the BPM of the track to which the effect is to be applied and the effect timing in milliseconds. It looks basic, but it tells you everything you need to know at a glance.

Tap button
If the effects unit's BPM counter hasn't correctly identified the BPM of the track, you can tap the Tap button in time to the beat to set the correct BPM. The Quantize button here is specific to the DJM-900NXS.

Cue button
You can preview some effects in your headphones. Do this by activating the cue button.

Effect selector
Twist the effect selector to choose the effect you want to use.

Channel selector
Twist the channel selector to apply the effect to a specific channel, the microphone input, either side of the crossfader or the master channel.

Time
Use this to fine-tune the timing in case the BPM counter is close but not quite exact.

Level/depth control
Use this to control the amount of the effect that is applied to your mix. Twist it to the right to hear more of the effect and to the left to subtly apply the effect.

On/off button
Press this to engage the effect and press it again to turn it off.

How To Use
Hot Cues

Hot cue buttons are an essential part of breaking up tracks to create your own edits and remixes, so you need to master them

▼ Virtual DJ provides three hot cues per deck, which enough to edit tracks on the fly

MAW presents India
To Be In Love (Full Intention Vocal Mix) - 5A/4A - 127
127.00 BPM
ELAPSED 01:32.4   REMAIN 04:48.1
GAIN 0.0dB   KEY Cm   PITCH +0.0

EFFECTS   P.1 P.2   SAMPLER
Flanger   siren   VOL
FILTER   KEY
LOOP
1 2 4 8 16 32
SHIFT
IN   OUT
CUE II ▶ SYNC
BROWSER   SAMPLE

+ Computer
+ Desktop
  NetSearch
  GeniusDJ
Search: to be in

Have you ever gone to a club or listened to a mixtape and wondered why a track you know inside out doesn't play as you expected? Perhaps it breaks down too early or breaks down for one or two bars before kicking back in to the chorus. Is it a remix? Possibly, but it's more likely that the DJ is using hot cues.

Hot cues are an essential tool for rearranging tracks on the fly so that they play in a different order to what your crowd expects. There are many reasons why you'd want to do this. The first is to create a new and original edit that no other DJ has or can perform, something that separates you from everybody else. Another reason is to shorten sections of a track so that you can more easily mix them into something else.

As an example, imagine you have a track playing in deck A and one cued up in deck B. You want to mix them together at those exact points, but the track in deck A ends before the track in deck B breaks down. You can set a hot cue at the point at which the track in deck B breaks down, and then trigger it just as the track in deck A ends.

You can also use hot cues to jump momentarily from one part of a track to another. Perhaps you want to play the last bar of a 16-bar phrase in the middle of a phrase for effect. You could either trigger hot cues on just one deck, or you could have the same track in a second deck. This way, you could trigger the hot cues, slam the crossfader over to the other deck so that the crowd can hear them, then slam the

crossfader back over to the other deck once you've played that bar in the second deck.

Hot cues are extremely versatile, and how you use them is limited only by your imagination. The best way to use them is to set hot cues at the start of events within tracks, whether they're the start of a phrase, breakdown, acapella section or an exciting piece of percussion. When you first get a track, prep it by setting hot cues at such places. Them, if you get a bit of inspiration while practising, you can try out some on-the-fly editing without interrupting your flow. If you have to pause and interrupt your flow to set hot cues, it's easy to lose focus and

enthusiasm for it, or forget what it is you wanted to achieve in the first place.

Hot cue drumming
Another great way to use hot cues is as a drum machine or sampler. To do this, you'll need to have some clear drum or vocal samples. These could be actual samples you've recorded from a drum machine or they could be hot cues set on a track that features some clear drum sounds.

Arrange them in your hot cue slots in a manner that makes sense. We find it's better to place sounds that you use frequently next to each other, so that we have a bass drum

▲ Traktor Pro 2.5 provides eight hot cues, which gives you plenty of scope for cutting up tracks

◀ Organise your hot cues wisely, so that you can quickly jump to different points in a track for effect

the first hot cue button, a snare on the second, hats or handclaps on the third and s frequently used sounds on the others. deck loaded with drum samples fantastic way of displaying a little showmanship when playing live. Suppose you've got a track with a long, spacey breakdown and you want to get the crowd excited with anticipation before the track kicks back in again. Start doing a bit of gentle drumming on the hot cues, perhaps tapping out an ultra-funky breakbeat. You'll be doing something visual, and the audience will know that you're performing for them and respect you for it.

How To Use
Loops

If you want to make your own edits and on-the-fly remixes, mastering looping is essential. We give you the skills you need

Looping has been around for a long time, but only in recent years has it been possible to use loops that don't quickly fall out of phase with everything else you're playing. Before that, you could set a loop and it would be decent enough to listen to, but mixing it in to other tracks would be a nightmare, because it wouldn't be a perfect loop.

Software systems such as Traktor and Serato Scratch have made perfect loops a reality, as have hardware devices such as the CDJ-2000 and CDJ-900. It's now possible to set a four-beat loop and leave it playing in the background while you focus on triggering samples or setting effects.

Put simply, a loop is a segment of music that repeats itself. In DJing, a loop has a

loop-in point and a loop-out point, both of which define a loop's length. You can set the loop-in and -out points yourself, but most applications and a lot of hardware devices provide auto-loop buttons that automatically set a loop of a specific length. Traktor Pro 2, for example, lets you set auto-loops between 1/32 of a beat and 32 beats in length. This gives you lots of flexibility and it means you can quickly set a loop. Too busy talking to your mates instead of mixing and the currently playing track's about to run out? Don't panic: just set a four- or eight-beat loop while you get the next track mixed in to it. It might not be the best mix you've ever pulled off, but at least you won't have to endure heart-stopping embarrassment as silence hits the floor and everyone looks at you, wondering what's happened to the music.

Using loops to remix

You may not have a top studio, but if you have decent software you can use loops to create some inventive edits and live remixes. The best way to do this is to use software with at least four decks. If you're using Ableton, the world's your oyster in terms of decks, but if you're using softwa based on the traditional deck-to-deck mixing paradigm then you need four deck You can get away with two, but you'd have to rely on hot cues more than loops. If you're using software such as Traktor Pro 2 or Virtual DJ, the best approach is t combine loops with hot cues and effects.

As with hot cues, you need to identify exciting parts of a track, such as verses, choruses and breakdowns. Then you'd ne to create loops that capture these parts o a track and place each one in a deck. You

▼ Software such as Virtual DJ makes it easy to combin loops with hot cues and effects

CREATING STUTTER LOOPS

A neat technique for mixing out of one tune and into another is to create a ½-beat loop and then decrease it until the incoming track hits a breakdown. At that point, you can then slam the crossfader over to the incoming track. You could even apply an echo, reverb or other post-fader effect to the outgoing track to create a more dramatic mix.

n either play them one at a time, blending
em in to each other with the use of effects
d some decent fading, or you can select
ops that play well together so that you
n bring in a decent stab and play it over a
ssline or drum loop, moving from section
section and using filters and effects to
eate breakdowns and build-ups.
Created a breakdown but need a drum
ll to excite the audience before you kick
ck in to the track proper? No problem.
mply set a one-beat loop on a clear bass
um, let it play over the breakdown and
en gradually reduce the beat fraction of
e loop, going from one-beat to 1/16th
a beat. Each reduction of the fraction
ll increase the excitement. Make sure
u take it out of the mix as you kick back
to the track. This technique apes the
ammoth breakdowns and subsequent
ild-ups of classic Hardfloor remixes such
Yeke Yeke's *Mory Kante* and New Order's
ue Monday, so check out those tracks to
ar the effect we're trying to emulate.
The best way to learn how to use loops
to use them. You'll naturally come up
th ideas for using loops as you mix, but
so think about how you can use loops
eatively when you're in your home studio.
looping multiple sections of a track
d bring them in and out of the mix to
mic the structure of a regular song. Think
out sections of different tracks and try
mbining them to see what works. This
where harmonic mixing becomes helpful
e p50), so use your harmonic mixing
stem to see which tracks are compatible.

Harmonic Mixing

Harmonic mixing ensures smooth and natural-sounding transitions between tracks. Don't know music theory? Don't worry, there's software to help you

Ever performed a mix and thought it sounded bad, even though you had your tracks perfectly beatmatched and in phase? The sad truth is that some tracks just don't sound good together, and there are a number of reasons why that might be so. Perhaps the drums and percussions clash too heavily, or maybe the basslines of both tracks are too pronounced and flow the whole way through the tracks.

Another reason why tracks may not play well together is that their musical keys may not be compatible. No matter how well you set up the phrasing, beatmatching and phasing of tracks with incompatible keys, your mixes won't sound natural or smooth. There'll be something jarring about them.

Harmonic mixing is a technique that involves identifying the musical key of your tracks and then mixing tracks with compatible keys to achieve smooth and natural-sounding mixes that don't sound 'off'. It has grown in popularity in recent years because of the large number of DJs producing sets that play lots of different tracks at the same time.

You're not limited to using tracks within a single musical key. You can switch to other compatible keys within a mix, giving you and the audience some variation over the course of your set, which makes your set interesting and defeats boredom.

Using musical keys

For those unfamiliar with musical keys, trying to pin down exactly what one is can be a challenge. The Oxford English Dictionary defines it as "a group of notes based on a particular note and comprising a scale, regarded as forming the tonal basis of a passage of music". This means that each track is based around a specific set of notes, and there's a specific note that is most relevant to the group. This is called the tonic note, and each musical key is named after this note. To further complicate things, there are major and minor keys.

What that means for DJs is you have to mix tracks in to each other that are in the same key, such as A major, or mix tracks with compatible keys such as, in the case of A Major, F sharp minor. This may sound difficult, but there are tools to help you identify which tracks should be played

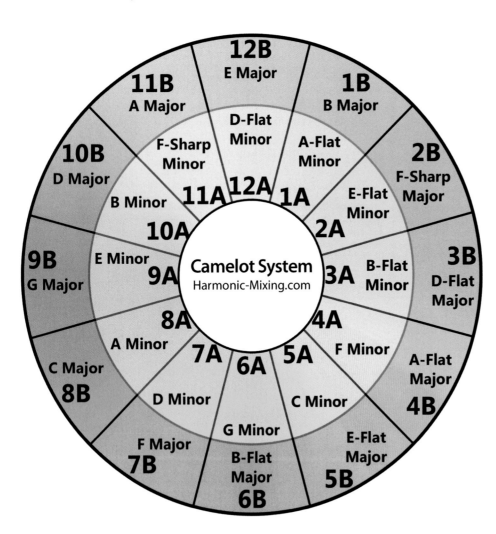

USING RAPID EVOLUTION 3
TO IDENTIFY KEYS

1 Decide if you want to import folders or files.

Rapid Evolution 3 beta 58

Import   Export   Options

- Audio File(s)
- Folder
- Playlist(s)
- ITunes
- Traktor
- Mixmeister
- RE2
- RE3

Song Description   Ratin

2 Select the folders or files you want to import.

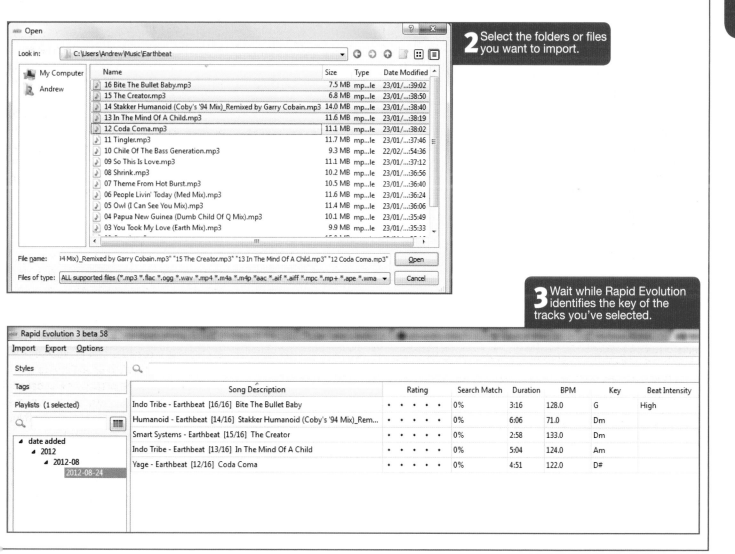

Open

Look in: C:\Users\Andrew\Music\Earthbeat

My Computer
Andrew

Name	Size	Type	Date Modified
16 Bite The Bullet Baby.mp3	7.5 MB	mp...le	23/01/...:39:02
15 The Creator.mp3	6.8 MB	mp...le	23/01/...:38:50
14 Stakker Humanoid (Coby's '94 Mix)_Remixed by Garry Cobain.mp3	14.0 MB	mp...le	23/01/...:38:40
13 In The Mind Of A Child.mp3	11.6 MB	mp...le	23/01/...:38:19
12 Coda Coma.mp3	11.1 MB	mp...le	23/01/...:38:02
11 Tingler.mp3	11.7 MB	mp...le	23/01/...:37:46
10 Chile Of The Bass Generation.mp3	9.3 MB	mp...le	22/02/...:54:36
09 So This Is Love.mp3	11.1 MB	mp...le	23/01/...:37:12
08 Shrink.mp3	10.2 MB	mp...le	23/01/...:36:56
07 Theme From Hot Burst.mp3	10.5 MB	mp...le	23/01/...:36:40
06 People Livin' Today (Med Mix).mp3	11.6 MB	mp...le	23/01/...:36:24
05 Owl (I Can See You Mix).mp3	11.4 MB	mp...le	23/01/...:36:06
04 Papua New Guinea (Dumb Child Of Q Mix).mp3	10.1 MB	mp...le	23/01/...:35:49
03 You Took My Love (Earth Mix).mp3	9.9 MB	mp...le	23/01/...:35:33

File name:)4 Mix)_Remixed by Garry Cobain.mp3" "15 The Creator.mp3" "13 In The Mind Of A Child.mp3" "12 Coda Coma.mp3"   Open

Files of type: ALL supported files (*.mp3 *.flac *.ogg *.wav *.mp4 *.m4a *.m4p *aac *.aif *.aiff *.mpc *.mp+ *.ape *.wma   Cancel

3 Wait while Rapid Evolution identifies the key of the tracks you've selected.

Rapid Evolution 3 beta 58

Import   Export   Options

Styles

Tags

Playlists (1 selected)

▲ date added
  ▲ 2012
    ▲ 2012-08
      2012-08-24

Song Description	Rating	Search Match	Duration	BPM	Key	Beat Intensity
Indo Tribe - Earthbeat [16/16] Bite The Bullet Baby	• • • • •	0%	3:16	128.0	G	High
Humanoid - Earthbeat [14/16] Stakker Humanoid (Coby's '94 Mix)_Rem...	• • • • •	0%	6:06	71.0	Dm	
Smart Systems - Earthbeat [15/16] The Creator	• • • • •	0%	2:58	133.0	Dm	
Indo Tribe - Earthbeat [13/16] In The Mind Of A Child	• • • • •	0%	5:04	124.0	Am	
Yage - Earthbeat [12/16] Coda Coma	• • • • •	0%	4:51	122.0	D#	

together. One such tool is the Circle of Fifths, which is a wheel upon which all the different keys are listed. Another more DJ-friendly tool is the Camelot wheel, created by Mark Davis (see p50). It looks similar to the Circle of Fifths, but is labelled from one to 12, like a clock face. The Camelot wheel is further divided in to inner and outer wheels. The numbers on the outer wheel are labelled with a B and the inner numbers are labelled with an A. To mix harmonically, you simply have to move from a number to the one before it or the one after it. This means that if you're playing a track in F sharp minor, which is 11A on the Camelot wheel, you could mix in to a track with the key B minor, which is 10A on the Camelot wheel.

That's all well and good, but it doesn't help us identify the key of our tracks. Thankfully, software is available that identifies the key so that we can consult charts such as the Circle of Fifths and the Camelot wheel and mix harmonically.

Keying software

Traditionally, identifying a track's musical key involved tapping keys on a piano or keyboard, and it was a time-consuming process far beyond the ability of many DJs. Fortunately, many talented software developers have produced applications that identify musical keys for us, so that we don't have to. Not only does this software identify the key, it also writes it to the MP3 tags of our tracks so that we can quickly see it within our software. This means we

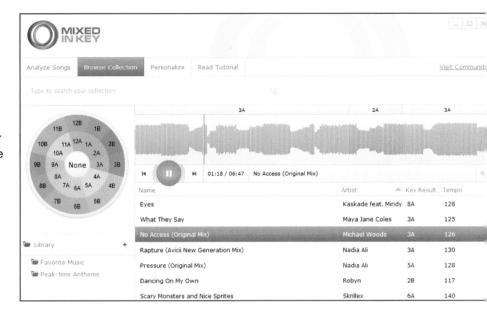

can sort our tracks by key so that we don't have to search too far to find a compatible track that fits in to our set.

One popular keying application is Mixed In Key, which is now on its fifth version. Mixed In Key adopts the Camelot wheel way of doing things and once it's identified the key of your track it will tag it with its Camelot code, such as 4A or 10B. You can tag the filename, track name and add an MP3 tag, whatever makes it easier for you to identify a track. We've used Mixed In Key since version 4, and we find it easy to use. It costs $58 (around £36) and is available from **www.mixedinkey.com**.

Another decent bit of software of is Rapid Evolution 3. It's a free-to-use piece of software that can be downloaded from **www.mixshare.com**. It's still a beta version so it looks rougher than Mixed In Key and has a home-brew feel about it. Even so, you can quickly select tracks or folders of track to analyse. Instead of the Camelot system favoured by Mixed In Key, Rapid Evolution 3 provides the actual keys of the tracks, such as C and F sharp. Of course, you can still use the Camelot wheel with Rapid Evolution's results.

Feeding tracks in to your keying software still takes time, but it's not your time you're wasting. You can ask the software to find the key of your tracks and leave it to it while you get on with something more interesting such as mixing or slapping zombies in Resident Evil 6.

Use it

Harmonic mixing is an important weapon in the fight to get you booked as a DJ before someone else. Thanks to software such as Mixed In Key and Rapid Evolution 3, all it involves is a little bit of preparation and a little bit of thought. Even if you're skint, Rapid Evolution 3 means you can get your tracks keyed and create harmonically correct mixes for nothing.

However, it's important not to rely on the software too heavily. It isn't bullet-proof, and you still need to use your ears to make sure your mixes sound good. Our advice? Practise and keep practising until you know your tunes inside out.

MIKE WEATHERLEY MP & THE LAST NIGHT A DJ SAVED MY LIFE FOUNDATION PRESENT

DJ VACANCY

16 - 25 YEAR OLD REQUIRED TO WIN NATIONAL COMPETITION.
NO PREVIOUS EXPERIENCE NECESSARY, ALL GENRES OF MUSIC WELCOME.

PRIZES TO INCLUDE:

▸ FINALIST TO PLAY A HISTORIC SET WITH 'A' LIST DJ
AT **THE HOUSE OF COMMONS TERRACE**, LONDON, MARCH 2013
▸ FULL AUDIO PRODUCTION DEGREE SCHOLARSHIP AT **THE SAE INSTITUTE**
▸ DJ SET AT **WE LOVE...SPACE** IN **IBIZA** 2013 SEASON
▸ WIDE RANGE EQUIPMENT & EDUCATIONAL AUDIO / DJ COURSES FOR HEAT FINALISTS

WWW.HOUSETHEHOUSE.ORG

FOR MORE INFO OR TO OFFER SUPPORT EMAIL: INFO@LASTNIGHTADJSAVEDMYLIFE.ORG

FIND US ON
FACEBOOK

THE LAST NIGHT A DJ SAVED MY LIFE FOUNDATION REGISTERED CHARITY NO. 1142478 IN ENGLAND AND WALES

Using Ableton Live

Ableton Live is incredibly popular with a vast army of digital DJs, and for good reason. Even though it's intended for music production rather than DJing, Ableton Live has many elements that let digital DJs create spectacularly creative mixes that combine lots of different tracks, samples and instruments.

With Ableton Live, you can create perfect mix tapes that have different parts of many different tracks playing at the same time. You can easily create your own edits and remixes by chopping tracks into bite-size chunks that you can rearrange in a way that'll keep your audience excited and interested. It's also great for augmenting tracks with your own production, such as backbeating a track with a break, or adding your own strings.

Ableton Live is notoriously complex for the beginner to get into, so in this chapter, we show you how to mix with Ableton Live, how to use effects and EQs to make your mixes more interesting, and how to rearrange tracks with loops and clips. We'll give you the skills you need to take your DJing creativity to the next level.

CHAPTER THREE

How To DJ With Ableton Live

Ableton lets you flex your creative muscles like no other app, but at first glance it's scary as hell. Fear no more – here's how to use it

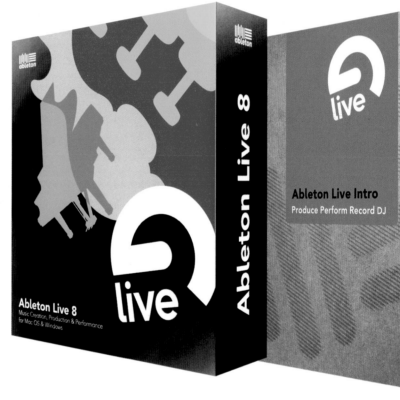

Ableton Live 8 is an incredibly powerful piece of software. Not only does it let you mix tracks, it also lets you split them up in to bite-size chunks so that you can remix and edit them live. You can create your own beats, basslines and melodies using MIDI instruments and play them alongside audio, creating truly unique sets. Because of this, many top DJs such as Paul Van Dyk, Deadmau5 and Amit ignite dancefloors the world over with Ableton Live week in, week out.

Unfortunately, for some people, one look at it is enough to make them jump through the nearest window in fright, and learning how to use efficiently can be made all the more difficult because of the many approaches you can take. Thankfully, we can tell you everything a DJ needs to know about Ableton Live, and nothing you don't. If you want to break free of the same old deck-to-deck, A-to-B DJing, read on.

Paradigm shifting

Most software applications take the traditional two-decks-and-mixer DJing approach and apply it to software. They might combine it with high-level features such as looping and effects, but you're still mixing from one deck to another.

In contrast, Ableton Live gives you a different way of building a set. Instead of

decks, you have audio tracks into which you can place individual clips. Clips can be full tracks or parts, such as loops. Think of each audio track as a channel on a traditional DJ mixer into which you can load tracks. You can stack an incredible amount of tracks in to an audio track, and although they're stacked vertically and you can only play one clip at a time, you can play them in any order.

Although you can only play one clip from an audio track at a time, you can play as many tracks simultaneously as your computer can handle. If you have a full tune in the first audio track and a full tune in the second, you can play them together, play the first tune until you want to mix out of it, start the tune in the second audio track and then cut off the outgoing track, just as you would with

ABLETON MIDI CONTROLLERS

Although you can control Ableton with a mouse, a dedicated Ableton MIDI controller makes DJing with Ableton a far more natural experience. In particular, you should invest in a MIDI controller that lets you trigger and stop clips, so you can combine loops and tracks quickly whenever you want.

Akai APC40
Price: £309

The Akai APC40 gives you everything you need to get started with Ableton Live, including the software itself. It's a cut-down version of the Ableton Live, but you still get enough audio and MIDI tracks to DJ. You can trigger scenes or individual clips, and it also has a crossfader and channel faders.

Novation Launchpad
Price: £129

The Novation Launchpad is a cracking modular controller that lets you easily combine and trigger clips. At £129, it's relatively inexpensive, too. It gives you a massive 64-button clip launch grid with multi-coloured buttons so you can easily see the state of the clips at any one time.

▲▼Getting your hands on a quality controller can make all the difference when using Ableton Live

ditional decks. There's nothing stopping u mixing tunes traditionally, like this, but e opportunity's there to do that and add er elements and effect alonside them. ur imagination is pretty much the limit. To make the transition from traditional software easier, Ableton Live provides signable crossfaders, should you wish use them. This is sometimes handy, but en Ableton's approach to mixing, it's en easier and more natural to just use the annel faders.

prepared

dly, we were banned m the Cub scuts, but e thing we did take ay from our brief time under the wing of ela and co. was the tto 'be prepared'. Although that rallying cry s intended to help the vival instincts of Scouts ould they end up being nt over the top to face emy machine guns, it's ually good advice for

anyone embarking on a DJing career with Ableton Live. It's vitally important for any DJ to know their tracks inside-out, but with Ableton Live you also need to prep them before you start your set.

When you first add a track to Ableton Live it's analysed to determine its BPM and its initial starting point, the point from which the track plays when you press start. Unfortunately, it doesn't always get the BPM right or set the play marker at the right point, so you need to check and correct it. Because Ableton Live lets you play many different audio clips and tracks at the same time,

there's mileage to be gained by going through your tracks and ripping out loops and vocals to use as independent tracks. This is what will enable you to create unique mixes further down the line.

This can seem like hard work, but you only have to do it once, after which Live will create an

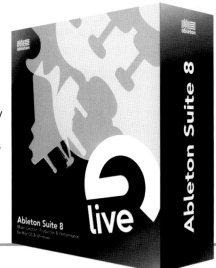

accompanying file with every track with your work saved to it. After that, you're free to use your tracks as creatively - and in as many different forms - as you want. To make it as easy as possible to get into Ableton Live, we've broken down the process of DJing with live into handy bite-size chunks.

Which version?

There are many different versions of Ableton Live. All of them offer the same core features, but more expensive versions expand on that core feature set. Some versions let you import more file formats, some let you use more audio and MIDI tracks, and some let you incorporate video in your Ableton Live sets. The version you choose depends on how much you have to spend and the features you actually need. The best way to decide this is to download the demo from *ableton.com/free-trial* and check it out before you buy.

At the time of writing, there are three versions of Live:

- Ableton Live 8 Intro (£89 from amazon.co.uk)
- Ableton Live 8 (£299 from decks.co.uk)
- Ableton Suite 8 (£499 from decks.co.uk)

MAKING SENSE OF THE SESSION VIEW

If you're a DJ, the Session View window is the most important, although the Arrangement View is handy to touch up any sets you've recorded. This is where you place all your clips.

Master track
The master track lets you set the overall volume of the Ableton set. It also contains scene launch buttons that let you trigger a whole horizontal row of clips with one one click.

Master BPM
You use this box to set the BPM of *all* clips in your Ableton Set. You can change it whenever you want.

Nudge buttons
These behave just like pitch bend buttons on a controller or software such as Traktor. The Nudge buttons speed up or slow down your entire Ableton mix so that you can get it in phase with CDJs or turntables.

Transport controls
The transport controls work just like the deck controls of other DJ applications, except they control the entire Ableton set and not just individual decks.

Quantisation menu
For DJs, this menu lets you select the beat length that passes before the clip you've just triggered kicks in. If it's set to one bar, for example, you'll have to wait until the end of the bar before the clip starts.

Audio tracks
You store clips in the audio tracks. Clips can be full tunes or parts of tunes, such as drum loops or vocals. Clips are stacked vertically.

MIDI tracks
MIDI tracks work in a similar way to audio tracks, except they contain MIDI data generated by MIDI instruments such as synths and drum machines. This makes it easy to add your own production work to your DJ sets in order to create unique live remixes.

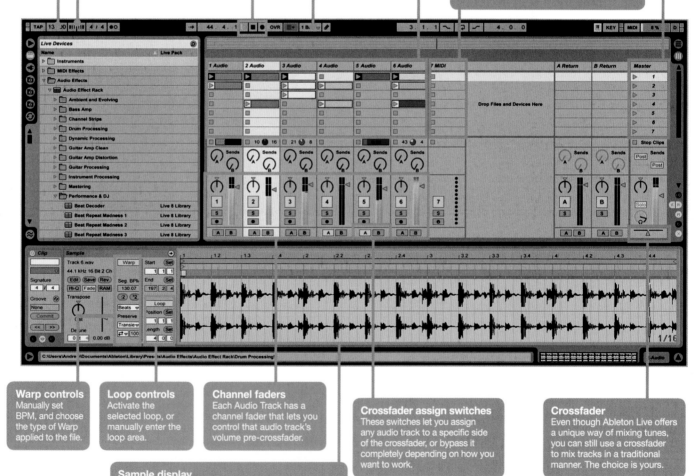

Warp controls
Manually set BPM, and choose the type of Warp applied to the file.

Loop controls
Activate the selected loop, or manually enter the loop area.

Channel faders
Each Audio Track has a channel fader that lets you control that audio track's volume pre-crossfader.

Crossfader assign switches
These switches let you assign any audio track to a specific side of the crossfader, or bypass it completely depending on how you want to work.

Crossfader
Even though Ableton Live offers a unique way of mixing tunes, you can still use a crossfader to mix tracks in a traditional manner. The choice is yours.

Sample display
The sample editor displays a waveform of a clip. You can zoom in and out of the clip so that you can see the whole clip or just an enlarged portion of it for fine-tuning. You can set loops, warp markers and define the first beat using the Sample Editor.

Using Effects

Ableton Live's effects are sophisticated and comprehensive, but they're not as scary as they look at first sight

As DJs, we're used to mixers and software having effects units, but none are as sophisticated or flexible as Ableton Live's. It doesn't just provide you with a flanger, an echo and a filter, it lets you apply more than one effect on a channel in any order you choose, creating unique combinations and sounds.

Effects are applied to individual audio tracks, and each audio track can have more than one effect. To apply an effect to an audio track you simply have to select the audio track to which the effect is applied and then double-click an effect within Ableton Live's Device Browser. The effect is then displayed within a tab next to the Sample Editor's tab. This tab is automatically displayed when you add an effect to a track.

If you apply multiple effects, they link in 'chains', where the output of the first effect is fed in to the input of the second, and so on. For this reason, it's important to think about the order effects are arranged in. You can re-arrange a chain, should it be necessary,

by clicking and holding its title bar and moving it to a different place in the chain.

There are so many options that the best way to see how they transform your clips is to get stuck in and use them, noting down what does what and your preferences.

EQs

Unlike many other software audio applications, you must add equalisers to an audio track as an effect. One such effect is EQ Three, and another is EQ Eight. As implied by its name, the EQ Three effect provides a three-band equaliser. You also get kill switches for each band, so you can press a single button to kill all bass frequencies in an instant, for example. The individual bands are controlled by virtual potentiometers. In contrast, EQ Eight provides an X/Y pad to which you can add one or more filters. The more filters you add, the more you're able to shape the sound how you want. You can even choose from one of six filter types for each filter. This gives you

immensely sophisticated control over your audio track's equalisation settings.

Effects racks

Ableton Live now lets you combine multip effects into self-contained chains, called 'Racks'. To create a Rack, you simply hav to highlight each effect you want to includ in the Rack by clicking each effect's title bar while holding your keyboard's Shift button and then right-clicking one of then Choose the Group option from the menu and your Effects Rack will be created. You can then expand the Rack's Macro controls and map individual functions from each individual effect unit to a Macr pot. This means that if you're happy with your flanger's settings, for example, and only want to control the flanger's rate and depth, you can assign these functions to the Macro controls so you can adjust then easily, along with essential controls form other effects.

It's worth remembering that you can assign effects to the master channel, too, and Effects Racks are a great way of giving you access to your favourite chains of effects, and the parameters you tweak the most, that you can easily apply and use to manipulate all output channels at once.

060

APPLYING AN EFFECT

Applying an effect to an audio track is straightforward.

1 Select the audio track to which you want to apply an effect.

2 Double-click an effect in the device browser to apply it to the track.

3 Alter the effect's settings at your leisure. Happy tweaking.

CREATING EFFECTS RACKS

Effects racks let you combine many different effects units in to one large effects unit for easier management and use. Once created, you can map specific functions to easily accessible Macro controls so that you don't have to hunt for them.

1 Highlight each effect by clicking its title bar while holding down the Shift key on your keyboard.

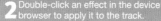

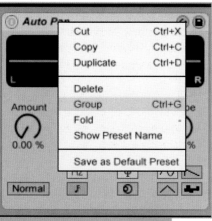

2 Right-click any effect's title bar and select 'Group' from the menu.

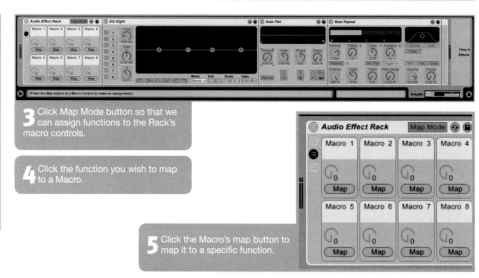

3 Click Map Mode button so that we can assign functions to the Rack's macro controls.

4 Click the function you wish to map to a Macro.

5 Click the Macro's map button to map it to a specific function.

Warping Clips

It's essential that Ableton Live knows the correct BPM of your clips. Sometimes it needs a helping hand

When you first load a track into Ableton Live, the software analyses it and attempts to determine its BPM and the location of the first beat. Even if you load a happy hardcore or breakbeat track, Ableton Live pretty much gets this right more often than not. Sadly, there are instances where it isn't so perfect and you have to give it a helping hand. It could be that the track you're importing's too complex, or perhaps it has a down-tempo intro which eludes any attempt to pinpoint the 'one'.

If Ableton has determined a BPM you know is wrong, you have a couple of options. You can either type the correct BPM into the clip's BPM box or you can place warp markers on each beat and have Ableton determine the BPM from the position of those markers. Don't panic, though: warping isn't as difficult as it at first seems, and once you've warped all your clips you won't have to do it again.

Notice those yellow markers above the waveform? They're warp markers. The number of warp markers employed by Ableton is dependent on the track it has analysed. Simple clips might just have one marker at their start. You place warp markers by double-clicking the thin line just above the waveform. In fact, if you hover the cursor over this line a grey warp marker appears.

To make sure Ableton's correctly identified the BPM of the track, place a yellow warp marker on every beat. Look at the BPM of the track and it might possibly change in response to your marker placement. Once you've placed your markers, right-click the marker that's furthest to the right of the sample editor and select Warp From Here on the menu. Ableton Live then adjusts the track's BPM accordingly.

Warp options

There's more to warping than setting warp markers, though. There are a number of options to consider, like whether or not to warp the clip at all. If the Warp button is activ and illuminated yellow then the clip will play at the master tempo for the entire Live set. I it's inactive, the clip will play at its native BP and you'll have great difficulty beatmixing it with other tracks. If you're using Ableton Liv to beatmix, you need all your clips warped.

Another consideration is the warp mode you employ. You have six different modes to choose from, and each treats the audio clip a different way. Experiment with the differen warp modes to see which suits your set or individual clip best. Indeed, top DJs such as Amit use specific warp modes on specific clips because of the different ways in which the algorithms alter the sound of the music.

▼ The yellow markers above the waveform are warp markers to show the beat of the track

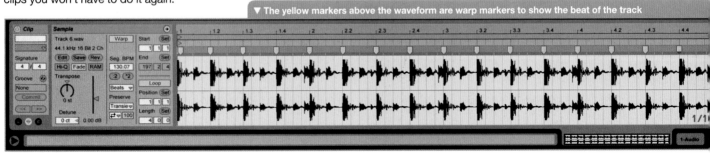

Using Loops And Samples

Loops and samples will form the basis of your live edits and remixes. Find out how to master them in Ableton with our help

Loops are an essential tool for creating live edits or customising the another track with a hot vocal, bassline or drum beat. Although creating loops in Ableton Live isn't as instantly straightforward or obvious as creating loops in other applications such as Traktor or Djay, it isn't difficult. Better still, Ableton Live provides excellent looping facilities and a number of different ways to create loops.

One method of looping is to use the loop controls in the Sample box. To activate a loop, simply press the Loop button. If the Loop button's illuminated yellow, the loop's active and will play until you deactivate it. You can activate a loop at any time by pressing the Loop button, and when you do activate it the loop the loop will play at the end of the next beat, keeping the loop in sync with other clips, keeping the mix smooth.

You can control the size and start point of a loop using the Loop Position and Length controls. The Position controls set the start point of the loop and it's best to think of them as a more precise version of a CDJ or controller's Loop In button. The Length controls set the length of the loop, predictably enough, but Ableton Live lets you set loop lengths with much more precision than most other software.Both the Position and Length controls provide three fields in which you can set bars, beats and sixteenths, with the left box being bars and the right being sixteenths. This gives you a tremendous amount of control over your loops.

Another, possibly quicker method of setting a loop is to use a clip's loop braces. You can drag these to the desired length and then click the Loop button to activate it. You can also use the loop braces to re-size the loop when it's active.

An even quicker method if you want to create a brief loop is to press the left-mouse button, keep it pressed and drag the cursor along the clip's waveform. The section of the clip you've selected is the coloured orange. Simply right-click the selected portion of the clip and choose Loop Selection to create and activate the loop there and then.

One of the strengths of Ableton Live is the ability to cut up sections of tracks and combine to create edits or unique mixes, and loops make it easy to rip new clips from existing tracks. As an example, you might just want the drum-beat from a trac so you can play it alongside another track or your own production. To rip the sample from the full track, all you have to do is create the loop, right-click anywhere on the clip's waveform and then choose Cro Sample from the menu. It's that simple.

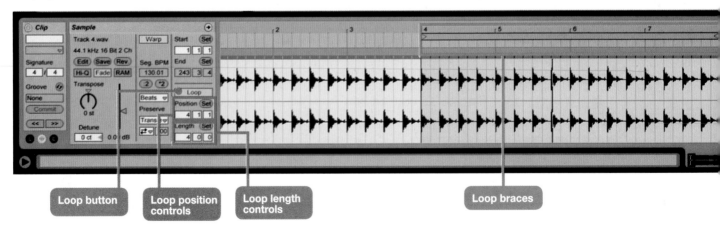

Loop button

Loop position controls

Loop length controls

Loop braces

RIPPING SAMPLES

Triggering samples and combining short clips with longer phrases or full tracks is what makes Ableton Live a fun and powerful and system for DJing. Thankfully, you can rip samples out of existing audio files within Ableton Live – you don't need any other application. Here's how you do it.

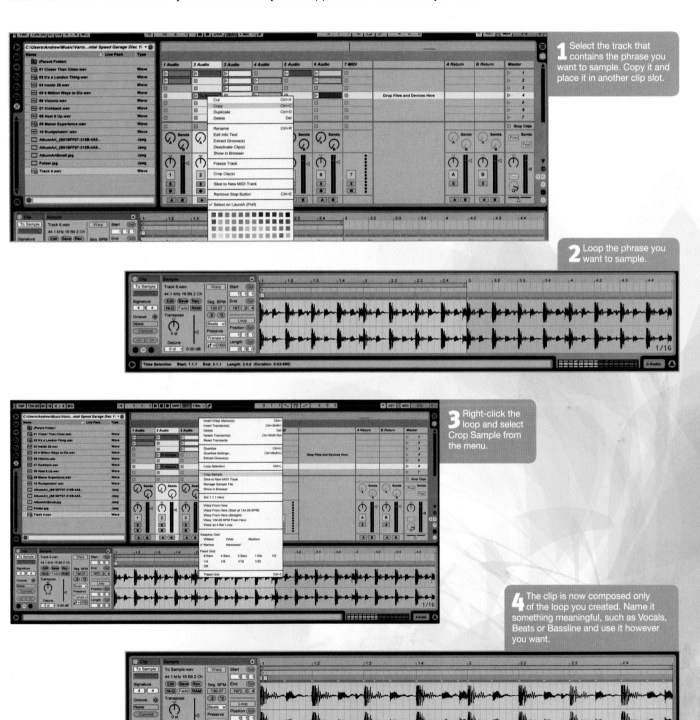

1 Select the track that contains the phrase you want to sample. Copy it and place it in another clip slot.

2 Loop the phrase you want to sample.

3 Right-click the loop and select Crop Sample from the menu.

4 The clip is now composed only of the loop you created. Name it something meaningful, such as Vocals, Beats or Bassline and use it however you want.

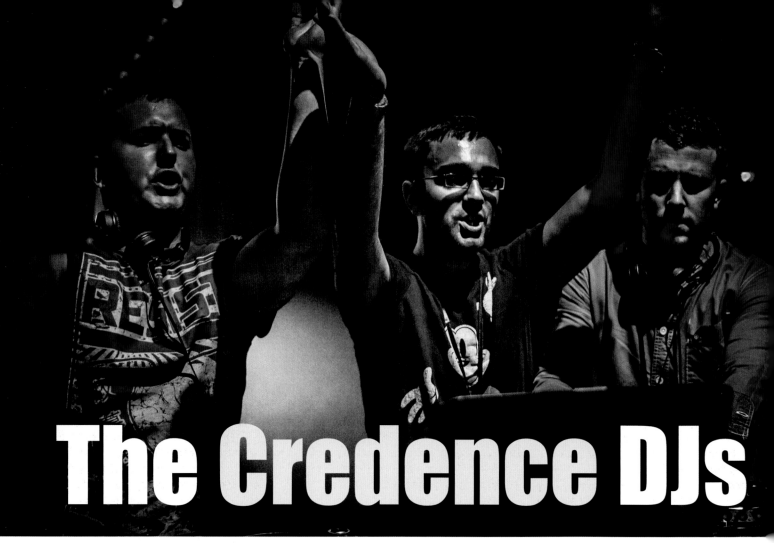

The Credence DJs

Afraid of using Ableton Live in the club?
Let the Credence DJs tell you why it's
good for business

Credence is a trio of DJs who came together, after having served time at various clubs across the country, in order to make a bigger impact on the London club scene. Using a combination of traditional DJing methods and Ableton Live, Credence has quickly made a name for itself as a provider of fun and creative mash-ups and live remixes. Not for the sake of it, but as a means of igniting the audience and giving them something no other DJs can.

Credence is composed of Sean Linney, Olly King and James Bickerton, and between them they've played alongside top acts such as Pendulum, Chase &

Status, Freemasons, Example and Danny Byrd. We caught up with Credence to ask them about using Ableton Live in the club and how they create their mash-ups.

H2DJ: You're well known for combining lots of different samples and loops to create something unique. What kind of reaction do you get from the audience?
Credence: We played a gig on a boat party to celebrate the Olympics, and we played to a huge crowd as we went up and down the Thames. The DJ that was on before us came behind the decks, saying "guys, guys, what's that remix you're playing?"

It was a track called *Miami Vice*, quite a techy house track, and we'd put an acapella of Azealia Banks's *212* over the top. He said: "What's that remix, it's amazing! I need it!"

We just turned to him and said "Mate, this is live!" He immediately got out his card and gave it to us, and he was like, "Give me a shout". He was just dumbfounded that we were doing that mash-up live, there and then, and I was like, "Hang on, just watch because the next drop's coming".

Olly faded out the acapella as the next drop came and then kicked the acapella back in. The crowd went wild, which is a massive buzz, because that reaction's exactly what we're trying to achieve.

H2DJ: So it's that element of going the extra mile that's bringing in the club gigs?
Credence: Yes, we reckon so. We see a lot of DJs just playing from one CDJ to the other, and there's nothing wrong with that, we just like that extra element. It really helps with bookings. As an example, the promoter of that boat event said we give it that bit extra. He put us on just before the headline DJ and he loved it.

We bring nothing but energy and enthusiasm to doing what we do, and we reckon half the reason the crowd goes crazy is not because of all of this technical wizardry that we're doing, but the fact that it's three guys absolutely loving the music they're playing. When that enthusiasm goes in and you put that enthusiasm into your mixes and your mash-ups, it carries across to the audience. Then we meet a club manager, they see that energy and they think, "If they can bring that energy to my promotion or my night, then that's what I want".

H2DJ: So chopping up, rearranging and layering tracks works in a club?
Credence: Yes, we think there's a lot of glamour in doing the hard work and it can really help to unite different tribes in your audience. We play a lot of house music with commercial vocals, but you really want to play to your crowd. If you have people that aren't really into house music but you play a loop of acapella from the charts along with your track, that'll get the girls dancing because they recognise it. If you get the girls on board then the guys will start dancing, but then underneath all that we've got a really cool underground track, music that we love.

▲ Preparation is everything for Credence

That keeps us doing this, and there are people in the crowd who listen to what we do and think, "This is really good". People see you doing the traditional style of DJing and combining it with Ableton Live, and that creates a massive buzz. You really can please both sides of the crowd. Now that's a fundamentally very simple thing for us to do, but it makes such a difference to the crowd.

H2DJ: Do you guys just use Ableton Live?
Credence: We use one laptop that's linked up with Serato Scratch Live and Ableton through The Bridge, which is a technology that lets the two apps communicate. We did discuss, when we were coming up with our concept, playing with two laptops so that one would have much more control over the acapellas and vocals, and things like that, but there

▼Creative mixing can unite diverse crowds

were other complications with connecting two laptops and using a midi-clock to synchronise them. So we're just using one at the moment.

We take it in turns to chop and change between the different systems, with two guys doing the track selection and mixing and the third guy layering acapellas on top. The CDJs and mixer are almost always supplied by the venue at which you're playing, but we do have a DDJ-S1 just in case we don't have a mixer or decks. It's highly convenient when you have to use your own equipment at a gig, and we can always adapt.

H2DJ: Do you think modern technology makes it easier to perform live remixes?
Credence: Definitely. Even at the simplest end of the spectrum you've got looping functionality on the CDJs that was once the stuff of dreams. There's so much more that you can do now, which is great. We've got so many ways to make ourselves stand out from the next guy, because ultimately that's what's going to get you booked.

H2DJ: Any advice for our readers?
Credence: Learn the basics and how to DJ by ear. Once you've nailed the skills you can progress on to the modern technology that automates those processes.

BOOKING
If you want Credence to rock your party with their technical wizardry, check out the Credence website at *www.credencedjs.co.uk*.

10 iOS Apps You Can't Live Without

Make killer beats and mixes on the move with 10 of the best iOS apps you can buy

Developers realised the music-making potential of the iPad soon after its release, and even the iPhone lets you create killer beats and save ideas on the move. DJs love augmenting tracks with their own productions, and iOS makes it easier than ever to do that. It's also the number one mobile operating system for DJ apps. We've chosen 10 of the best apps you can't possibly live without.

Djay
Price: 69p for iPhone, £13.99 for iPad
We're massive fans of Djay, and recommend you buy and download it now. Whether you use the iPad or bargain iPhone version, Djay provides one of the best laid out interfaces of any app. It adopts the two-deck paradigm, but that's not bad thing. Whatever you want from a DJ app, Djay's got it.

iMaschine
Price: £2.99
iMaschine lets you sketch out beats and grooves on the move using 16 drum pads, two keyboards and an audio recorder. Once you've created your catchy killer groove you can export it as an audio file.

The gain, panning and volume of each section can be modified to suit your needs, and you can easily select and apply up to two effects to your track, such as chorus, delay and flanger. Buy it. Buy it now.

Vjay
Price: £6.99
Vjay is a fantastic way of capitalising on your collection. Each deck has a video monitor, and you can mix your videos just as you would your tunes, except you choose transition effects to be applied to the videos as you mix them. Extremely fun and a bargain

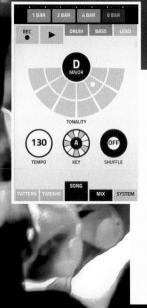

Propellerhead Figure
Price: 69p
Propellerhead's Figure is a new and innovative way to create music. You don't even need any prior musical knowledge, you simply swipe and tap keyboard and drum parts to express the direction you want the music to go. It's an iPhone app only, but you can still use it on your iPad. You can choose from different types of drum, lead and bass sounds, use a basic mixer to set volume levels and change tempo – all for less than £1. A real bargain.

thedjguide.co.u

Akai SynthStation
Price: £1.49

Akai has drawn on its synthesiser know-how to bring you SynthStation – an app that provides many functions that let you transform and alter sounds as you see fit. It features adjustable LFOs, oscillators and much more. There's also support for crafting your own beats, and given its low price it's a bit of a bargain. This is easily a contender for best-value iOS music production app of all time.

iDJ
Price: £1.49

Numark's iDJ lets you select tracks to be included in a playlist and then iDJ mixes them for you, allowing you to select the type of mix used and the length of beat mix. This is a simple but immensely fun app.

Korg iElectribe
Price: £13.99

The Korg iElectribe is the iOS version of Korg's popular hardware-based drum machine and synth box. In fact, iElectribe's interface looks incredibly similar to the top panel of an Electribe ESX1, so if you're already familiar with the Electribe way of doing things, you can easily get in to it.

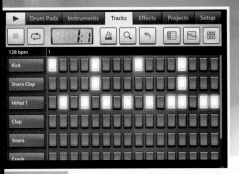

FL Studio Mobile
Price: £10.49

FL Studio Mobile is the iOS version of Image Line's excellent FL Studio digital audio workstation. It can create beats, melodies, basslines or whatever you want using the virtual keyboard or the 'piano roll', which lets you draw key presses onto the screen, handy if you struggle to play chords on the virtual keyboard. It's a bit fiddly, but it's fun.

Deckadance
Price: £2.49

Deckadance finally comes to the iPad, and it's a pretty good conversion form the desktop. You can use effects loops and hot cues to great effect, but there's no proper cueing system.

ReBirth
Price: £1.99 for iPhone, £10.49 for iPad

Roland's TB-303 bassline synth, TR-808 and TR-909 drum machines are classic instruments venerated the world over. Now you can experience the classic bubbling and pounding sounds of these instruments on your iOS device.

edjguide.co.uk

For Drum & Bass producer Amit, Ableton Live provides a path from studio to DJ booth that takes him exactly where he wants to go. If you're a producer looking to create a 'live' presence, it could be just the thing for you, too

Selected Amit Discography

- **Killer Driller/Colour Blind,** Metalheadz, 2012
- **Exit EP,** Exit Records, 2012
- **9 Times LP,** Commercial Suicide, 2011
- **Propaganda/White Trash,** Commercial Suicide, 2008
- **Suicide Bomber,** Commercial Suicide, 2007
- **Never Ending LP,** Commercial Suicide, 2006
- **Immigrants/Second Cut,** Bingo, 2005

AMIT

Drum & Bass legend Amit has long been a pioneer of Ableton Live. This is a DJ that doesn't just play records, he remixes them, creating truly unique and one-off sets. We found out how.

H2DJ: When did you first decide to swap the studio for the DJ booth?

Amit: I got to the point where I'd released a significant amount of music under the Amit artist name and I was just about to deliver my first album. I knew that there were friends and colleagues who were travelling the world and playing my music, and it was great. I'd wait for the feedback, I'd ask them how it sounded, and they'd tell me what it was like.

Initially, I just wanted to be a Producer who'd be in his studio, creating music and supplying it to the bloodstream so it would hit the scene and people would hear it. I was happy doing that, but then something twigged. I think I was in the car one time, with [fellow D&B producer] Calibre, and he said, "Don't you want to see the world?"

It dawned on me that there are all those people out there that listen to my music. How could I deliver my music to them without jumping on the DJ bandwagon? Because, at the time, there lots of producers who made one hit, got some decks and were suddenly international DJs. I said to DJ Randall "I'm gonna have two main events for the LP, one where I play for the first time and another where I launch the LP. I want you to be there." He said, "Amit, don't worry. If you want to learn DJing I'll come round and teach you."

That was kind of tempting at the time. He said he'd coached Andy C, and he could do the same for me. I said to him, "You're a real DJ, I don't want to step on your toes".

H2DJ: Why do you use Ableton Live?

Amit: Ableton Live is geared towards the person who doesn't just want to mix records. He might have a 32-bar loop of an unfinished track, but he strips it down into bass, drums, vocals and so on and manipulates those. He creates a track out of that loop, giving fans a unique experience.

I just want to be a creative person and do something original. Someone showed me what Ableton could do, and it was amazing. I was like, 'this is it'. Ableton Live gives you ultimate control. You can go in any direction, you can add as many sounds and layers as you want - it's just a massive program that allows you to be creative.

The first gig I did was with Goldie. I was told that for your first gig you might get 100 people, but there were 1,400 people there. It was a big thing. The second was the launch in London, and I played with Randall for that one. I never looked back, because for me performing with Ableton made perfect sense.

H2DJ: How accepting are people of you using Ableton Live instead of decks?

Amit: There's definitely a new wave of music listeners that don't mind. It's up to you what you want to do, and as long as it sounds good and people are enjoying themselves, they're up for it. Then you've got your purists. I guess, for the right reasons, they see DJing and turntablism as being an artform they don't want to see disappear. That's okay, but there are different views and different tools.

▲ For Amit, Ableton Live made perfect sense

H2DJ: So DJing with Ableton Live is a natural and creative experience for you?

Amit: Yeah, I might get a track that I'm really into and start it from the second drop of the track, then loop that section. With Ableton I can do that and it becomes a special experience within itself, especially within music that I've created. There might be a certain loop of a track that I just want to run as an interlude between tracks.

You've got loop markers and start points and all sorts that you can really use to your advantage. You can trigger stuff and pitch clips down, pitch them up and really get creative.

As another example, I'll take an old track that people know, take the lead sound out, take another thing out and have it all stripped separately. Then I'll manipulate it like it's a remix and perhaps fuse it with something else. Basically, you're creating a musical journey out of work you've created, work you might never finish, and reprises from old tunes with new beats. Then you can bring in a track that has greatly influenced you.

The great thing with Ableton is that you can slow things down, so you can go from 170bpm to 140bpm and then down to 100bpm. You know, for me as a Producer it takes the whole timing element out of it so I can just focus on being creative. I don't have to quartz lock this then quartz lock that. Forget that, it's all gonna be fine; use your production techniques to create your live experience.

The one thing I will say is that once you can use it you have to show that you're performing. Traditional DJing is quite active. You're picking up vinyl and putting it on a turntable; you're animated. There's a kind of ritual to it. With laptops, you really have to work on the performance side of it to show that you're actually doing something. Initially, when using a computer, you can be stiff, but I've learned some things you can do to combat that. You can use controllers to show you're actually changing the sounds in real-time and not just playing tune after tune as if it's iTunes.

H2DJ: How do you plan your sets?

Amit: I tend to do a bit of homework before a gig. I ask the promoters what it's like in that club, what the system's like. If it's a big system, I know I can start off with tracks that are big in the low-end regions, whereas if It's a small system I might go in another direction initially. I try to make each experience different, and I also try to cover past work, present work that I'm just releasing and new work that hasn't materialised and is kind of maturing.

I'll brim my laptop with loads of stuff, then when I get there I get a vibe on the night for what I'm going to do. What I will do is have a set of notes of what I want to play. For example, I might want to play a specific track because it's coming out. Maybe 90% of the stuff I play will be mine, and then 10% of the tracks will be from colleagues of mine who are putting out music that I really like, and I'll play those a well. I'll also try to include some classics that have really influenced me.

Sometimes, I'll also play atmosphere beds from films. When I went to Japan, I kicked o with the opening score to Akira Kurosawa's *Throne of Blood*. Going to Japan and seeing everyone respond to that was just amazing, really was a great moment.

H2DJ: Are you rigid with your set list or do you adapt it to suit your audience?

Amit: I'll have a list of things that I definitely know that I'm going to play, but the order may change and I may not play some of them.

When I first started playing I could just do what I wanted, like playing non-stop hardcore but now I enjoy that special relationship with the crowd. For instance, you have points where you say "right, now it's my turn, now I'm going to educate you" or "I'm gonna show you what I want to play."

Sometimes, you get people on mobile phones saying, "have you got that cause I really wanna hear it," or sometimes I'll throw them something obvious that I know they really want to hear. It's really that relationship, the to-ing and fro-ing, my turn your turn. I mean, ultimately they've put money in your pocket, so you want them to leave happy.

072

H2DJ: How do you organise your sets?

Amit: I warp all the individual clips; with the simple ones you just warp the entire track from start to end. For unfinished stuff, or if you want to create a live version of a track, you can warp the individual stems, so you'd warp the bass section, the drums, vocals, lead and so on. Then, you can bring them up on faders so you can mix them individually.

I use Re-Pitch mode which simulates the pitch of a turntable. There are many [Warp] modes, though, and another pitch mode I use is Complex mode. If I'm just synchronising rhythm and there's no bass layered on it then I might use Complex mode, because when you pitch down you can actually hear the grains of the pitch. It becomes a kind of robotic sound.

In terms of launching, with the Vestax [VCM100 controller], you can even launch just by clicking play or stop or you can drag and drop particular scenes, the problem is with, if you have all the tracks set up so you're hitting start and stop, the problem there is that you're kind of rigid to that set, whereas, when you're dragging stuff, you can move stuff out/in, you might not want to follow the format that you might have set before you left, so I'll have a order of tracks that I want to play. I'll have two decks, like Deck A and Deck B, which I can

Looking cool under pressure, Amit goes to work

drag stuff and mix between, then I'll have five or six lanes that have got bass drums, lead and so on for each individual track, so that's five lanes of that and then at the end on the master track, you can click global play, for the whole thing and then you can manipulate the individual stems, so I'll go between those two depending on where I am and how I feel.

H2DJ: What equipment do you use?

Amit: I've got a Vestax VCM100 and a couple of Faderfox boxes. The Vestax is my primary mixer and I've got the boxes to trigger sounds. I've got a Korg Kaoss pad, too.

H2DJ: Do you use the Faderfoxes to control effects or just the Kaoss pad?

Amit: I use the Kaoss for effects, but I also use the Vestax, which has quite a lot

of controls on it, so I can send reverbs and delays, pitch stuff up and down, and really play with the music. I also use the Faderfox controllers to control reggae/dub effects.

As for my favourite effects, I use the Auto-Filter, the Ping-Pong Delay and various reverbs. What I'll do is make a chain, so I have a bus with reverb, ping-pongs, EQs and stuff and then use the pan pots to control them. I don't really like the EQs in Ableton Live, I find them really harsh and brutal, but there's a guy who's made this third-party EQ effect called EQ3.8 v2, which is really good. The guy's name is Tarekith, and lots of producers use his custom EQs when they perform live because they're a lot smoother than the three-band EQ that comes with Ableton Live.

H2DJ: What do you like about the VCM?

Amit: The VCM is brilliant. It's really heavy, but it's sturdy and as strong as any in-house mixer. I've had mixers in the past and a lot of them are really flimsy. You'll do a quick move from the EQ to the mixer and have things flying around and pan pots disappearing, but the Vestax is quite sturdy. Honestly, you need to go to the gym to be able to carry one of those around!

H2DJ: Does the Kaoss pad sit on the master output?

Amit: Yes, the soundcard's output goes into the input of the Kaoss pad. The only drawback is that it manipulates the whole set; you can't add effects to individual channels.

H2DJ: How would you change your setup?

Amit: I wish I didn't have to use a laptop. I'd love to be able to use an iPad instead, and then manipulate virtual control surfaces over Bluetooth or Wi-Fi. Being in front of a computer creates a barrier between you and the audience, so that's what I'd change.

H2DJ: Do you ever have any problems setting up your equipment?

Amit: Not really. I tend to soundcheck an hour before the club opens and check it over the PA. With clubs like Fabric, you don't need to do that because they've got a fantastic sound engineer who talks you through it. If you're doing an Ableton Live set they'll put you on the stage and on a completely different signal path to the main DJ set up.

USING ABLETON

073

Tripping The Face-palm Fantastic

There's an old adage stating that 'the only person who never made a mistake, did nothing', but it's a sentiment that can ring hollow when it's you who's just ejected the wrong CD, precipitating an immense, all-consuming silence that seems to last an eternity. Re-inserting the CD takes mere seconds, but when you're being given the evils by a silent club of unimpressed revellers, entire galaxies could expand and collapse in the same timeframe.

All DJs make mistakes, so if you're going to pursue a DJing career you may as well get used to it. You'll be in good company, too, as these quotes testify...

▶ At one of my first gigs, I played at a friend's birthday party at a Scouts Hut. A few minutes into my set, the amp went up in flames and I had to put it out by wafting it with a vinyl sleeve in front of everyone! Not ideal! ⏸

Jordan Suckley

▶ There are actually two embarrassing moments. As a club DJ, there was falling downstairs and my record box opening up and the vinyl spilling everywhere. The other one was stopping the wrong record. ⏸

DJ Spoony

▶ Worst moment? In Bangkok running a PC with Windows XP, getting the blue screen of death and everything crashing. ⏸

Amit

Equipment Reviews

The most important weapon in a DJ's arsenal is music, but that's no use if you don't have anything to play it on. In this section, we're going to show you the software, apps, controllers and headphones that could take your digital DJing to the next level.

Want to expand your setup, but not sure what you should look for? Don't panic – each section has its own buyer's guide so you can decide what's important to you and your workflow. Whatever your needs or budget, there's something for you here.

To give you the best consumer advice straight from the experts, we've teamed up with DJ Worx, the internet's best site for DJing equipment news and reviews. Its reviews are highly respected by manufacturers and the industry, so you can depend on them for honest opinions on the latest equipment. Check out more great reviews at **www.djworx.com**.

REVIEWS BY
DJ WORX

TRACK
Coma Cat - Tensnake

RING MOD

TRACK
Libre (Axwell Vocal Mix)

POWER

CUES

Software
Buying Guide

Software is the cheapest way to start your DJing career, but finding the right package can be tricky unless you follow our advice

Not only does software give you greater control over your mixes, and flexibility in what you do with them in between, than traditional hardware, it can also offer a much cheap option for beginners.

You can buy good quality, professional-grade software for as little as £50, and some fun-for-a-while iOS apps from less than £1, which means you can give mixing a try mixing without dropping hundreds (o thousands) of your hard-earned pounds on hardware. In fact, if you go for VirtualD Home Free you won't have to pay a thing, providing you have a computer to run it o

The first decision you need to make when buying software is whether or not you need a digital vinyl system (DVS). Although this is a pretty straightforward question to answer, if you already own turntables or CDJs and want to control your software with timecode you should get a DVS. If you do need a DVS, make sure it supports enough inputs and outputs for your setup. The more I/O ports you have the more expensive your hardware will be, but the extra expense will be worth it.

Out of control
Do you need MIDI control of your software? Even if you don't need it now, if you choose software that allows MIDI control, you have the option to it with a hardware controller at later date. Check that your software lets you use different kinds of MIDI controllers, and it also preferable to use software that lets you edit controller mappings to suit your needs, and change them as those needs change.

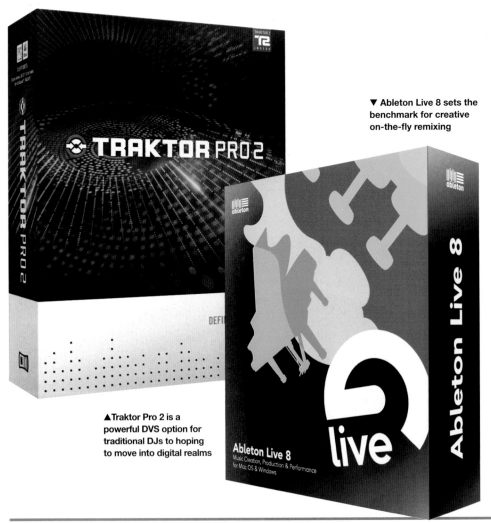

▼ Ableton Live 8 sets the benchmark for creative on-the-fly remixing

▲Traktor Pro 2 is a powerful DVS option for traditional DJs to hoping to move into digital realms

Next, think about the number of virtual
decks you want to use. Most people will
be happy with two, especially if you just
want mix from one track in to another or
control a DVS with two turntables or CDJs.
Four decks, however, will let you get a bit
more creative with looping. Traktor pro 2.5
goes one step further and lets you swap
regular decks with remix decks so you can
augment a conventional set with some full-
on mash-up action. If that isn't enough,
VirtualDJ lets you use up to 99 virtual
decks; we can't think why you would need
to, but you could.

If you want to get truly creative, or if you
want to combine your own productions with
regular tracks or loops, you should check
out Ableton Live
which also
allows many audio
channels to run
simultaneously,
but alongside
MIDI channels,
too. It also allows
tracking of shorter
audio clips for the
purpose of live
mixing.

All this comes
with a steep
learning curve, but
if you're willing
to invest the time
you'll get excellent
results.

On the move

For just 69p you can download the simply
fantastic Djay to your iPhone and learn how
to use effects, loops and hot cues in any free
time you may have. Like more expensive
software, it's not limited to the traditional two-
decks-and-mixer, making it possible to create
mixes every bit as sophisticated as those
produced by desktop applications.

Apps like Numark's iDJ provide a fun way
of introducing new people to DJing, where
all that's required is to tell it which tracks to
mix and what type of mix it should use to
do it. If you're new to DJing, this is an ideal
way to quickly learn the philosophy and
process of mixing music, before moving on
to more involved apps.

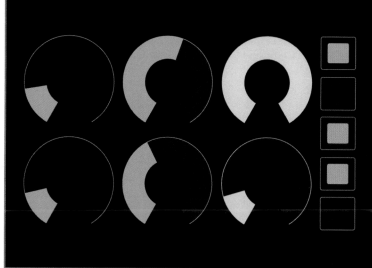

▲ Software functionality is almost limitless. VDJ, for
example, combines audio and video mixing

▲ Touch OSC is not a mixing app in itself, it's a
handy iOS-based controller for Ableton Live

Some apps are designed to support
desktop DJing applications. Good examples
are Cross DJ Remote, which lets you
control the Cross DJ Free software direct
from your iOS device. Another great iOS
app is Touch OSC, which lets you wirelessly
control software such as Ableton Live. It
gives you lots of different controls, such as
faders, drum pads and even an X/Y pad. It
looks great, too, having something of the
movie *Tron* about it.

Whichever software you choose, you
should endeavour to learn every inch of it.
This is the best way to get your money's
worth and maximise your creativity.

▼ Traktor is a fully-featured DVS system that allows
you to control digital files with physical decks

Serato Scratch Live 2.4

Price: From £349 **Supplier:** decks.co.uk **Manufacturer:** Rane **Website:** rane.com

Control modern software with your decks and CDJs

Serato Scratch Live is a digital vinyl system (DVS) that unites traditional DJ hardware with digital DJ technology. A Rane SL2, SL3 or SL4 audio interface will let you take a laptop full of tunes to a club and mix them using the club equipment. For bedroom DJs, Serato offers the opportunity to DJ without using real vinyl or burning lots of CDs.

The software itself is easy to set up. Once you're registered at Serato.com you can download the latest version of Serato Scratch Live; it's free, but you can't use it until you connect one of the SL interfaces to your computer. Without the interface, you still can arrange your playlists and plan your night's set, but you can't play tunes. In either case, Serato Scratch Live quickly locates your iTunes library and playlists.

The hardware setup is similarly simple, and you just need to connect your decks and mixer to the audio interface. The SL 2, 3 and 4 units all have a bypass button that lets you use your equipment in the normal manner when pressed. The older SL1's bypass requires twice the amount of wiring, but is still relatively simple.

Scratch Live's interface looks incredibly clean and is simple to navigate. When mixing with two decks, a vertical side-by-side waveform view of your tracks makes it easy to beat match visually, without headphones. The amount of decks available to you depends on the SL box used. SL1 and SL2 allow two-deck mixing, while SL3 allows three-deck mixing and the SL4 allows four-decks.

Scratch Live has all the features that have now become standard in DJ programs and high-end CDJs. That means that elements such as manual looping, quantised looping, slip-roll, hot cues, a sampler, highly accurate BPM readings and a range of effects are all at hand.

Scratch Live also has a 'bridge' function that lets you operate Ableton Live from within the software, which could be employed to create some unique sets. It doesn't have a sync function, but many purists buy it for this very reason.

In use, the joys of Scratch Live really become apparent. The minimalist interface lets you focus on your mix, the software's very responsive and you can search for tracks very quickly. Scratch Live's timecode vinyl is high-quality, and it feels just like regular vinyl in use. Scratch Live is well known for its stability, and this was reflected in our club test, where it performed brilliantly and didn't crash.

Serato's main competition is the formidable Traktor Scratch, which is loaded with features and effects. Both applications are excellent, but Scratch Live's interface may prove less distracting for you than Traktor's. Scratch Live isn't cheap, but its price feels warranted when you experience its sheer quality.

Traktor Pro 2.5

ice: From £79 **Supplier:** decks.co.uk **Manufacturer:** Native Instruments **Website:** native-instruments.com

raktor Pro 2.5
s packed full of
eatures, but is it
user-friendly?

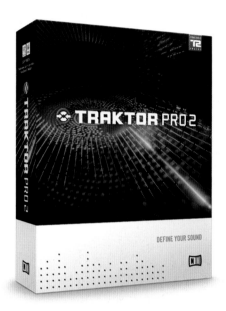

ince its first release many, many
years ago, Traktor has gone
through quite a number of different
carnations, all of which have oozed
uality and come packed with high-end
atures. Although we're primarily
viewing Traktor Pro 2.5 here, it bears
oting that there are many different
ersions of this application, some of which
e 'lite' versions with a reduced set of
atures and others are full-on digital vinyl
ystems (DVS) that include audio
terfaces. We'll mention DVS use later in
e review.

Traktor Pro 2.5 looks intimidating when
ou first boot it up due to the wealth of
atures it offers. You get four decks,
ach with eight hot cues, an advanced
oping system and a colourful, informative
aveform. Each deck also has a pitch slider
at you can set to a number of different
nges, between 6% and 100%.

Unlike some other applications, such as
cratch Live and VirtualDJ, you can't see
ack waveforms side by side. Instead, each
eck has a phase meter that shows you the
eat of a track in relation to the master clock,
you can adjust the speed of the deck to
t it in phase. The master clock can be the
PM of one of Traktor's decks, or entered
anually. We find the phase meter to be a
eful tool for mixing, because while we can
y on our ears most of the time it offers help
en we need to get tracks in phase quickly.

Hot cues, and these are arranged in
a line under each deck. Sadly, they're
not very big, and it's far easier to use a
controller to set and trigger them, than
work onscreen. Each deck also gets a
loop strip, and you can set loops between
$1/32$nd of a beat and 32 beats in length with
just one click of the mouse. Each deck
also has loop in and out buttons so you
can create loops manually. Again, using a
controller, whether modular or all-in-one,
will get the best out of these features.

If there's one thing that Traktor's does
better than all other DJing applications
it is effects. They may lack the studio
sophistication of Ableton Live's, but they're
perfect for DJs and they're easy to exploit.
Traktor Pro 2.5 gives you four effects banks,
and each effect bank can either have a single
effect in it or up to three combined effects. If
you choose to have a single effect you'll have
more control over it, and the way it alters the
sound. For example, the delay on its own
offers controls for Rate, Feedback and Filter
parameters; choose to have three combined

effects, you can only control one aspect of
each of those three effects.

In addition to the main effects, each
channel gets a filter and 'key' control. The
key control is a fantastic effect that affects
the pitch of the track playing through it,
so it either sounds low-pitch and scary or
high-pitched and silly. Used sparingly, you
can create some truly dramatic effects with
these two controls.

The mixer section itself is as fully featured
as the rest of Traktor Pro 2.5, with each
channel having an accurate peak meter and
crossfader assign switches. You can adjust
the crossfader, too, letting you have either
a smooth transition from one side of the
crossfader to other or a fast cut for scratching.
Annoyingly, you have to go into Traktor's
settings menu to adjust the crossfader curve,
which means you can't quickly set it to a fast
cut if you want to perform a quick scratch
before the next beatmix and vice versa.

If you use Traktor, a MIDI controller really is
a must, so check out **www.djworx.com** and
www.thedjguide.co.uk for suitable models,
but it's also a great choice if you want to
use timecode control media with your CDJs
and turntables. At the time of writing, you
can get Traktor Scratch Pro 2.5 with a three
stereo-channel audio interface for just £235,
which is an absolute bargain. If you need an
incredibly powerful and comprehensive DJing
application, buy Traktor Pro 2.5.

VERDICT

>> Traktor Pro 2.5 offers DJs all the
features they could ever need, and it's
easy to use

KILLER FEATURES

>> Four highly configurable effects
decks that are easy to control
>> You can map it to many controllers

VirtualDJ Pro 7

Price: Free to around £219 **Supplier:** virtualdj.com **Manufacturer:** Atomix Productions **Website:** virtualdj.com

Mix videos and MP3s with VirtualDJ

VirtualDJ is incredibly popular with mobile DJs; two big reasons for this are its low cost and its ability to mix video. This also makes it ideal for karaoke.

Fundamentally, it's a two-decks-and-mixer application, imitating a traditional DJ set up. Below these is a pane that works as a track browser, sampler, video and audio effects section and a mix recorder. Its default appearance, or skin, is dark but easy to comprehend – though this can be customised, should you wish, and there are many skins available on the VirtualDJ website.

Each deck has three hot cues buttons and an auto-loop strip from which you can choose a loop of a specified length with one press. The hot cues are handy, but there can be an uncomfortable delay between pressing one and the deck playing from the relevant track location. As well as the auto-loop strip, you can manually create loops using loop in and out buttons. Loops are pretty tight and you can have two four-beat loops playing for as long as is practical without them falling out of phase. The auto-loop strips only display loops of one to 32 beats, but you can use an arrow button to create loops of less than one beat.

Each deck has a pitch slider, a virtual jog wheel and pitch-bend buttons. The pitch-bend buttons work brilliantly, but the jog wheel is of limited use. The pitch slider's handy, but most people will use the sync button to beatmatch tracks.

In addition to the above features, each deck also has a built-in effects unit with a filter pot and a key pot. Traktor offers similar functionality, and we think it sounds better than VirtualDJ, but these are handy enough, and the filter has a decent amount of resonance. The effects are standard stuff

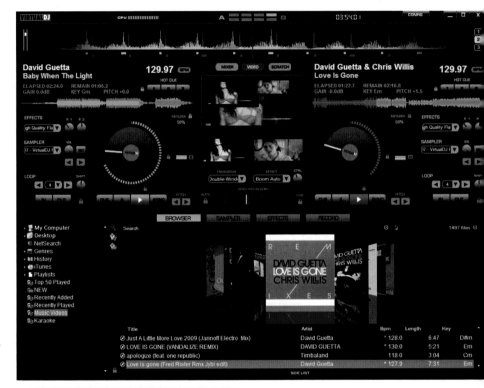

like flanger and echo. Disappointingly, though, the echo can't be used post-fader. Again, the quality of the effects doesn't match Traktor, but they're useful. You also get a sampler, which is great for one-shot sounds.

The killer feature of VirtualDJ, though, is its ability to mix video. When doing this, you lose the mixer section but gain three monitors: one for the left deck, one for the right and one showing the output. You also get a video crossfader, which you can link to the main crossfader (to mix videos and audio simultaneously) or operate separately.

The decks remain the same, so mixing with videos is the same as mixing with audio. You can even scratch the videos in to your set or beatmix them. To add more variety, VirtualDJ

includes a number of transitions, such as Cube – that paints videos on to different faces of a cube, which spins as you push the crossfader from one side to the other.

VirtualDJ isn't as highly polished as Scratch Live or Traktor, but it's feature-packed and perfect if you want to do more than mix MP3s. Video mixing quickly becomes addictive, and you could end up buying as many videos as MP3s. There are quite a few different versions, from a free version to around £219 for the full version (which also lets you use timecode). VirtualDJ is perfect for mobile DJs or those looking for free software in order to get in to DJing.

Control
Your Destiny

Unsure which controller suits you best? We guide you through the different options and arm you with the questions to ask

I f you want to get those ravers raising the roof on your club, you need the good sense to play the right record at the right time. To create the mixes you have in your mind's eye means mastering the tools of your trade, and for the digital DJ, that probably means learning to work with a decent controller. The right model won't just allow you to mix one track in to another using ergonomic, intuitive buttons and faders, it will allow you to access features which give you the ability to rip tracks apart using hot cues, loops and effects to create something truly original, on-the-fly.

Controllers can range from basic models with two channels, to hardcore Ableton Live controllers with more flashing lights than ET's washing machine. Whatever your budget, though, the chances are there's something for you – but before you bust out the plastic and hit the checkout, we're going to walk you through the things you need to know.

Over the next few pages you're going to meet some of the hottest and best-value controllers currently available, but should your perfect controller not be here, be sure to check out **www.thedjguide.co.uk** and **www.djworx.com** to see a wider selection.

Modular or all-in-one?

You would be forgiven for wondering what the differences between modular and all-in-one controllers are. Well, an all-in-one gives you virtual decks, an effects unit and a mixer, whereas a modular controller is designed to support a specific task, such as tweaking effects, triggering hot cues or ripping samples.

If you only have a laptop, you're better off with an all-in-one controller. It will give you virtually everything you need, and most all-in-ones come with software, so you can be scaring next-door's cat within minutes of getting it home. If you already have a setup, especially an Ableton setup, going modular should let you use your software more effectively and intuitively.

A small keyboard and trackpad isn't the best control surface with which to control something as complex as DJ software, but a modular controller lets you assign essential functions, specific to your software, to physical faders, knobs and buttons.

If you already have decks, some all-in-one controllers let you attach them so that you can still mix when the laptop's unplugged. Having this get-out, or even just an iPod plugged in, could be a real life-saver if your laptop crashes. Some controllers, such as the Traktor Kontrol S4, also let you use traditional decks to control software with timecode, without the need for an expensive audio interface.

Jog on

The next question you want to ask yourself is do I need jog wheels and if so, what kind do you need? These perform a dual function: they let you momentarily speed up

slow down tracks so that you can get
m in phase with another track, while also
ing you scratch and beatjuggle.

f you simply want to mix, you may not
ed jog wheels at all. Modern DJ software
s you pitch bend tracks into phase using
ttons, and you can quickly move to
erent parts of a track using cue points.
f you scratch, consider your controllers
efully. Not only does scratching punish
ur kit more than mixing, it also requires
ch more responsive jog wheels and
tware. Better, scratch-oriented, jog wheels
ve tighter integration with the host software
n MIDI offers, and should also have high-
ality, touch-sensitive, platters.

fects

ou want to create effective and original
undscapes, you need to master your
ects units. When it comes to controllers,
re are those with built in effects – usually
xer/controller hybrids like the Pioneer
M-900NXS or Allen & Heath Xone:DB4
nd those which simply provide controls
your software. Almost all all-in-one
ntrollers have a set of configurable dumb
ntrols, which make sense if you're working
clusively with software. You'll need to
sure compatibility with your software,
ough, and you should also make sure
t there's room sufficient room around
e effects controls to be comfortable, and
ough of them to do what you want.

ders

rhaps most important of all are a
ntroller's faders. Effective use of the faders
s you build tension, gradually introducing
t killer track until just the right moment
en you fully open one fader and drop the
t. To do this well, you need smooth, fluid
ders that move freely and don't jump to a
erent position with the slightest touch.

If you're into scratching, it's all about the
crossfader. Does it have a sensible fader
cap? How responsive is it? Some controllers
provide crossfader curve controls, while
others make you adjust crossfader curves
within the software you're using. The Native
Instruments Kontrol S4 is particularly well-
suited to scratching.

Hot cues

The best part of digital mixing is that you
never have to play a track the way the
producer intended. Hot cues are perfect for
rearranging on the fly and jumping straight
in to a specific part of a tune. Most modern
all-in-one controllers have a set of hot cue
buttons, but if you foresee yourself using
these controls often, you should get a
controller with large, durable ones as they
will take spankings you won't give to other
controls. Most controllers provide four hot cue
buttons, along with some means of setting
and deleting the cues, but if these are hot
cues are important to your style, search for
more. You should also want to get a controller
with the biggest hot cue buttons you can, the
larger they are, the less likely you are to miss
one and mess up a mix.

Looping

Looping is another function intrinsically linked
to live remixing and editing, and an area that
can make or break your relationship with a
controller. You need to know how you want
to trigger loops: do you want to set auto-
cues with one press, or define the size of a
loop manually or even change a loop's length
while you're in the middle of it? These are
all questions you need to consider; better
controllers provide all of these options, but
you still need to make sure there's enough
space around the controls and they're suited
to the way you play. As an example, we're
particularly fond of setting a one-beat loop

and gradually reducing it to ¼- or ⅛-beat
loop. We prefer to do this with a pot, and find
buttons to be slower when changing loop
lengths. On the flip-side, it's a lot easier to hit
the loop length you need when using buttons;
when the adrenaline's flowing, it's easy to
twist a pot too far and set a ¹⁄₃₂-beat loop
instead of the ¼-beat loop we wanted.

Global controls

Often overlooked, global controls are
those essential features you can't live
without, such as track selection and loading
controls. DJ has traditionally been a very
tactile thing, and using dedicated hardware
to control software brings this element of
the artform back a little. Using a controller
to select and load tracks is a much more
natural and effective than using a trackpad.
Some controllers even provide controls
for audio recorders and audio-visual
mixing. Controllers designed for a specific
application are much more likely to have
such features, but they may be redundant if
you later switch apps.

Which software?

This last consideration probably has the
biggest bearing on the future cost of your
setup than any other. Which software do you
get with your controller, if any?

High-quality DJing software isn't cheap, and
switching to a different application will involve
a good deal of re-training. You may need to
spend time re-analysing and reorganising your
track library, too. If you can, check out demos
of different software applications to see which
one suits you best and then buy a hardware
controller that comes with that software. This
is much easier said than done, but even if
the controller comes with a 'lite' version of
your favourite software, it'll probably be much
cheaper to upgrade from this version than buy
the full version of the software off-the-shelf.

Numark iDJ Pro

Price: £309 **Supplier:** decks.co.uk **Manufacturer:** Numark **Website:** numark.com

VERDICT
>> A fantastic controller, as long as you have an iPad and Djay

Unleash the full power of the Djay app on your iPad with the iDJ Pro

The Numark iDJ Pro is a fairly large controller that uses an iPad to provide the software, rather than a laptop. It's compatible with Algoriddim's excellent Djay app, although you'll need to buy that separately, which adds extra expense. You could use the ultra-cheap iPhone version of Djay and still make use of all the controls – including effects, hot cues and loops – but you'll have to live with iPhone version's interface. If you're already paying out for the iDJ Pro, it's probably false economy not to buy the iPad version, though.

You view Djay vertically. Across the top of the interface, you'll see a selection of effects, loop activation and settings controls. In the middle, you have spinning platters and peak meters, and at the base of the interface you have effects pads that switch between Djay's Instant FX and X/Y pads. The interface therefore shows everything you need to see.

One quirk of using the iDJ is that you have to insert the iPad into it upside down, which in turn means you must also enter your pass-code and navigate to the Djay app upside down and that you can't lock your iPad when you're away from the iDJ Pro, not ideal if you're using the unit at a venue or party.

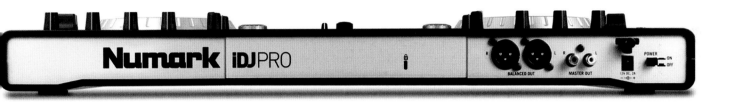

The unit itself is light but sturdy. There's very slight flex in the centre, but only you press very hard. The controls feel sturdy enough, and we feel the build quality matches the iDJ pro's price. It doesn't scream high quality, but neither does it feel low quality. Our only concern is that there's quite a bit of play in the unit's pitch slider, but gave us no cause for concern.

What it does do is give all the controls you could possibly need in order to exploit Djay fully, including track selection controls, hot cue buttons, loop buttons, effects controls and even a record button. You also get a Shift button that lets you delete hot cues or create loops of a specific length.

The rotary channel faders give the iDJ an old-school feel; they're pleasing large and smooth, though, and surrounded by LEDs that illuminate and extinguish as you move them making it easy to see how loud your track is.

You do get a conventional 45mm crossfader, though, and when Djay's set to a sharp cut it's great for scratching. You have to push the crossfader slightly by around 2mm before you hear anything, but then the sound of the opposite deck kicks in fully. The crossfader has some resistance to it, but not enough to impede your cutting.

Also unlike many controllers, the iDJ Pro's EQ pots are located at the top of the unit, above either deck. It isn't an ideal location, but they're well spaced and turn fairly smoothly. Importantly, the location is just far enough away from the loop controls,that you'll only hit them if you're clumsy.

Cueing controls are located on the front of the unit, not the top. We don't like this and found them awkward to use. We also think they're too low profile. An ability to extend and contract them, as you can on the Traktor Kontrol S4, would be better. What is good is the inclusion of both 3.5mm and 6.3mm headphone jacks, which means

▶ The jog wheels are wonderfully large and have just the right amount of resistance to them ‖

no more tantrums because you've forgotten your headphone adaptor.

The jog wheels are wonderfully large and, for us, have just the right amount of resistance to them. They're light enough to perform smooth spinbacks but have enough resistance to perform smooth pitch bends. Annoyingly, you must choose between scratching and pitch-bend modes. You can't do both. Happily, each deck has a pair of pitch-bend buttons, so you can use these to get your tracks in phase and use the jog wheels for scratching.

As long as you choose a tight pitch range, the pitch slider lets you increment the BPM of a track in small steps, which is great for pulling off tight beatmixes. The pitch sliders don't have a centre detent. Instead, they have a blue LED that illuminates at the zero point. Each deck also has a Sync button should you want to let the iPad match tempos.

You get three hot cues per deck, which is enough to let you jump around the track and create your own live edits. Once created, the hot cues are saved and you can use them straight away. The hot cues are incredibly responsive, and you hear the hot cue as soon as you press the button.

The iDJ Pro has a very comprehensive looping section, as befits a Djay controller. You can set loops manually using the loop in and out buttons, you can create loops of specific sizes using the auto-loop controls and you can use the Reloop button to re-enter a loop. If you use the Shift button with the loop controls you can also perform some accurate and addictive slip-roll loops.

These let you perform a loop of a specific duration and when you release the control the track plays from the location it would have been if you hadn't entered the loop. Each control is large and easy to hit. The iDJ pro really does have an excellent looping section.

Sadly, you only get one effect control and a button to switch it on or off. The effect control adjusts the rate of a specific effect rather than the amount of effect applied (except for the Bit-Crusher effect), but you can use the X/Y pad and Instant FX on the iPad should you wish. This is probably the best approach given the tactile nature of Djay's effects.

We were sceptical of the iDJ Pro, but it proved itself to be a fantastic controller, as long as you have an iPad and a copy of Djay that you can dedicate to it. Mind you, it's no good having an iDJ Pro if you can never use it because your mum or missus needs the iPad for a spot of internet window-shopping.

If you have a dedicated iPad, or sole access to one, you'll find the iDJ Pro a fun, versatile and powerful controller that really does let you make the most of Djay.

KILLER FEATURES

>> **No need for a laptop**
>> **Well integrated with Djay**
>> **Excellent loop controls**
>> **Responsive jog wheels**
>> **Well built**

Traktor Kontrol S4

Price: £699 **Supplier:** scan.co.uk **Manufacturer:** Native Instruments **Website:** nativeinstruments.com

Can NI's own hardware controller tame Traktor for you?

VERDICT
>> **The Kontrol S4 is the best Traktor controller we've ever used**

The Traktor Kontrol S4 is an incredibly versatile DJ MIDI controller that lets you mix and scratch tracks together, loop portions of a track, jump straight to specific part of a track using hot cue buttons and even control the included Traktor Pro 2.5 software with timecoded CDs and vinyl records. There are enough features here, to warrant making the Kontrol S4 the centrepiece of your setup and a replacement for older vinyl and CD-based setups.

The most eye-catching element of the S4 is its uncluttered and incredibly smooth fader area. There's plenty of space between each fader, which means you can adjust track volumes without accidentally nudging other faders. The individual fader units are fairly smooth and have quite a heavy resistance. We'd have preferred smoother faders, but you can easily and quickly move them without impediment. Each channel fader has its own peak meter to show you a track's level visually. The peak meters are pretty accurate and are a valuable and useful feature. With lesser controllers you must look at your software to check levels, which divides your focus rather than keeping your attention on the job at hand.

The Kontrol S4's crossfader is great for mixing or scratching. There's quite a bit of friction in comparison to scratch-oriented crossfaders such as Ecler's Eternal crossfader or the DJM-T1's crossfader, but we had no problems performing scratch techniques such as crabs and flares.

088

▶ This is one of the best MIDI controllers we've ever used, and certainly the best Traktor controller ⏸

Modern DJ controllers only need jog wheels to scratch, so if a controller has them they need to be good. Thankfully, the Kontrol S4's jog wheels are excellent. Because Native Instruments manufactures the Traktor software as well as the Kontrol S4, the integration between the two is extremely tight, meaning that the jog wheels control Traktor using a bespoke protocol rather than the less well defined MIDI method, so moving the jog wheel has a near-instantaneous effect on a track.

This responsiveness means you can perform your scratches and beatjuggles naturally without having to compensate for any latency. You can also use the jog wheels to speed up and slow down tracks momentarily to synchronise them, and the very low latency and responsiveness helps here too.

Our only criticism is the size of the jog wheels. Larger jog wheels would let us perform scratches more naturally, but you do soon get used to the size and you can always attach a regular turntable or CDJ to the Kontrol S4 if you want to scratch on a larger platter.

An important part of digital DJing is the ability to use hot cues, loops and samples, and the Kontrol S4 provides an effective array of controls for these functions. It has four hot cue buttons, four sample buttons and two loop control buttons. It also has one rotary pot that lets you set the loop size and activate the loop and another that lets you move the position of the loop.

The loop in and out buttons are great for setting irregularly sized loops for effect, but the most useful loop control is surely the rotary auto-looper. This is especially handy if you need to create a panic loop because you've lost track of time and one of your songs is eight beats away from silence. The auto-looper's also brilliant

for decrementing a loop, so that you can progress from a ½-beat loop to a ⅛th-beat loop, for example.

The hot cue buttons are made from rubber rather than plastic, and they're comparatively large. This makes them easy to hit and stops your fingers becoming fatigued if you press them often. They're large size makes them great for hot cue drumming, which is where you set hot cues on drum beats or special sounds so that you can trigger them as if you're tapping away a drum machine or Akai MPC.

The Kontrol S4 is one of the best MIDI controllers we've ever used and is certainly the best Traktor controller we've used. It has everything you need to make the most of the Traktor software and your creativity. The fact that you can

attach regular turntables and CDJs further increases its value.

NI has perhaps packed too much in to the Kontrol S4, and many people would be better off with the Kontrol S2, a two-channel version of the S4 that doesn't let you use external CDJs and turntables. Even so, if you want to get into DJing or integrate a digital controller into a traditional setup, this a great place to start.

KILLER FEATURES

>> Comes with full version of Traktor Pro 2
>> Incredibly responsive jog wheels
>> Uncluttered fader area
>> Large rubber hot cue pads

Akai APC20

Price: £159 **Supplier:** Akai 01252 896000 **Manufacturer:** Akai **Website:** akaipro.com
Required Specification: 1.5GHz processor, 512MB RAM, Windows XP or higher, OS X 10.3.9 or higher, ASIO or Windows compatible soundcard, USB port

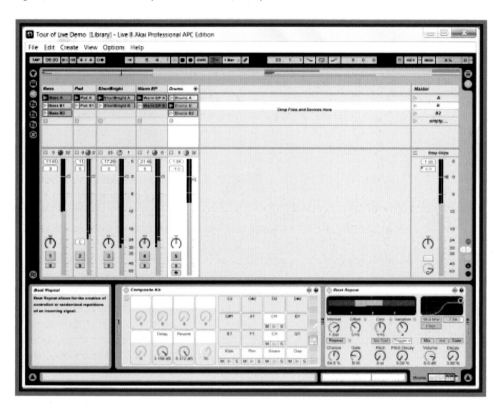

VERDICT
>> A bargain controller for new or experienced computer musicians

Take control of your DAW with Akai's compact controller

Computers have had a place in the recording studio since the 1980s, but modern Digital Audio Workstations (DAWs) are much more than mere note sequencers. They provide you with a range of virtual instruments to play, let you arrange music using drag-and-drop and feature virtual mixers for creating a final edit.

Producers and musicians are no longer limited by what their production software – or the PC running it – is capable of, but more-often-than-not their inability to control it effectively using a keyboard and mouse. That, in short, is why the APC20 was invented.

Looking as if it has just been ripped from the flight deck of the Millennium Falcon, the APC20 is a compact mixture of illuminated push buttons and silky smooth faders. It's designed to work with any DAW that supports MIDI learn, but from the start Akai's intention was to make the APC20 work with one DAW in particular: Ableton Live.

Ableton Live has not only come to dominate home and semi-pro studios, but also DJ booths the world over because of the novel way in which sections of music can be arranged and triggered on the fly. MIDI tracks and audio files can be triggered alongside each other, in real-time, via Live's onscreen Clip Matrix, which is mirrored in hardware by a 5x8 array of pads that dominates the main surface of the APC20. Each of these pads illuminates in one of three colours, depending on

The Clip Matrix gives you the power to arrange and remix a track as it plays

virtual instruments. Sadly, the Clip buttons don't detect velocity, which means any melodies or rhythm tracks produced with them will sound artificial and synthetic. Below the Navigation section is a series of buttons that arm the record function for a channel, solo a channel and activate it. At the base of the APC20 are nine faders, with each fader controlling the volume of an individual audio channel. The faders are smooth and have quite a bit of resistance when pushed. This means you can make small accurate movements with them in the safe knowledge that they won't hurtle to the end of the rail at the slightest touch.

Just to ice this particular cake nicely, there's no need to fret about the additional cost of buying the software itself, as every APC20 is bundled with Ableton Live 8 Akai Edition. This makes the entire package excellent value as well as technically impressive. While it doesn't have the solid, industrial feel of professional studio equipment, the APC20 is durable enough to survive your home studio and a limited life on the road.

state of the clip in the software: een if a clip is present but not playing, ange if it's playing and red when the hift button is pressed to access other atures. The benefit of this is that you n't have to look at the screen to see hat's happening in the Clip Matrix, as u're getting real-time information from e hardware directly.
Each row of the Clip Matrix features a parate Scene Launch button to the right it. Pressing the Scene Launch button uses the entire row of clips to play.

Suppose one row contains all the musical elements for a breakdown. Pressing the Scene Launch button for that row will stop the currently playing clips and start the breakdown. The Clip Matrix gives you the power to arrange and remix a track as it plays. This is impressive enough, but below the Clip Matrix things just get better.

Nine illuminated push buttons let you control essential transport controls, such as play and record. The APC20 also features a Note Mode button that lets you use the buttons in the Clip Matrix to play

KILLER FEATURES

>> Designed for Ableton Live
>> 40 clip launch buttons
>> Scene launch buttons
>> Comes with Ableton Live 8 Akai Edition

Headphones
Buying Guide

There's more to
a good pair of DJ
headphones than
how cool they look

The DJ world has changed beyond all recognition in the last decade, but there has been one constant throughout: headphones. These seemingly simple pieces of kit must perform some very specific duties, which we'll outline below.

Build quality Headphones will be abused; roughly thrown around your head and shoulders, the DJ booth and your kit bag. So, ideally, the model you choose will be repairable when the world gets too tough. Most designs conform to an established blueprint, using a lot of plastic with swivel and pivot engineering for comfort. This combination sees many casualties, so be sure to look out for simplified construction. It's also important to consider if parts can be replaced. Spare cables and ear pieces should be readily available, although generally they're not that cheap.

Looks DJs are surprisingly conservative, while also being image conscious, which explains why so many headphones look so similar. Times are changing, though.

In some cases, this interest in style comes at the expense of quality, but headphones designed explicitly for DJs should mean that the necessary boxes have been ticked.

Sound quality While you need to hear what the crowd is hearing, that doesn't always mean a need for audiophile quality. Thus, the audio characteristics of DJ cans are more

bass heavy. Sound however is very subjective, and should try as many models as you can.

The drivers (or speakers) are generally 50mm with some notable instances coming in at 40mm. Larger drivers are often marginally louder, with perhaps more bass. 40mm ones are more compact and expensive, but compensate accordingly in terms of sound. Your ears are better than numbers when it comes to judging sound quality; make sure that they're loud enough, and then trust your instincts.

Comfort Making headphones to with a universal fit just isn't possible. Thus circumaural (over-ear), supra-aural (on-ear) or the increasingly popular in-ear design cover the multitude of differences in human biology. Hinges and pivots help make headphones comfortable, as do headbands – just make sure that they actually fit.

Isolation There's no point having all manner of sound control if all you can hear is what the crowd is dancing to. That sound needs to stay on the floor and out of your ears.

Compactness DJing is a nomadic job. Throwing a controller into carry-on hand baggage may not leave room in your bag for much else. So smaller headphones can be a major advantage. While hinges and pivots can be a weak point, they can be good in terms of folding neatly into a bag.

Conclusion

Buying DJ headphones is about more than just listening. You'll get through numerous pairs in your DJing life, so it comes down to a trade-off between cheap pairs, that will sound okay and break in a short time, expensive models that could last longer and sound better, but represent a bigger outlay and risk.

092

Sennheiser HD25-1 II

Price: £149 **Supplier:** amazon.co.uk **Manufacturer:** Sennheiser **Website:** sennheiser.co.uk

They're not pretty, but Sennheiser's cans come with a reputation for quality

VERDICT

>> A leader in the DJ headphone market, and with good reason. They're sturdy, comfortable and easily repaired

The HD25 headphone series has many fans, and for good reason. In a sea of very similar headphones, the 25-1 IIs are unique in so many ways, so let's take a deeper look at them.

You don't get much in the box, just a screw adaptor and a bag. A harsh nylon bag, mind you – not the usual soft touch type. The headphones also only have a 1.5m straight cable, which feels short. In fact, the HD25-1 IIs do look a little like something you'd get for free in a cereal packet. The exposed wires, small cups and all-black plastic components don't exactly ooze 'bling', but on your head they certainly scream DJ. It's that whole minimalist cool thing.

They may look flimsy at first glance, but everything about these headphones is solid. There are no covers over hollow components to hide ultra-thin wires. Everything is moulded from solid durable plastic, and the 25-1 IIs can be pretty much broken down to a component level, with spares are available for just about every part as well. A definite bonus.

Having a smaller driver in a small cup doesn't seem to affect the HD25-1 II's audio quality one bit. They push out a lot of bass, but remain bright in the mids and top-end. They're very good at lower volumes, too, and we suspect a lot of thought has gone into making the most out of the small driver.

Headphones that sit on your ears generally provide better isolation than over-ear ones, and this is very true of the HD25-IIs, which offer better isolation than any other headphone we've used. The soft cup sits comfortably and seals like a dream. If you're using them in a public place, don't push them too hard because sound does leak from them a little, though, made worse by their bright sound characteristics.

These headphones are incredibly comfortable, though, and the soft cup mould to your ear. They have a pleasingly wide range of adjustment: a full 55mm per side, and let's not forget the split headband. If you can't get these to fit your head and be comfortable, then nothing will. The fantastic overall design keeps them glued in place, too. You can happily swivel one ear out of the way and they still remain stable on your head. Nothing is perfect, though, and the compact design means that wedging them between your head and shoulder is a struggle. Sadly, they're not very compact, either. They don't fold, but with the cups pushed all the way up, they do take up a little less space.

Despite the almost clunky construction, the Sennheiser HD25-1 IIs have a well-deserved top-of-the-food-chain reputation. They're amazingly comfortable, isolate like no other and sound great. Given the fact that everything is replaceable, it's hard not to put the HD25s head and shoulders above the rest of the market.

KILLER FEATURES

>> Excellent sound isolation
>> Excellent sound quality
>> Very comfortable

Pioneer HDJ-500

Price: £79 **Supplier:** decks.co.uk **Manufacturer:** Pioneer **Website:** pioneer.co.uk

Can the basic model in the HDJ range hold up its good name?

There's no denying Pioneer's pedigree in the headphone department. Its HDJ-1000s have such a reputation that there are many counterfeits floating around and you're more than likely to see a pair sat on your favourite DJ's head.

Pioneer then surpassed itself with the even higher-spec HDJ-2000s, but of the people unable or unwilling to drop hundreds of pounds on a pair of headphones? Well, that's where the HDJ-500s come to the party. Part headphone and part lifestyle statement, the HDJ-500s are about looks and features at a budget price. Well, as budget as Pioneer gets, anyway.

In the box you'll find a straight 1m cable for regular use with media players such as iPods, and a coiled 1.2m cable for DJ use alongside the obligatory size adaptor. There's no bag, though, you'll have to buy your own.

In terms of looks, Pioneer's obviously going in a new direction by avoided hinges wherever possible. These on-ear cans definitely imitate their cousins, the HDJ-2000, while employing far more plastic to do it – bar flashes of decorative metal, and a metal strip inside the headband. That said, they still look classy. There's nothing clunky about them at all and they feel substantial. In terms of style, you can also choose from three different colours: black, red and white. The HDJ-500s are all plastic, but this particular pair did seem to withstand a good amount of over the top bending and twisting.

We were, however, pleased that the cable is removable and locks in place. Because it's

VERDICT

>> The HDJ-500s are comfortable and well-priced, but there are better DJ-specific headphones out there

a less popular 2.5mm microjack connector, I have a feeling that you may be limited to buying Pioneer specific cables to replace it. Firstly to have them lock, and secondly because it's a very narrow barrel. The earpieces appear to be replaceable as well.

We found the HDJ-500s to be really good at the bottom and mid-ranges, but slightly lacking at the top end. When driven hard, they had a tendency to distort, but overall they perform as well as we'd expect: very good at lower volumes, but not handling a heavy load as well as higher priced units.

Isolation is crucial, of course, and in this respect the HDJ-500s perform well; much better than expected, in fact. We also found them very comfortable. The foam-lined

headband was especially welcome, and its narrowness increased its comfort.

From a space saving point of view, the HDJ-500s aren't that good because you can't push the cups into the headband. There's no bag or case to put them in either, further reducing their easy portability.

All things considered, though, the HDJ-500s are good value – a funky yet functional set of cans that should give reasonable service if you look after them. They're represent a good bridge between lifestyle and DJing camps, and are priced very competitively – quite low for something with a Pioneer logo on it, in fact. Having a choice of colour is pretty cool, too. If you're on a budget, these add up to an excellent choice.

KILLER FEATURES

>> Excellent sound isolation
>> Excellent sound quality
>> Very comfortable

Top 10
Accessories
Every Digital DJ Needs

USB Drive

Whether you're plugging it in to a CDJ-2000 or loading tracks on to your MacBook Air, you need a fast, reliable and high capacity USB flash drive if you want to be a digital DJ. A drive such as the 64GB Kingston DataTraveler HyperX 3.0 pictured here. At the time of writing, you can get the 64GB version for around £76. That's a massive amount of music on such a small device.

Griffin DJ Cable

The Griffin DJ Cable is ideal if your controller fails and you need to use your iPad as backup. Designed for Algoriddim's Djay, this short cable lets you cue tracks in your headphones while your audience hears the live mix.

All you have to do to rock a party with your iPad is plug the male end in to your iPad's headphone socket, enable split output and you're away.

Griffin Studio Connect

DJs have been augmenting other people's tracks for decades, usually with a drum machine or sampler, and there's no reason why digital DJs can't do the same. Especially when Griffin Technology has created Studio Connect, an audio and MIDI interface for the iPad.

It also charges your iPad. Studio Connect is expensive, but it's a great device if you use your iPad for music production.

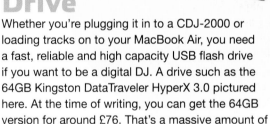

External Effects Unit

You can never have too many effects, by which we mean the DJ can never have too many effects. Your audience will be just as happy without them, but hey, you're just being creative. The Korg Kaosspad Quad pictured here currently costs just £200.

Decksavers

Decksavers are made from ultra-strong polycarbonate and can withstand punishment that would destroy lesser covers. Each cover is designed for a specific product, such as a Denon MC-3000 or Pioneer CDJ-2000, and its lipped sides ensure a snug fit that prevents dust being blown through it and on to your gear. Need proof? Check out this video at produced by our friends at DJ Worx (**tinyurl.com/bsqztkd**).

Microphone

We'd all love to stand behind the decks, looking moody and dropping phat beats, but that isn't practical. Whether you're DJing in a club or bar, you need a decent microphone.

You could spend hundreds on a top of the range radio mic, but it's unnecessary if you're in the DJ booth. Instead, get something like a Shure SM58 or SM48.

DJ Headphones

Look online or in the shops and you'll see a thousand cheap headphones claiming they're for DJs just because they've got a few dodgy hinges on them. Be warned – if you want a decent pair of DJ headphones you need to know how good they sound, whether not they block outside noise and how durable they are. Examples of good DJing headphones are Sennheiser HD-25s (**www.sennheiser.co.uk**), Pioneer HDJ-2000s (**www.pioneer.co.uk**) and Shure SRH750DJs (**www. shure.com**) pictured here.

Kensington Lock

No-one wants to go back to the old days of lugging heavy record boxes around, but the problem with laptops is that they're incredibly easy to nick. Protect it with a Kensington Security Lock (**www.kensington.com**).

Smartphone

No matter what our opinion of taking requests, there'll always be times when we need to quickly download that latest killer track.

And if you've got decent DJ apps on there, it can also be handy backup if your main controller goes down. The iPhone is still the best choice for DJs, but the cheapest iPhone 5 is currently £529 for a 16GB model. If you just want a mobile jukebox to patch in to your mixer, then you could go for an Android model, with decent devices starting from just £100.

Laptop and Controller Bags

You may not need to take your vinyl to the club any more, but you do need to take your laptop, headphones and controller. To help you carry all this gear with ease, Magma (**www.magma-bags.de**) has produces bags for specific controllers or for a combination of your laptop and gear, such as the DIGI control trolley XL pictured here.

Getting Gigs

You can walk on the moon, cradle your new-born baby for the first time or rescue a giant panda from a burning building, but nothing compares to the euphoria and unbridled ecstasy of pulling off a perfect mix in front of a live audience of hand-waving ravers.

Practise your mixing, nail those techniques and amass that mammoth collection of killer tracks, because there will come a time when you need to leave your home studio and step in to the DJ booth or radio studio to prove you have what it takes to make people move.

Ready to make that leap? No problem. In this chapter, DJ Spoony shares his vast club and radio DJing experience, we show you how to set up an internet radio station and we tell you how to get your first club gig. We also show you the best music download sites, how to promote yourself online and where to further your DJ training. This is it. This is where your hard work pays off.

CHAPTER FIVE

Getting Gigs

Playing live could be the biggest rush you'll ever experience. So why not break out of your bedroom with our guide?

No matter how much fun you have in your home studio, nothing compares to performing live in front of a club full of people. The feeling you get when your audience whoops with delight and throws their hands skywards because of something you've done is as addictive as it is euphoric.

Unfortunately, breaking out of your bedroom and in to the clubs often seems like an impossible mission, yet the clubs are full of DJs who did just that. How did they do it? Was it luck, hard work or did they simply know the right people? To be honest it was probably a combination of all three.

Unless you practise your art and develop your own style, your mixes will sound terrible or boring. You've got to put in the hard work and nail all those mixing techniques, no matter how frustrating it might be.

Make new friends

You also need to know the right people, but that doesn't mean you should give up just because your mum isn't best mates with the local club owner. What it means is you should branch out and make as many new contacts as you can. At first, that might be difficult if you're the only person you know who's interested in DJing, but you'll be surprised how many promoters or friends of promoters your existing friends already know. All you need to do is ask.

Social media has made this task a lot easier, and Facebook and Twitter can be great ways of extending your network of contacts. Be careful, though. Never give

ur address to or meet someone you've
ly met on Facebook and that none of your
er friends know.

outh clubs
ve you got a local youth club? If so, go
d check it out. Youth clubs often have a
t of decks and a mixer that you can use.
tter still, many run free DJing courses and
mpetitions. Not only will you get expert
tion in mixing, you'll also get to meet new
d existing DJs, which further increases your
ances of playing live and making a career
t of DJing. Also, why not host your own
ub night at your local youth club?
Remember, DJ Spoony cut his teeth at
local youth club, and even though he's
ayed all over the world to thousands of
ople, he'll still tell you that one of his best
ing moments was tearing the dancefloor

▲ Social media is an essential tool for building a fanbase that will support you when you play live

apart while representing his local youth club many, many years ago.

Record shops
It may be harder in this age of digital downloads, but it certainly pays to be pally with your nearest record shop. Become a frequent buyer, haunt the aisles of your favourite genre and speak to shop staff. Many DJs still buy physical media, either out of habit or because they still prefer to play upfront vinyl or CDs. They typically visit the same record shops and have a good rapport with the staff there because they buy so much music. If you make friends with shop staff they'll be in a position to introduce you to DJs. Once you're friendly with a DJ they'll be much more likely to introduce you to a promoter, ask you to play at their night or cover them when they're can't make a gig. Ask DJs and shop to listen to your demos, too, to get valuable constructive feedback.

Even with social media, record shops are a fantastic place to hear the latest news about the DJing scene in your local area. Also, make sure you regularly pick up flyers and get in contact with the promoters.

Play at your local pub
Pubs and bars are a great place to learn the craft. You're right up close to your audience, which means you see its reaction to your song choices in pristine high-definition reality. If your crowd doesn't like the obscure Drum & Bass tracks you've been playing they'll certainly let you know, and there's no stronger hint than people walking out. Equally, if they go mental to the latest commercial R&B track they'll let you know by storming the dancefloor and staying in the pub all night long. This is good for you and the landlord.

Many promoters, such as Steve Nash pictured ere, are DJs themselves

▲ Always remember that a DJ's job is to draw in customers, and keep them in the venue

If you DJ at a pub or small bar, you'll probably have to take your own equipment, so be careful. In that kind of environment it's easy for people to spill their drink on your controller or CDJs, so get your setup insured against such eventualities.

DJing in pubs and small bars is a good way of learning how to read a crowd. You may not be playing your own personal favourites, but you DJ for your audience, not yourself, and learning that early on is a good thing. You may need to play for free initially, especially if you've approached the landlord and suggested they let you play, but if it's a success and brings money in to the pub or bar it should start to pay you.

Contacting promoters

Perhaps the best way of getting a club gig is to contact promoters directly. Promoters are always looking for new and original DJs who can get people through

the doors to party all night and, of course, part with their hard earned money at the bar. We'd all love to play the main room at the Ministry of Sound, but you're much more likely to get your big break playing for local promoters putting on nights at local clubs.

The best thing to do is see which promoters specialise in your style of music and email or phone them to ask if you can play at their club nights. Offer to send them a demo CD or point them in the direction of your Mixcloud or Soundcloud demos. Expect rejections, but have the tenacity and confidence to continue and you'll eventually land your first gig.

Remember: it's a business

Music may be your passion, but clubs are a business. They exist to make money and to do that they need to draw people in, and convince them to stay. Your job is to make that happen, so treat your DJing as a business and be as professional as you can be before and during your gigs. Play for the crowd, not yourself. If you're in to dubstep but it's 80s classics that's keeping the dancefloor packed, play 80s classics. Similarly, don't be afraid of asking for mon if a club's business has improved because you're keeping people in it.

TOP TIPS FOR GETTING GIGS

↻ **Promote yourself on social networking sites, and websites such as Soundcloud and Mixcloud**

↻ **Practise DJing to become as technically brilliant as you can be**

↻ **If you're young enough, visit your local youth club. It might have DJ courses or a set of decks on which you can practise. It might even let you put on your on your own DJing events**

↻ **Check out club nights put on by local promoters. Visit the club nights, enjoy them and become a known face.**

↻ **Get friendly with the regulars at your local record shop. Staff there will know other DJs and promoters, and will stock flyers of local clubs and promoters that you could potentially contact**

↻ **See if you can play at your local pub or bar. This is a great way of learning how - and how not - to please a crowd, and it will mentally prepare you for bigger gigs, should they arise**

↻ **Remember that running a club is a business. Play for the crowd, not for yourself and keep them in the club. That will get you more gigs.**

102

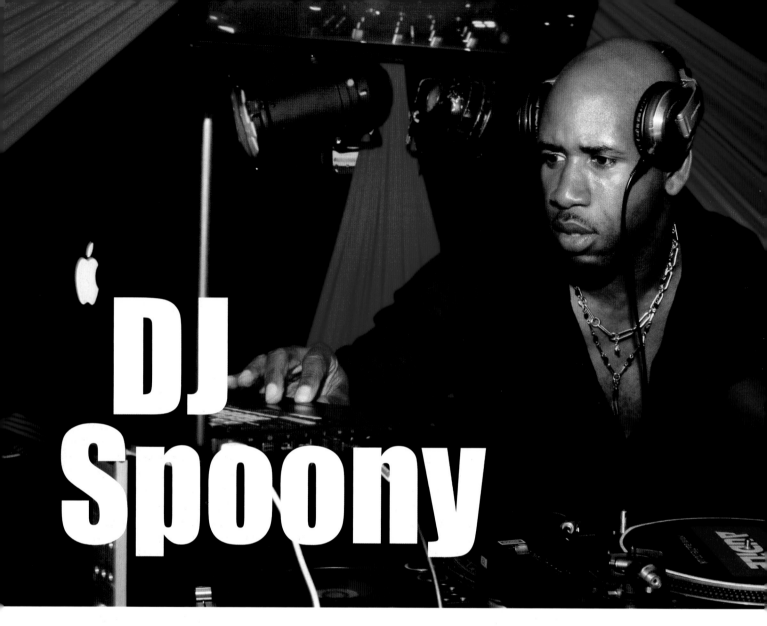

DJ Spoony

DJ Spoony is a UK Garage legend who conquered pirate radio before making his name on BBC Radio 1. Who better to drop some science on getting airborne?

Jonathan Joseph, better known by his DJ name, Spoony, is no stranger to hard work or the success that can spring from it. In a short space of time he went from bedroom DJ to club and radio DJ, honing his presenting skills on London-based pirate radio stations before migrating to commercial radio and the big time. He was instrumental in bringing the exciting sound of underground UK Garage (UKG) to a wider audience and recorded big-selling mix CDs for legendary club night Twice As Nice, at which he was resident DJ for seven years.

Although he's a seasoned and talented club DJ, Jonathan has an over-riding passion for broadcasting, and this unceasing need to entertain over the airwaves earned him a Sony Radio Award as part of Dreem Team, a prestigious slot on Radio 1's Weekend Breakfast show and a Five Live show in

which he combines his love of sport with his love of broadcasting. His radio experience is comprehensive and versatile, giving him a national profile beyond the UKG persona that we all know and love. So how did he break out of his bedroom in Hackney to become a national broadcasting treasure?

H2DJ: When did you first realise you wanted to be a DJ?
JJ: I was 15. The guy who taught me to mix was a guy called Steve Howard, who I first saw mixing at my local youth club. Another influence was a guy I went to school with called Maurice, and then there was DJ Ron, who went on to become a very big Drum & Bass DJ. These are guys I went to school with, but they were a little bit older than me.

Norman Jay is another name I used to look up to. KCC were also peers of mine

thedjguide.co.

o I used to go to carnival to listen to, and
n I eventually got to play alongside them.
 a little bit weird, do you know what I
ean? They're very big names for me, even
ough they're names that may not roll off
erybody's tongue. Most people will have
ard of Norman Jay MBE, but they may not
ve heard of KCC, who have been just as
uential in my professional career as maybe
rman Jay has.

Rap Attack was a big sound system at the
e, so I was very into Rap Attack, too.

DJ: What's happened to Rap Attack now?
: I think he's still involved in the music
ustry. It's really weird; I used to be resident
 at a club night called Twice As Nice in the
e 90s/early 2000s, and he used to come
ery week. That was quite surreal because
pent so much time wanting to do what he
s doing.

DJ: How did you kick off your career?
: I started at home, with one deck and a
ne recorder. I got my first pair of decks
en I was maybe 17 or 18, and then I just
actised, practised, practised, and did a little
 of pirate radio.

DJ: Is pirate radio good for a fledgling DJ?
: Well, there are two things about pirate
dio: the promotion you get from it, and then
ere's the question of whether you want to
 a broadcaster. Some people, like Carl Cox,
ver really did radio, he wasn't a radio man,
t Pete Tong has got where he is by being a
ry successful radio DJ and club DJ.
 liked talking about the music I was
aying and people liked hearing what I was
ying about the music. So, I thought, 'well,
eople want to hear me I'll keep talking',
en though in the end I'll be a broadcaster
 music. Other people might not be as
nfident and don't mind just mixing and
aying records, or they don't mind mixing
d making records in the studio.
Eric Morillo isn't a radio DJ, he's a very
ccessful DJ and prolific producer, so that's
e route that he went. Many, many years
o he was a [sound] engineer on some of
e early Masters At Work records. He was
e engineer, so he would've been making
e beats, programming, all the stuff like that.
entually he thinks he'll do this himself.

▲ The Dreem Team, Spoony's DJ crew

H2DJ: How did you get your radio gig?
JJ: Friends of mine were running the station
and knew I was DJing. It was largely a Drum
& Bass station, but they said they wanted to
have some house shows. I was playing house
music, so I got in as a house specialist. That
was years ago. I did that for a little while, and
went on to another big underground station.
It was called London Underground, and
it was all house and garage. That's where
myself, Timmi Magic and Mikee B linked up
and became Dreem Team.

**H2DJ: Did you get in to pirate radio to
promote yourself as a club DJ, or is
broadcasting your passion?**
JJ: Radio has become my passion. I used to
love listening to radio at the time, but I didn't
realise I wanted to become a professional
radio DJ. At the time I was listening to Greg
Edwards, Chris Tarrant, Kenny Everett, David
Rodigan and Tony Blackburn. That's what I
used to listen to. I loved being entertained
by those guys. They're consummate
professionals. I just loved to play music.
The actual skill of radio broadcasting came
later on. At the time I just wanted to mix and
scratch my way through my two-hour slot.

**H2DJ: Did your broadcasting skills come
naturally to you?**
JJ: Maybe because I had the desire it came
naturally. When you put yourself in a state to
study and receive information it becomes an
easier process. Because I loved it and enjoyed
it, I was able to absorb that knowledge.

**H2DJ: What are the essential skills
needed to be a radio DJ?**
JJ: You need to be willing to learn, and listen
to your producers. That is very important
because they see it from another perspective.
You've got to get a good team, and trust your
team, because you work together closely.
   I see it as being a relay, and I've got to
carry the baton across the line. I couldn't
carry the baton across that line unless
everyone else completes their leg. That
includes the assistant who is getting phone
calls lined up, the producer who is making
sure that not only do they do their bit, making
sure we work on the right features, and
getting me the right records to play at the
right time. I then carry the baton across the
line. It's very, very much a team effort.

H2DJ: Who influenced you as a radio DJ?
JJ: Chris Evans is someone who had a
massive influence on me as a broadcaster
because I used to listen to him and you'd
just think, it's like watching a film. I could've
listened to Chris Evans and never watched
TV, because it was that entertaining. That's
how good it was. He was the best of the
next generation. After the likes of Tarrant and
Everett, Chris Evans was - for me - the next
one in line. He was the best of our generation.
When I listened to Chris Evans I thought
'now I want to do radio'. Chris Tarrant, Kenny
Everett, David Rodigan and Greg Edwards,
I loved listening to those guys, but when I
heard Chris Evans doing it, I was like, 'I want
to do *that*'.

H2DJ: What advice would you give DJs wanting to get in to radio?

JJ: It's a difficult one that. Some people want to do it because they want to be famous, some do it because they have a passion for it. If you've got real passion, you'll do pirate radio, you'll do hospital radio, you'll perfect your craft, you'll read, you'll know your music inside-out and you'll do whatever it takes. If people are going to do that, I say follow your nose and follow your instincts.

If someone wants to get into it because they want to be famous it's difficult for me to give them advice because I come at it from a purist angle. I can't see it any other way and I'm not ashamed to say that, either.

For me, it happened naturally because I loved what I was doing and I would've been happy doing what I was doing. The longer you stay in it and the harder you work, the luckier you get. Just like Gary Player [the top golfer] said: "the harder you work, the luckier you get."

I used to travel all over London to buy my records. I'd sit down and make notes on them; the release date, what other stuff that label had released, what other stuff that artist had released. I did this for pirate radio, so when you listened to my show it didn't sound like someone had just run up there with a box of records. It sounded like Chris Evans doing a house music show on London Underground. That's what I wanted it to sound like, so there's a bit of humour, there's some jokes, there's bits where I didn't talk, there are bits where I play jingles. You didn't hear that on every pirate radio show, and that's probably what made it sound different to some of the other shows. Then you get a bit of luck, where someone goes "I was in my car and I heard that show, I like what the guy was doing, I'm gonna get him to come over."

H2DJ: Do you get other established DJs coming to you for advice?

JJ: Not really. It's one of those weird industries where people don't want to go and ask others. Some times when you're out, and you talk to people, they pick your brain a little bit, but I couldn't say 'such-and-such from that radio station asked me for advice'.

That said, there was one DJ that I was pretty instrumental in getting on the radio. He didn't want to do it, although I knew he was

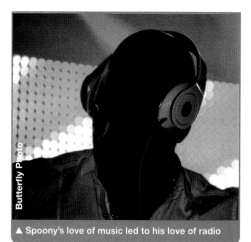

▲ Spoony's love of music led to his love of radio

good enough to do it, but I think he was put off by the thought of not being accepted. I gave him the confidence to do it by saying "you know, what's the worst thing that can happen? They can say you're not good enough or we don't want you, and that's exactly where you are now, so you might as well go for it."

I gave him a little bit of coaching; just a few tips that I'd been given. The best radio shows and the best broadcasters keep it simple. I told him to do that and he ended up making a very successful radio career for himself.

H2DJ: Do you get people on social networks asking advice and so on?

JJ: Yeah, bits and pieces. It's very flattering. I suppose that's recognition of the work I've done over the years, you know what I mean?

H2DJ: Can you still make a radio career for yourself in your forties?

JJ: Yeah, why not? As long as you're getting your message across, as long you're not becoming a dinosaur. If you don't evolve you become extinct, so I'm cool with it.

H2DJ: Is musical heritage important to you?

JJ: I've got a 16-year-old daughter, so we sit down and speak about music. She might say to me in the car, who's that record by dad? I might say, who's that one by? But we can have that conversation. I don't go, "oh, take this off, it's a load of rubbish."

Some of it *is* rubbish, mind you, but I suppose some of that's to do with music becoming disposable to a certain degree, but we have fantastic conversations about music. Again, from a young age when I was updating

her iPod for her I was making sure she had music on there with a bit of culture and not just current stuff that she wouldn't want to listen to the next year. There would be Prince some Michael Jackson on there, whether she asked for it or not.

I'm lucky. I was brought up as a black guy Hackney, so I had my peers at school listening to Madness, Bad Manners, The Specials and Blondie and then I'd go home and listen to Calypso, Marvin Gaye and Dorothy Moore. It was a complete mixed bag, so I grew up listening to and loving all kinds of music.

I didn't want my daughter to just want to be into one particular style, so I got her listening to garage mixed with a little bit of funky house. She can listen to her pop, the stuff on the radio, and then 'this was what Nan used to listen to', so she ends up with a broad taste in music too.

H2DJ: What's your best DJing moment?

JJ: There's one special moment when I was really young, just 15. It was one of my first DJing experiences. We lived in Hackney and we had a soundclash against some guys from Islington. We went to Islington to do it, and when we got there it was absolutely packed. It soon became my turn to go on the decks. I said to one of my partners, "what do you think I should do?" He asked "what are you confident you can do? There's a lot of people here if you don't get it right."

I'd been practising for this moment for two to three weeks, so I just did what I'd been practising at home. The place just went off. I had goosebumps. All the time I was practising it, I did so thinking the place was going to be packed, so I was in that zone. I was able to relive those moments practising at home, and I coped under that intense pressure.

The other moment was with Dreem Team. We did a gig for Radio 1, an outside broadcast in Cyprus, one of the first we did, and it was just a great day. All three of us were on air, having fun. The sun was beating down on us and we had about a thousand people in this lagoon on the beach. I had to close my eyes and think 'I've gone from my bedroom in Hackney, where my decks are on concrete slabs and crates, and now I'm on national radio.' I wouldn't have swapped places with anyone in the world at that point.

3 ISSUES FOR £1
on any of these great magazines

MacUser

If you use an Apple Mac, then MacUser is essential reading for you. Packed with buying advice, world exclusive reviews, breaking news and practical features, it helps you maximise the potential of your Mac.

3 issues for £1
then £17.95 every 6 months payable by Direct Debit

WebUser

Web User is packed with fantastic free software, must-visit new websites, PC and web tips, brilliant money-saving tips, easy-to-follow workshops and comprehensive hardware and software reviews.

3 issues for £1
then £19.99 every 13 issues payable by Direct Debit

COMPUTER SHOPPER

Computer Shopper tests more products than any other magazine in the UK. Packed with features, workshops and in-depth advice Computer Shopper will keep you ahead of the latest developments in technology.

3 issues for £1
then £21.99 every 6 months payable by Direct Debit

PC PRO

PC Pro is the UK's number one magazine for IT enthusiasts and professionals. Stay ahead of the latest developments with essential news, reviews and insight.

3 issues for £1
then £19.99 every 6 months payable by Direct Debit

CUSTOM PC

Custom PC is the ultimate magazine for PC enthusiasts with a passion for performance hardware and customisation. Each issue is delivered with wit, style and authority and is a must-read for anyone serious about customisation.

3 issues for £1
then £15.99 every 6 months payable by Direct Debit

If you enjoy your first three issues for £1, your subscription will continue at the low rate quoted above with great savings on the shop price. If you are not completely satisfied, you can write to cancel your subscription within your trial period and pay no more than the £1 already debited.

CALL 0844 844 0053

quote code G1201PMB

Want to get yourself heard? Why not set up your own internet radio station?

Start Your Own Online Radio Station

There was a time when starting your own radio station meant acquiring a broadcasting licence or setting up shop on a boat somewhere in international waters. These days, although pirate radio stations still exist, there's an easier option that won't cost you an arm and a leg and won't land you in prison either: the internet.

Thanks to the internet, it's never been easier or more affordable to get yourself heard. However, you're going to need some equipment to get started and, depending on how many people you want to reach and what kind of show you want to produce, the costs range from practically nil to thousands of pounds.

The absolute cheapest option would be to simply plug a microphone into your PC (or even use a mobile phone with a recording app), and then upload the resultant recording to your own website. Assuming you have all the hardware already, the only cost would be your web hosting. Even that could be offset by uploading it to a free third-party service such as Podbean (**www.podbean.com**).

However, that's a podcast rather than a radio station, and this example assumes you don't want to play any music. What we want is a streaming station, where listeners can't pause, rewind, fast-forward or download our broadcast, and we also want to be able to play music. We'll look at the licensing implications and financial burden of playing music later. First, let's look at how we create a radio show and get it online.

Hardware

As we've already said, you can record a radio show simply by plugging a microphone into a PC. That's all well and good if you're not fussy about audio quality or things like fading out songs playing pre-recorded clips. If you'd rather aim a bit higher, then you'll need some kind of mixer. If you're really serious, you might want to pay for a hardware mixer, with all the fantastic knobs and dials that such a solution comes with. This is also a particularly good option if you plan to broadcast live.

You could just plug a microphone directly in to your PC, or via an audio interface, and then use software for mixing. Assuming you're pre recording your show before, then you can use Audacity (**audacity.sourceforge.net**) to put it together. It's free, and easy to use.

▶ A condenser mic is good investment, and USB models such as this one from www.inta-audio.com add an extra layer of convenience

▲ If you want to broadcast music, then you're highly likely to need a licence from the PRS

Whichever option you choose, it's best to invest in a decent condenser microphone (or two if you're going to be chatting to guests). This should mean your recording won't need cleaning up so much in software afterwards. It's also worth bearing in mind that USB models are available, so you don't necessarily need to buy any extra hardware to hook them up to your computer. You're also going to need a decent pair of headphones, so you can hear what you're recording. If they leak sound, then there's the risk of feedback, but you'll need to consider your budget before you invest. All the equipment you need can be found from stores like **www.gear4music.com** or high-street shops such as Maplin.

Getting online

There are a number of different ways to get your show online, including getting on the iTunes radio list - though you'll need to fulfil all kinds of criteria, and possibly hand over your first-born child to achieve

You can pick up a simple mixer like the Alto Zephyr ZMX52 for less than £40

this. It's certainly not a good option for those just starting out.

Instead, we're going to look at the popular Shoutcast service. Created by Nullsoft, the company behind the media player Winamp, Shoutcast radio stations can be accessed by a huge number of media software applications (including iTunes and Windows Media Player) and hardware players. To get on Shoutcast, you'll need a server to stream your show from. While it's possible to host your station on your own server at home, this isn't recommended for most people, due to the costs and the technical complexity involved.

If you don't mind having ads inserted into your show, then you can sign up with one of the many free Shoutcast servers that can be found online, such as **www.caster.fm** or **www.listen2myradio.com**. Another good option is **http://freestreamhosting.org**, which puts either text or

image-based adverts on the web page for your station, but doesn't use audio ads at all. Free services often have premium deals as well, where you pay a few quid a month to remove ads and increase your bandwidth - which determines how many people can listen to your station at once - and possibly the bitrate at which your station is streamed. Of course, there are also plenty of company that only offer paid-for services, which might be worth considering if they meet your requirements. A good example is **www.zfast.co.uk**, which allows you to create a package according to your needs. On its website, there's a calculator with three sliders covering number of listeners, streaming bitrate and bandwidth per month.

As an example, we chose 150 simultaneous listeners, the highest bitrate of 128kbps and 60GB of bandwidth per month. The total was a pretty reasonable £6 per month. There are plenty more hosting companies around, though, so we definitely recommend have a scout about before putting any money down.

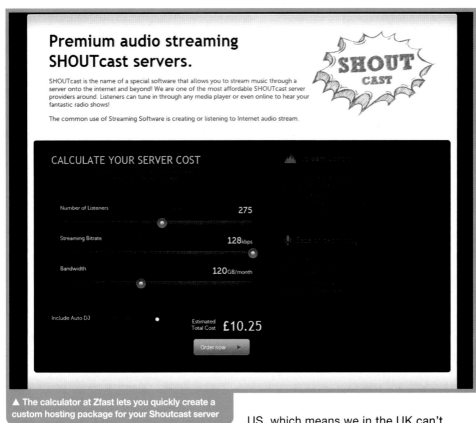

Premium audio streaming SHOUTcast servers.

SHOUTcast is the name of a special software that allows you to stream music through a server onto the internet and beyond! We are one of the most affordable SHOUTcast server providers around. Listeners can tune in through any media player or even online to hear your fantastic radio shows!

The common use of Streaming Software is creating or listening to Internet audio stream.

CALCULATE YOUR SERVER COST

Number of Listeners   275

Streaming Bitrate   128kbps

Bandwidth   120GB/month

Include Auto DJ

Estimated
Total Cost   £10.25

Order now ►

▲ The calculator at Zfast lets you quickly create a custom hosting package for your Shoutcast server

Other options

Shoutcast isn't the only way to get your show online. An alternative is Icecast, which has some advantages but ultimately won't get you same level of exposure. Another option is the peer-to-peer based solution Peercast which, like BitTorrent downloads, does away with the need for central servers.

For sheer simplicity, though, you could try **www.live365.com**. While it offers a range of Pro packages for the creation of live broadcasts, with more control over things like advertising, there are also a range of personal packages for less demanding users. It's an American site, though, so prices are in dollars - ranging between $3.95 per month for 250MB of disk space and five simultaneous listeners right up to $99.95 for 6GB and 250 listeners. Your broadcast will be available on Live365 website as well as via the Android and iOS apps.

Live365 is particularly interesting, because it pays royalties to artists and record labels on behalf of the users. Unfortunately, this is only valid in the

US, which means we in the UK can't technically use it. Which brings us to what is probably the biggest and most expensive hurdle in the way of someone wanting to creating their own internet radio station: licensing.

Music licences

Anyone who wants to broadcast music in the UK, irrespective of the medium, will have to pay for licences from two industry bodies: the Performing Rights Society (PRS) and Phonographic Performance Limited (PPL). The PRS represents the rights of artists, while PPL represents the recording companies and each of them will require separate payment.

The only way to avoid paying these costs is to play music from unsigned artists, with their permission, or music that is in the public domain (out of copyright). There's also the option of playing music protected by a Creative Commons licence. This enables you to copy and distribute artists' work, while protecting their copyright. You don't have to pay, but you do have to give credit and fulfil any condition specified by the artist.

Assuming that you don't want to do that, though, then you'll have to get in touch with the relevant bodies and get your wallet out. How much you pay will depend on what kind of broadcast you're providing, how many people listen to it and how much music you're using. For example, the cost of a podcast with

▼ A free computer program like Audacity could be all you need, especially if you're on a tight budget

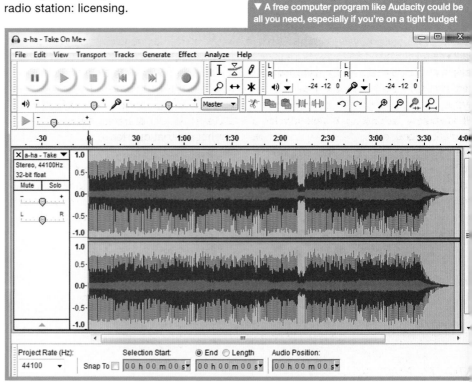

usic in it will differ greatly to a live radio ow. Also, if your show is 'interactive' . users can pause, rewind, etc) or downloadable, it will cost more to oadcast music.

For the PRS, you should head to ww.prsformusic.com, where you can e the various costs and also pay for a ence there and then. The Limited Online usic Licence (LOML) is designed for all online services, which generate less an £12,500 per year in revenue. Earn y more and you'll need the full licence the LOML+.

There are five bands of LOML, from A to ranging from £118 plus VAT to £1,176 us VAT per year. What you get for that pends on what you're providing, but pure webcasts with no interactive ement, the breakdown of costs is own in this table:

and	A	B	C	D	E
st (£)	118	235	588	882	1,176
nits	180,000 streams	360,000 streams	900,000 streams	1,350,000 streams	1,800,000 streams

Unless you get hugely popular, you should okay with band A. Whichever band you for, though, the costs are reasonable. The PPL isn't quite so generous. The nimum you'll pay is £189.41 plus VAT per ar for Small Radio Service licence. That's suming you're making less than £5,000 per ar in revenue. This limits you to 270,000 rformances' per year, and doesn't include eractive services. If you want to provide ything like that, you'll have to contact L at radiobroadcasting@ppluk.com for ormation about cost.

It's also important to consider what PPL fines as a performance in the context internet radio. According to its official cumentation at tinyurl.com/czr6pyg a rformance is "one recorded music track eamed to one user." For example, if

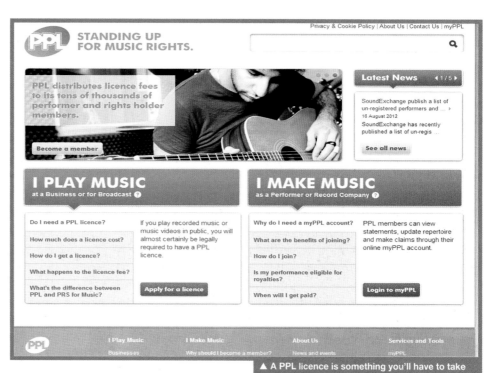

▲ A PPL licence is something you'll have to take into account if your show includes music

you play one track on your show and 50 people listen to it, that's 50 of your allowed performances gone. Suddenly, that 270,000 limit doesn't seem so good. It should be fine when you start, but any kind of success could mean you soon need to purchase a more expensive licence. A standard licence will cost you a non-refundable advance of £790 plus VAT per year, recoupable against a rate-per-performance of £0.00061.

On top of the financial responsibility to PPL, you're also obliged to provide it with a quarterly Webcasting Report, detailing the total number of listener hours your station has attracted as well as the average number of tracks you've played per hour in that quarter.

The PPL licence allows broadcasting to mobile phones, providing that the website broadcasting the music has a licence. Many Shoutcast stations are easily accessed on phones, so it's worth clarifying this before you start broadcasting.

What next?

Clearly, starting a radio station that plays commercial music is going to cost you a couple of hundred quid, and that's before you consider buying any equipment to ensure the quality of the final product. If you're not confident of making money from your efforts, or you're not prepared to make a loss to get your show on the air and benefit from the promotional opportunities it affords, it might be worth considering the Creative Commons route, playing unsigned bands, or a talk show.

Once you've chosen a show format, it's time to consider the many different ways to get online. Some of them can be quite complex, though, so beginners should consider using a hosting service that provides its own software and simple setup (http://ubroadcast.com, for example, has its Station Manager program). Whatever you do, think carefully about your requirements so you don't overspend or end up with a service or equipment that doesn't meet your needs. Research all your options carefully and you should be fine. All you need to do then is think of something to put on your show - and that is where you can really make yourself stand out from the crowd by doing something original.

► The cost of a podcast with usic in it will differ greatly to a ve radio show ❚❚

Jordan Suckley

Radio 1's Jordan
Suckley is the
consummate DJ,
combining top-notch
production skills with
a seemingly natural
ability to ignite a
crowd. How does he
do it? We found out…

ordan Suckley was winning DJ
competitions aged 18, and was picked
as 'One To Watch' by Beatport in 2010
d *MixMag* in 2011. Now rated as one of
e top Trance/House DJs in the world, he's
o produced tracks that have been picked
by Cream - and many others - for mix
Ds. He is also known for his mixing skills:
ing three decks, live effects, scratching,
tting and looping tracks to encapsulate his
erest in both production and performance.

**DJ: How old were you when you
alised you wanted to DJ?**
: Around 17 years old.

DJ: Who were your influences?
: The DJs at the clubs in my area at first,
en as my taste developed I was inspired
the likes of The Scratch Perverts, Eddie
lliwell, Sander van Doorn and many others.

DJ: How did you get your first gig?
: I handed in a mix CD to my local club,
stiny & Elite, then went back the week
er and the DJ said he liked it and would
e me a set! I instantly fell in love with it
er my first set. I just used to turn up every
ek pretending I thought he'd told me I
uld play again. Sneaky!

DJ: What was the first kit you bought?
: I got ripped off with my first setup. I had
Gemini mixer and these Gemini turntables
h no pitch, so to beat match I had to
ve the vinyl with my finger to keep it at
same speed. It was ridiculous!

**DJ: What's the essential skill of DJing?
xing, tune selection or showmanship?**
: A mixture of everything. Also, I love to
a passionate DJ really getting involved.
ere's nothing worse than a DJ turning
, stringing a few tracks together and not
eracting with the crowd. Do the damage
d the promoter will get the DJ back.

**DJ: Some say modern equipment makes
xing too easy. What's your opinion?**
: It's all a load of rubbish, you don't get
y brownie points for beat matching,
expected of you! The people who are
rried about sync buttons must be very
erage DJs! For me it opens many doors!

**H2DJ: How do you think DJing will evolve?
Will it die out as an art?**
JS: I think most DJs breaking through
spend more time mastering the art of
production than DJing these days, so
maybe we will see less technical DJs in the
future? In terms of technology for DJs, it's
a very exciting time and I can't wait to see
what new innovations come out over the
next few years.

**H2DJ: What's your favourite technique for
mixing out of a tune?**
JS: I love to mix over breakdowns, so as
the breakdown of one track is playing, it
builds up and as its about to drop, I like
to drop another track or bassline so they
drop together. Of course, this only works
if the drop is techy. I also like scratching
and then catching the last scratch on the
Pioneer RMX Beatroll and mashing it up!

H2DJ: What do you reckon to Ableton Live?
JS: I love Ableton because you can layer so
many tracks/loops, although I haven't used
it in any clubs, it's more just for fun at home!

H2DJ: What's in your home studio?
JS: 27in iMac, Logic 9, MIDI keyboard,
Focusrite Pro Soundcard and synths
such as Sylenth, Massive, Logic's Plugins
and Zebra. I like to keep my plug-ins to a
minimum so I know them inside out.

**H2DJ: You're known for live remixing.
How do you come up with your ideas? Do
you plan them or do you have a sudden
flashes of inspiration when playing live?**
JS: I'm too indecisive to plan anything, so
I always just make things up as I go along.
That's how I approached my Pioneer DJ
Sounds video on YouTube. I just picked a load
of tracks and then made it up as I went along.

H2DJ: What tools do you use to remix live? Is it just CDJs or do you also use samplers too?

JS: I was recently given the new Pioneer RMX FX unit. You can load your own samples in to it. I love it! Also, I make my own DJ tools, loops & sounds, which I layer over mixes in the clubs!

H2DJ: Do DJs need to produce their own tracks or, if DJing's their passion, should they just concentrate on just that?

JS: You 100% need to make tracks, but make sure they're on the right labels because releasing on small labels will only get you so far. As for DJing, to get gigs you need your own music for promoters to take note.

H2DJ: When you sit down to create a track, how do you approach it? As a producer looking to make a great track, or as a DJ thinking "this'll send the crowd nuts"?

JS: I always try to make my tracks dancefloor friendly because, at the end of the day, you want people to dance, don't you? Driving bassline, techy stabs and a nice riff. These are the elements I focus on with my tracks.

DDJ: Which is your favourite remix or edit?

JS: I think my favourite is my remix of *Not Over Yet* by Grace. I made the whole track from scratch and got the vocals re-sung.

H2DJ: How do you create a track? Do you play around with beats or maybe jot down the melody you have in your head?

JS: I always start with the melody first. That's the most important element in Trance: a killer riff. So I get a nice melody down first and then build the track around that. I don't move on with the rest of the track until I am happy with the melody.

H2DJ: What nonexistent piece of tech would improve your setup and why?

JS: I'd love a touchscreen iMac for using Logic. I think that would be pretty good fun!

H2DJ: What advice do you have for DJs looking to get their first club gig?

JS: Lock yourself away for a few years, say goodbye to your friends and family, master your own production technique and try to make some killer tracks!

H2DJ: Many promoters want DJs to sell tickets and only book DJs because they can sell tickets to their friends. What's your opinion on this?

JS: I had to do this when I started. I hated it, but I can understand why promoters do it, as they want the nights to be a success. It's all part of the stepping-stones: working your way up the ladder if you're just a DJ and not a producer at first.

H2DJ: Many established club DJs are complaining that nobody's getting paid because new and inexperienced DJs wi play for free. What do you think about this? Is it killing the scene or letting new blood through?

JS: No, I don't think it's killing anything. The smaller DJs may play for free, but they don't pull the crowds like the 'bigge DJs do.

H2DJ: What should our readers do to develop their own DJing style?

JS: Watch lots of YouTube videos and practise till your arms hurt.

H2DJ: You're a big name in the DJing industry, so what do you still want to achieve?

JS: I love to travel, so I'd love to travel to many more places around the world to experience different cultures and raves!

H2DJ: What can we expect from you in the coming year?

JS: A collaboration with Simon Patterson a remix for John O'Callaghan, a new voc track and loads of other new bits. Keep a look out on my Facebook page for news on those! Also, I'll be continuing my sho on BBC Radio 1, Thursday nights 9-10p on rotation!

114

Where To Download Music

Unsure which is the best download service for you? We take you through some of the best sites for tracking down tunes

Home taping may not have killed music in the 80s, but torrenting is proving to be a much more serious threat to today's music industry and the artists it supports. No matter how you argue it, your favourite artist suffers as a result of illegal downloads, and no matter what your opinion of illegal downloading may be, there are sound reasons for downloading your music legally.

If you're a digital DJ, the bitrate of your tunes has a strong bearing on their quality and should be a top concern of yours. Illegal torrents often provide songs containing dubious bitrates. That MP3 file with a 96kbps bitrate may sound okay through your iPod's earphones, but it's not going to sound great through a Funktion-One speaker system. Even the 320kbps MP3s you come across may have been re-encoded from a lower bitrate file. Downloads from legitimate sites, such as those outlined here, will be of much higher quality than those gained illicitly.

So, let's take a look at some decent music download sites.

iTunes

Where would this list be without the iPod and ITunes? A few years ago, songs purchased from iTunes had a low 128 kbps bitrate and DRM protection. This caused problems with some software applications such as Traktor and Serato, but times have changed and iTunes now offers 256kbps AAC files. To get these higher quality downloads, make sure you choose iTunes Plus.

An AAC file at 256kbps is roughly equivalent to a 320kbps MP3 file (it isn't called Advanced Audio Coding for nothing). Be warned, though. While newer Pioneer

▲ iTunes now offers high-quality, DRM-free options

▲ Spotify is a great streaming service with a fiddly method for purchasing music

Spotify

Alongside its various streaming services, Spotify also has a huge number of purchasable tracks. It only offers MP3s, but they're high-quality ones, at 320kbps. Of course, there's no need for a preview function, because you can stream tracks in their entirety before purchase. The selection ranges over every genre of music, and Spotify's a great place to go if you know exactly what you need.

The depth and breadth of available music is no-doubt Spotify's main selling point, but you need to download the program to trawl through its vast catalogue. The pricing isn't the clearest system in the world, though, and downloading tracks requires pre-purchasing 'downloads' - purchase tokens that are registered to your account. These are cheaper if purchased in bulk, but they expire if they aren't used within 30 days. This makes the process seem much more complicated than it need be.

Bleep

Moving on to the dedicated DJ download sites, Bleep offers digital DJs more specialist dance music than iTunes and Spotify. Releases are assembled cleanly in a grid layout, and cover art is clearly displayed. Searching for tracks is a pleasant experience and Bleep offers tracks in a wide range of formats. The formats available are high-quality 320kbps MP3 files and high-quality, uncompressed FLAC and WAV tracks. MP3s are slightly cheaper than FLAC and WAV tracks due to their lower quality.

DJs can handle AAC files with few or no problems, some older CDJs, such as the CDJ-800MK1 and CDJ-1000MK1 and MK2 variants may struggle.

The library of songs that iTunes offers is perhaps the most comprehensive of any dedicated digital download store, and searching for tracks is easy enough. iTunes provides the ability to preview a track for one minute and 30 seconds on longer tracks and 30 seconds on shorter ones. The song choice is undoubtedly impressive, but the iTunes store can only be reached through Apple's iTunes software. Although iTunes isn't a dedicated DJ download service (and it isn't trying to be), the sheer size of its library will be of some use to you.

▼ Bleep offer a high-quality DJ-friendly service

Bleep allows full previews of its tracks, which you can listen to in 59-second chunks. This prevents people using Bleep as a glorified MP3 player, but still lets genuine previewers assess a full track before purchase. Most tracks on the site are given a bio and mini-review that can aid customers.

Stand-out features include a blog, offering a look at new dance music, and a well-curated Recommended section. This is allied to a music choice spanning from the obvious to the obscure, and carries many sub-genres, such as 2-step, Dubstep, Electronic, Grime, Hip-hop, Beats and Indie.

Juno Download

Juno Download is the dedicated digital download site from Juno Records, one of the biggest online DJ stores on the web. It, as you would expect, offers a comprehensive music purchasing experience including solid Facebook integration, a regularly updated blog and a useful Juno Recommends section.

The homepage is chock full of features to the point of looking cluttered, but don't let this put you off, as the site offers a huge selection of tracks in a range of formats and bitrates (192kbps MP3s, 320kbps MP3s and uncompressed WAV files) all priced according to their quality. While home-studio DJs could opt for 192kbps MP3s to save money, club DJs should go for higher quality, because higher bitrates better suit a large sound-systems.

Juno Download, like Bleep, offers full song previews in instalments, but improves on its preview system. It offers a waveform view that allows the previewer to see where drops and breakdowns occur. With a huge selection of tracks, genres and an easy-to-use search system, you're likely to be highly satisfied by Juno Download.

▲ Juno Download is a massive online resource

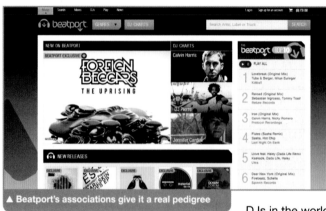

▲ Beatport's associations give it a real pedigree

Trackitdown.net

Trackitdown.net is a UK-based music download site specialising in dance music. You can download tracks as MP3s, or higher quality WAVs, and you can preview tracks using a preview player that's conveniently placed at the right-hand side of the website. It's large without

▼ Trackitdown.net was the first DJ download site

being obtrusive, and it even has a large and clear waveform so you can see how many breakdowns a track has and the size of them. Underneath the waveform is the cover art of the track you're currently listening to, along with a purchase button, social media links and even a ratings bar. The preview player also lets you create playlists. You can only preview it so long, but once that preview has ended you can start it again.

One neat feature of Trackitdown.net is the TiD Pro service created specifically for DJs. A monthly subscription reduces the cost of WAVs and MP3s to cost price, which means you can make some excellent savings, especially if you buy lots of tracks. If you like music you'll love Trackitdown.net.

Beatport

Beatport claims to be the "largest music store for DJs in the world", and its partnership with Native Instruments, Ableton, Numark and Pioneer gives it a firm grounding.

Beatport specialises in various types of dance music, and the site categorises music in sub-genres, such as Drum & Bass, Electro House and Nu Disco, among many others.

Beatport provides MP3 files with a bitrate of 320kbps, as well as uncompressed formats such as AIFF and WAV that typically cost £1 more than compressed MP3s. Song previewing is particularly impressive with Beatport because its preview player offers BPM, musical key info and a waveform view, which can be helpful when deciding a song's usefulness in your set. At two minutes long, you can preview a track for a decent length of time, but unlike Juno and Bleep, tracks can't be previewed in full.

Beatport's DJ Charts feature is particularly impressive, as professional DJs curate playlists full of their favourite tunes for purchase. Beatport sells royalty-free sample and loop packs for those wishing to spice up their sets without fear of copyright infringement. Beatport's pricing might seem comparatively expensive, but it's a fantastic site with high-quality material to download.

Take Your Skills Further

Every DJ can improve their skills with expert training

You may know how to beatmix, and you may be handy with loops and hot cues, but you can still benefit from the experience of other DJs. A great way of sharpening your skill set is to watch other DJs as they work their magic in the DJ booth. Be careful, though. If you're too distracting you'll annoy the DJ you're trying to learn from and risk being thrown out of the club.

An even better way is to enrol at a local college or specialist DJing or music production school. Your local college may have some free courses that you can undertake, and it'll probably have more than just DJing. Chances are you'll be able to learn about music production and audio engineering too, and both subjects are important subjects if you want to give your audience the best experience and further your DJing career.

A specialist DJing and music production school will have structured courses that lead to a specific qualification, such as a diploma or even a degree. One such school is the SAE Institute (*http://online.sae.edu*), which has campuses all over the world and does many different types of Creative media course - in film and animation, for example - not just DJing and music production.

SAE Institute courses include Ableton Live 101, a four-week course covering set-up and optimisation, mixing, recording and performing live - pretty much everything you need to get started with this software.

Another great place to learn DJing is the Ministry of Sound DJ Academy (**tinyurl. com/9f3oeyj**). It has a number of short courses taught by top DJ tutors at the world-famous club.

Hardcore Euphoria

There's no greater pleasure than sending a club full of eager revellers in to ecstasy because of something you've done, but every DJ has that one moment that eclipses all others for sheer, exquisite bliss. Here, some top DJs share their experiences with us...

▶ We did a gig for Radio 1, an outside broadcast in Cyprus, and it was just a great day. The sun was beating down on us and we had about a thousand people in this lagoon on the beach. I wouldn't have swapped places with anyone in the world at that point. ❚❚

DJ Spoony

thedjguide.co.

▶ There are two! The first is at Red Zone when I played with Goldie. That was my first gig. The second was supporting Sonic Youth. I'm a massive fan of Sonic Youth, so that was truly special. ❚❚

Amit

▶ Rather than picking a specific event, I'd say I have great DJ moments every week, especially when I play the right track at the right moment and can see all the clubbers going crazy! ❚❚

Jordan Suckley

Ed Real has been promoting and performing since 1992 and is well known in the dance music industry for his work as A&R at Nukleuz Records, Music Week Dance Label of the Year in 2002. He was also a founder of Trackitdown.net which, in 2004, was the first dedicated dance music download store to launch in Europe. He is still director of Trackitdown.net and helps to administrate *DJ Mag*'s Top 100 DJs Poll and Hard Dance Awards projects.

Get Yourself Noticed

From the bedroom to the dancefloor, DJ Ed Real gives us the essential guide to DJ marketing and promotion

Learning to master the art of mixing in the bedroom is great fun, but most people would love the chance to take these skills public. This is what makes DJing such a great hobby. There can't be many pastimes that can deliver a world of opportunity you can enjoy with a beer in one hand and a CD in the other.

122

Over my 20-year career as a DJ, I've met quite a few people who are truly gifted mixers. Their technical ability seems God-given, and certainly left me and my friends green with envy. Sometimes, amazing mixing skills aren't enough, though. If you want to take your beats out of the bedroom and into the club there are other things to consider.

De La Soul once famously rapped that "everybody wants to be a DJ"; 20 years down the line, that's as true today as it ever was, and it's easier than ever. For a start, digital DJing and cheap downloads have levelled the playing field and removed the need for someone to have a comprehensive, probably expensive, vinyl collection before even thinking about how to mix it. At one point, I could only afford one record per week, because they cost almost all the wages I'd earn for washing-up down the local pub. However, stepping out of the bedroom is more than just playing the right tunes, in the right order. It means adopting a persona and attitude that will win a following.

Getting the right DJ name

The most fun anyone can have is coming up with something to call yourself when you're behind the decks. Different styles and scenes have different perceptions, and differing levels of appreciation for the mystery

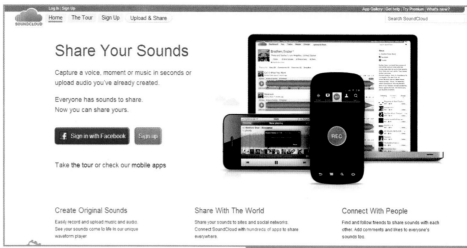

surrounding the names you'll see on a flyer or Facebook event page. More than ever before, what you call yourself becomes your brand and is intrinsically associated with how you market yourself. If you go to any large rave or festival, you'll see that the DJ line-up isn't just written, it's packed with logos that scream "I'm amazing – hear me spin!"

Not everyone goes in for this, though, and this is where the DJ needs to make an important decision. Put simply, some cool folk don't go in for snazzy graffiti style names. Sure, we know that all DJs are cool, otherwise we wouldn't be here, but as with most things in life, there's a societal hierarchy

▲ Soundcloud can provide a great platform to showcase your skills via social media

and there are different tribes. If you think that logos and DJ names that have more in common with a Manga cartoon strip than a nightclub are pretty naff, then you can use your full name and you'll be making one kind of statement. However, there's nothing wrong with adopting a space-age name at the weekend. After all, it's your spare time!

Promote yourself

Once you've decided on your identity, it's pretty easy to go public these days. Create a Facebook fan-page under your DJ name and a Soundcloud account to which you can upload mixes. Then you have firm foundations from which you can create a solid fan base. Unfortunately, this is where a lot of folk fail. A loyal fan-base gives you value in the eyes of promoters considering booking you for a set. It was the case for The Beatles when your granny and granddad were partying and it's still the case now. When you have fans, whether they're a group of friends who love to hear you mix in public or people beyond your circle who love your mixes and presentation, you'll start to be taken seriously by promoters. After all, they have to fill a dancefloor.

This part takes time, but can be fun. Upload your DJ mixes and share them with friends. People love to have a friend who's a DJ, and you can encourage them to recommend your mixes to their friends and so on. If you keep this up long enough, and if your mixes are good enough, then your fan base will grow. The more you practise and make those mixes, the more people you'll reach.

With a bit of hard work you'll become well known around school, college, town or beyond. Once you're confident you've got the skills and a group of friends who'll support you, it's time to start networking in the club and going after the gigs.

Making friends

As a DJ, there's a good chance you love going clubbing, and that's going to be a great help in this department. It's one great way to combine creating a fan base with a passion for partying, and it's one that's also going to give you a chance to spin too. Putting on your own events can be the most satisfying thing you could ever do, as long as you don't mind a lot of hard work and stress. That's where your crew and fan base come in to play.

DJing is a social activity that brings people together through a common love of having fun. If you've got a handful of friends who are as equally passionate about having fun as you, then you've got a great team in waiting. Not everyone needs to be a DJ, and if you're going to throw a party then having people who aren't afraid of handing out some flyers or invites and putting up posters all over college or town are just as important. Surround yourselves with good people who love being the centre of attention and you'll be surprised how many others will follow. They'll also be the first ones on the dancefloor when you hit the decks, getting the party started.

You can throw a party anywhere, and it's a good way to practise for your mixing, so

earmark a house, bar, field or school hall and spread the word. If you have a big gang of friends and they invite some more people along, you've got the start of a party. Learn from the experience of performing in public and if you enjoy it get stuck in and do it again.

Playing in front of crowds is different to mixing at home for your own amusement. It's great to see how people react to music and mixes, because you're playing for the audience and must react to the way they respond to your music. Don't worry,

though - every DJ's cleared the floor at least once in their time!

The more chances you have to play in public, the more people you meet and chances are you'll get a crew of like minded friends together who are up for seeing whether there are opportunities to throw bigger and better events.

Hitting the clubs

The step from private party to club night is a huge one, but every promoter started somewhere, and you can do it too. Don't get dazzled and bite off more you can chew and always remember that your first party is likely to be more successful than the second because everyone you know will want to support you, or be curious to see just what on earth you're up to.

Sometimes, that can give a sense of invincibility, but take it one step at a time. Chances are that a lot of the curious folk and those who came to your launch out of sense of duty will stay away when you try to repeat the experience. Pace your ambition.

Holding parties at a commercial venue like bar or club might bring a financial element to the proceedings and this can also turn things on their head. Try not to spend money you can't afford, though some expenses will need to be paid in advance, such as venue hire or decorations and lighting. Keep on top of this and there's nothing more disheartening than having to sell your own DJ kit because you've lost your shirt throwing a rave, leaving you back at square one with nothing left to mix on

In a proper venue, the opportunity now arises to meet your heroes by inviting well-known DJs to come and spin. This is an amazing experience and teaches us so much about the 'business'. Check out their fan pages on Facebook and either contact them directly or via their DJ agent if they have one It's best to find guest DJs who will go direct for starters because they'll be less expensive and you can network with them rather than having the buffer of a rude or offhand agent Play it cool and start learning.

Experienced DJs will give you lots of insight, but remember the saying 'never meet your heroes'. Sometimes, people can be a right pain to deal with. If that's the case, learn how not to act when you become famous, and young DJs ask you to spin at their event

5 free downloads from trackitdown.net

Want five free tracks from the web's greatest music download site? All you have to do is register at www.thedjguide.co.uk and we'll send you a voucher code to redeem at www.trackitdown.net

BUT THAT'S NOT ALL! Trackitdown.net is also offering one month's free TID Pro membership, giving you access to a revolutionary DJ membership service used by everyone from BBC Radio One DJs to club spinners worldwide.

For just £10 per month, TID Pro members buy their downloads for cost price - £0.99 for wav, and £0.79 for 320kbps MP3s - with labels and artists still receiving their full royalty, instead of taking a discount. This means DJs can make money go further and discover more music, and the labels benefit from more sales without losing revenue.

This is a fantastic opportunity to increase your track collection and see exactly why so many top DJs use Trackitdown.net to download music. To take advantage of the one month TID Pro offer, simply log on to **www.trackitdown.net** and enter this code: **H2DJ-AQ39PG726**

Competition
SAE INSTITUTE

WIN a music production course **worth £2,190!**

ow To DJ has teamed up with SAE Institute to give one lucky reader a free electronic music production MP) course worth £2,190. This is a tastic opportunity to get to grips with leton Live, audio engineering or one the many other subjects that the SAE titute offers.

You'll be taught by top, highly respected ors and network with other DJs and oducers. SAE Institute has many mpuses, so you won't be far from one. nd your answer to the question below to einstitutecomp@dennis.co.uk.

COMPETITION QUESTION

hat does EMP stand for?

. Electro-magnetic phenomenon
. Electronic Music Production
. Extra-musical productivity

TERMS AND CONDITIONS

The competition closes on 28th February 2013. Only one person may enter and any person found to be entering multiple times will be disqualified. The Competition is only open to residents of the United Kingdom who are aged 18 or older at the time of entry. By entering the competition the winner agrees to participate in such promotional activity and material as SAE Institute may require. The prize will not be transferable to another person. No part of the prize is exchangeable for cash or any other prize. SAE Institute reserves the right to cancel or amend the Electronic Music Production Certificate course at its sole discretion and without notice at SAE Institute requires the winner to claim their prize by 1st April 2013 and cannot be carried over. Failure to claim the prize within this time may result in disqualification and selection of an alternative winner.

DON'T RUIN YOUR BIG NIGHT

Pack these **5 essential items** in your kit bag. Now!

OUTPUT LEADS
They're awkward to carry around if you've done the right thing and bought a decent length, but you may need to bring your own output cables. You don't want to turn up at the venue to find a pair of 6.3mm jack plugs when your controller has XLR inputs.

HEADPHONES
Whether it's for reasons of hygiene, because they get nicked too easily or because club owners are tight-fisted is unclear, but most clubs don't provide headphones. You'll need a pair, but don't think a pair of iPhone earbuds will suffice either. They simply won't compete against a booming PA.

LAPTOP
Don't just make sure you've packed it – make sure your laptop's fully charged before you leave the house and that you take the charger.

TUNES
If you're mind's focused on the upcoming gig, it's all too easy to forget your batch of killer tunes. They're such an obvious requirement, it's easy to assume you've packed them. Don't. Assume nothing.

HEADPHONE ADAPTOR
It may be a diminutive bit of kit, but without it you're screwed - and don't expect the promoter to have one. It doesn't have to be a primo, military-grade model, so, for the sake of a couple of quid, buy one and put it in your bag.

thedjguide.co